AF600418

THE CATHOLIC UNIVERSITY OF AMERICA
CANON LAW STUDIES
No. 264

The Communication of Catholics with Schismatics

A HISTORICAL SYNOPSIS AND A COMMENTARY

BY
REV. IGNATIUS J. SZAL, A.B., J.C.L.
Priest of the Archdiocese of Philadelphia

A DISSERTATION

Submitted to the Faculty of the School of Canon Law of the Catholic University of America in Partial Fulfillment of the Requirements for the Degree of Doctor of Canon Law

THE CATHOLIC UNIVERSITY OF AMERICA PRESS
WASHINGTON, D. C.
1948

Nihil Obstat:

Ludovicus Motry, S.T.D., J.C.D.,

Censor Deputatus.

Washingtonii, die 31 martii 1948.

Imprimatur:

✠ D. Card. Dougherty,
Archiepiscopus Philadelphiensis.

Philadelphiae, die 2 aprilis 1948.

The Walther Printing House
Philadelphia

TO

MY MOTHER

AND TO

THE MEMORY OF

MY FATHER

TABLE OF CONTENTS

CHAPTER V

PAGE

CHAPTER VI

CHAPTER VII

CHAPTER VIII

PAGE

FOREWORD

The question of religious communication is one which is not restricted solely to the field of Canon Law; it is rather a canonico-moral problem. This is very evident from the fact that both canonists and moral theologians treat this matter, and in fact the moralists present a more detailed and comprehensive commentary on religious communication than do the canonists. The question of scandal and perversion from the faith is principally a moral consideration.

By reason of these facts, it will be difficult to treat religious communication solely from a canonical standpoint, for one will have to depend to a great degree on the writings of moral theologians. However, there will be no consideration of the sinfulness, be it mortal or venial, of religious communication. The purpose will be to determine whether a stated action is licit or illicit, whether the licitness of that action is intrinsic or extrinsic, and in virtue of what law, divine or ecclesiastical. These facts will give sufficient knowledge to the reader, so that he may easily apply the moral principles to the legislation of the Church and draw his own particular conclusions.

Although the present law in canon 1258 considers religious communication in respect to all non-Catholics, the present work is concerned solely with communication with schismatics. The principles governing religious communication remain the same in regard to all non-Catholics, but in the present treatise the consideration of the circumstances and occasions for religious communication will be restricted to those which are peculiar to schismatics.

This restriction of the discussion to schismatics is maintained not only in the canonical commentary, but likewise in the historical synopsis. In consequence of this, the historical background is of little significance prior to the XVI century. Religious communication in general has a very complete and detailed history when applied to all non-Catholics, but if it be limited to schismatics, one finds very little material in the early canonical sources concerning this particular form of religious communication.

In canon 1258, §1, the Code practically restates the divine law, although it is more comprehensive than the divine law, for it declares illicit not only the communication in rites which are of their nature non-Catholic, but also in rites which are Catholic in nature but exercised under the direction of a non-Catholic sect. However, the law is general and must be interpreted in the light of past interpretations and responses which have issued from the Holy See. These authoritative pronouncements of the Holy See have largely determined the principles to be followed in practice, and it is principally with these pronouncements that the present work is concerned.

The reader is finally cautioned against making an incorrect application of the principles presented in this work. It is to be remembered that two important factors which must be considered in every case of religious communication are the danger of perversion from the faith and of scandal to others. These two factors are determined principally from the accompanying circumstances. In consequence of this fact, what is licit in one locality may be illicit in another, and what is true of countries that are largely schismatic may be untrue where schismatics are in the minority.

The writer is very grateful to His Eminence, Dennis Cardinal Dougherty, Archbishop of Philadelphia, for the opportunity to pursue advanced studies at the Catholic University; to the members of the Faculty of the School of Canon Law for their counsel and direction; and to all those who, through their advice and encouragement, have made the completion of this work possible.

Part One
Historical Synopsis

CHAPTER I

THE EARLY COUNCILS AND THE DECREE OF GRATIAN

INTRODUCTION

The history of the Church is the history of its struggle to preserve the unity of its doctrine, worship, and discipline. Christ prayed for that unity and alluded to it also when He spoke of one flock and one shepherd.[1] For the Apostles it was not enough to spread the gospel of Christ among the infidel and to teach all nations. There was still the task of preserving the faith that had already been established. From the very beginning the Church had to contend with those who tried to disrupt its unity.

The greatest crime against the unity of faith was that of heresy, for it struck at the very foundations of the Church. Heresy was directly opposed to the true faith, for it denied that which the Church affirmed to be the teaching of Christ. But there was a crime, perhaps not quite so detestable as heresy, but still a source of great trouble to the Church — the crime of schism. Heresy was opposed to the unity of faith; schism was opposed to the bond of charity.

Article I — Preliminary Notions

A. *Notion of Schism*

The notion of schism is clear, for in law a schismatic is defined as one who, having received baptism and still retaining

[1] John, XVII, 21; X, 16.

the name of Christian, nevertheless refuses obedience to the Supreme Pontiff or refuses to communicate with those members of the Church who are subject to him.[2] There is here involved no denial of any article of divine or Catholic faith. Strictly considered, a schismatic professes belief in the sovereign power and primacy of the Pope, but out of malice refuses to be subject to him and to obey him as the Head of the Church and the Vicar of Christ on earth. Such schism is called pure schism.

To constitute the delict of schism in the strict sense, the following conditions are required:

1) One must withdraw directly (expressly) or indirectly (by means of one's actions) from obedience to the Roman Pontiff, and separate oneself from ecclesiastical communion with the rest of the faithful, even though one does not join a separate schismatical sect;
2) one's withdrawal must be made with obstinacy and rebellion;
3) the withdrawal must be made in relation to those things by which the unity of the Church is constituted; and
4) despite this formal disobedience the schismatic must recognize the Roman Pontiff as the true pastor of the Church, and he must profess as an article of faith that obedience is due the Roman Pontiff.[3]

As a consequence there is no schism involved if one separates from his bishop and the communion of the faithful of his diocese, but remains subject to the Roman Pontiff and the Universal Church. However, today such a position would be impossible to maintain in practice. Nor is there any schism if one merely transgress a Papal law for the reason that one considers it too difficult, or if one refuses obedience inasmuch as one suspects the person of the Pope or the validity of his election, or if one resists him as the civil head of a state.[4]

2 Can. 1325, §2.

3 Schmalzgrueber, *Jus Ecclesiasticum Universum* (5 vols. in 12, Romae, 1843-1845), Lib. V, tit. 8, n. 10 (hereafter cited *Jus Ecclesiasticum)*; Wernz, *Ius Decretalium* (2. ed., 6 vols., Romae et Prati, 1906-1913), VI, n. 356.

4 Reiffenstuel, *Jus Canonicum Universum* (5 vols. in 3, Maceratae, 1760, Lib. V, tit. 8, n. 5 (hereafter cited *Jus Canonicum)*; Schmalzgrueber, *Jus*

Pure schism, however, is rare. Though in theory or absolutely considered it can exist, in practice it is rarely to be found, for after a period of time most schismatics not only refuse obedience, but contend that they do not have to obey. This arises not from the nature of schism, but from the malice of the schismatic.[5] St. Jerome (ca. 342-420) stated that every schism invents some heretical doctrine in order to make it appear that the withdrawal from the Church was justified.[6] Pure schism is hardly possible except in individual persons.[7] Most authors hold that practically and historically there are few schismatics in the strict sense of the term.[8] Schism is ordinarily coupled with heresy, and in this form it is called mixed schism.

Van Espen (1646-1728) stated that schismatics are to be considered as heretics in regard to ecclesiastical censures, and he quoted St. Cyprian (+ 248) in support of his doctrine.[9] However, neither the text itself nor the *glossae* draw the conclusion expressed by Van Espen. He also stated that the canons of the Church and the sanctions of the Pontiffs treat of schism and heresy in almost the same manner. For though schism can

Ecclesiasticum, Lib. V, tit. 8, nn. 13-14; Ferraris, *Prompta Bibliotheca Canonica, Juridica, Moralis, Theologica, necnon Ascetica, Polemica, Rubricistica, Historica* (8 vols., Parisiis, Vol. VII [1857]), VII, p. 139, nn. 9, 10; Vecchiotti, *Institutiones Canonicae ex Operibus Cardinalis Soglia Excerptae* (2 vols., Augustae Taurinorum, 1867), II, 356; Vermeersch-Creusen, *Epitome Iuris Canonici* (3 vols., Vol. III, 5. ed., Mechliniae, Romae: H. Dessain, 1936), III, p. 310, n. 513.

5 Schmalzgrueber, *Jus Ecclesiasticum,* Lib. V, tit. 8, n. 6.

6 "Nullum schisma non aliquam sibi confingit haeresim, ut recte ab Ecclesia recessisse videatur." — *Commentaria Epistolae ad Titum,* c. 3, vv. 10, 11 — Migne, *Patrologiae Cursus Completus, Series Latina* (221 vols., Parisiis, 1844-1864), XXVI, col. 598 (hereafter cited *MPL); c.* 26, C. XXIV, q. 3.

7 Augustine, *A Commentary on the New Code of Canon Law* (2. ed., 8 vols., St. Louis, Mo.: B. Herder Book Co., 1918-1924, Vol. VIII [1924]), VIII, 278 (hereafter cited *A Commentary on Canon Law).*

8 Reiffenstuel, *Jus Canonicum,* Lib. V, tit. 8, nn. 7 and 9; Schmalzgrueber, *Jus Ecclesiasticum,* Lib. V, tit. 8, n. 5.

9 "Qui unitatem Ecclesiae non tenet, fidem non tenet." — c. 18, C. XXIV, q. 1; Van Espen, *Ius Ecclesiasticum in Epitomen Redactum* (5 vols. in 2, Bassani, 1784), Vol. II, pars. IV, tit. iv, c. 2, n. 29.

exist, absolutely considered, without heresy, it is ordinarily however conjoined with heresy. Though in the beginning it is free from heresy, it degenerates into heresy in the course of time.[10] The *glossae* in Gratian seem to uphold this view.[11]

Not every schism is at the same time heresy. This is true only of mixed schism. Otherwise it is difficult to explain why in several instances the law speaks only of schismatics, and makes no mention of heresy. There is an essential distinction between the two, as is evident from the fact that the canons of the Council of Laodicaea (343-381) treated separately of schismatics and of heretics.[12]

Despite all the foregoing arguments to the contrary, the term schismatic is in common usage in the law of the Church. When it is used, it has reference also to the Oriental schismatics, and not merely to a small group of individuals who refuse obedience to the Roman Pontiff.[13] It is with this group of Oriental schismatics that the present dissertation is concerned, and *a pari* the principles herein stated can be applied to other schismatics. Though one can safely say, in view of the common opinion of the authors, that practically all schism today is tainted with heresy, as is the case with various Oriental sects and the Old Catholics, still these groups of dissidents are commonly classed as schismatics in spite of the heretical doctrines which they are known to hold.[14]

[10] Van Espen, *Ius Ecclesiasticum Universum* (5 vols. in 4, Lovanii, 1778), Vol. II, pars. III, tit. iv, *De Delictis Ecclesiasticis*, c. 2, n. 52.

[11] "Hic videtur quod omnis qui non obedit statutis Romanae sedis fit haereticus." — *Glossa Ordinaria* ad D. XIX, c. 5, s. v. "*prostratus*." The use of the verb "*fit*" instead of "*sit*" seems to imply that the act of disobedience does not *per se* imply heresy, but leads one to become a heretic.

[12] Cc. 31-33 — Mansi, *Sacrorum Conciliorum Nova et Amplissima Collectio* (53 vols. in 60, Parisiis, Arnhem, Lipsiae, 1901-1927), II, 569 (hereafter cited Mansi).

[13] Herman, "Regunturne Orientales dissidentes legibus matrimonialibus Ecclesiae latinae?" — *Periodica de Re Morali, Canonica, Liturgica*, XXVII (1938), p. 9, n. 6.

[14] MacKenzie, *The Delict of Heresy in its Commission, Penalization, Absolution*, The Catholic University of America Canon Law Studies, n. 77 (Washington, D. C.: The Catholic University of America, 1932), p. 17.

However, there are others who hold that the Old Catholics are rather to be considered heretics, since their heretical doctrines predominate. Very shortly after their break with the Church they lapsed into the views of the Anglican Church, and thus departed further from the Catholic faith than would have been anticipated by a mere opposition to the Vatican Council.[15] The Polish National Church is also closely allied with the Old Catholic Movement, and is likewise more heretical than schismatic.[16] To consider the Old Catholics and the Polish National Church rather as heretics and schismatics is, in the writer's opinion, more in conformity with the truth. The denial of such fundamental dogmas as that of original sin, of the eternal punishment of hell, and of the necessity of faith for salvation[17] certainly brands the Polish National Church as a heretical body.

Perhaps due to the aforementioned difference of opinion among the authors, namely, whether the Orientals can rightly be called schismatics, especially after the Vatican Council which defined Papal Infallibility, several present-day authors forego the use of the term schismatic and speak instead of the Separated Eastern Church or of the Dissident Eastern Church.

An added reason for the use of the terms *dissident* and *separated* in referring to schismatics is the fact that these terms have a less odious signification. The decisions of the Holy See as a rule use exclusively the terms heretic or schismatic in referring to the Eastern Schismatics. The terms heretic and schismatic are also disciplinary terms. However, private authors prefer the less offensive terms *dissident* and *separated.* The terms heretic and schismatic have the added connotation of moral guilt, whereas *dissident* and *separated* prescind from any guilt. In the field of apologetics the latter terms are preferred, as they offer

15 Algermissen, *Christian Denominations* (St. Louis: B. Herder, 1945), p. 360.

16 Algermissen, *op. cit.*, pp. 360-363.

17 Algermissen, *op. cit.*, p. 362; cf. *Religious Bodies: 1936* (2 vols. in 3, Washington: U. S. Government Printing Office, 1941), II, 1377.

a more charitable approach in treating with our separated brethrent of the East.[18]

The Church had hardly been established before it was faced with the problem of dealing with heresy and schism. A division in the unity of the Church, or schism, was always considered a very great crime. Such divisions occurred in Apostolic times, though these were not perfect schisms, since they consisted in a division among the particular churches, and thus did not constitute a separation from the Roman Church.[19] St. Paul had to rebuke the Corinthians for the contentions that arose among them.[20] More emphasis, however, was laid on heresy, and the faithful were continuously warned against associating with those who were guilty of heresy.[21] But there is evidence of a similar admonition to shun dissenters.[22]

To prevent the spread of these evils and to punish the wrongdoers, the Church cut the guilty ones off from its Christian society, and forbade the faithful to associate with them. The faithful were forbidden to communicate with them not only in their religious rites, but also in civil matters. Such in general was the practice of the Church up until the XV century. There were specific exemptions granted in the case of those closely related to the delinquent, but the faithful in general were to avoid the company of those who were not in communion with the Church.

Following the Apostolic era, in the III century a schism broke out in the Church of Carthage under St. Cyprian (+ 258). The early Roman Councils under Pope Symmachus (498-514)[23] were

18 Jugie, *Theologia Dogmatica Christianorum Orientalium ab Ecclesia Catholica Dissidentium* (4 vols., Parisiis: Letouzey et Ané, 1926-1933), I, 19-22 (hereafter cited *Theologia Dogmatica Christianorum Orientalium).*

19 Wernz, *Ius Decretalium*, VI, n. 355.

20 I Cor., I, 10 ff.; XI, 18.

21 Tit., III, 10; II John, 10, 11.

22 Rom., XVI, 17; II Thess., III, 14.

23 Jaffé, *Regesta Pontificum ab condita Ecclesia ad annum post Christum natum MCXCVIII* (2. ed., correctam et auctam auspiciis Gulielmi Wattenbach curaverunt S. Löwenfeld, F. Kaltenbrunner, P. Ewald, 2 tomes in 1 vol., Lipsiae, 1885-1888), I, pp. 96-100 (hereafter cited Jaffé).

concerned with the schism occasioned by the election of Laurentius as antipope. At about the same time the controversy on the Three Chapters came into prominence. Under Acacius, the Patriarch of Constantinople (471-489), a schism broke out between the Eastern and the Western Churches, and it lasted from 484 to 519, when the breach was healed by Pope St. Hormisdas (514-523). However, in spite of the numerous schisms, there was little legislation in the early councils to regulate the matter of communication with schismatics.

It is to be noted that in the early Church a schism was very often coupled with heresy and was of a mixed nature. Thus the schism of Novatian in the reign of Pope St. Cornelius (251-253) and that of the Donatists in northern Africa were both mixed with a heretical doctrine.[24] This undoubtedly was the reason why the early councils spoke principally of heresy, the more serious of the two crimes, and only occasionally referred to schism.

In the VI century a very serious universal schism arose in northern Italy and other regions over the V Ecumenical Council (553), and is referred to in the letters of Pope Pelagius I (556-561).[25] The Middle Ages saw the schism of Photius (867), but there was also a division in the West in the XIV century through the election of antipopes and the controversies which arose as to who had been legitimately elected Pope led to the great Western Schism. Of course, all schisms in the Church are overshadowed by the Eastern Schism. The breach begun by Photius was never healed, and the final break between the Western and the Eastern Church came under Caerularius (1043-1058). Numerous settlements were attempted, but none produced any lasting effect.

It is only after this period, and even then not for some time to follow, that legislation regulating the communication with schismatics is found with any frequency.

Since the defection of the East there have been schisms of a lesser degree in the Church. In the XVIII century the sect of

24 Wernz, *loc. cit.*

25 Wernz, *loc. cit.;* c. 34 (S. Pelag.), C. XXIV, q. 1; Jaffé, n. 994.

freemasonry worked against the Church and was condemned scarcely ten years after its institution. Toward the end of the same century and in the beginning of the XIX century there were other schismatical movements, such as those abetted by Emperor Joseph II (1780-1790) and other princes, who on the pattern of the Anglican and of the Russian Churches subjected the Church locally to the civil powers and practically broke its connection with and dependence on the Holy See. Similar movements occurred in Germany, in Switzerland, and in Italy, but with much less success. In more recent times the Polish National Church was established as a schismatical group, but in a short time it degenerated into a heretical sect.[26]

B. *Status of Schismatics*

In the treatment of heresy the question of religious communication was given lengthy consideration in the Church's legislative enactments. Distinctions were made between the various degrees of communication. There were the *credentes,* the *defensores,* the *fautores,* and the *receptatores haereticorum.* However, the question of communication with schismatics was not directly considered, with the exception of a few particular cases. Bancroft states that the authors during the Middle Ages did not treat of religious communication with non-Catholics precisely as such, but that their concern was centered about the prohibition to communicate with the excommunicated on the one hand, and with the infidel on the other. He places heretics and schismatics in the class of the excommunicated.[27] This indeed seems to have been the common opinion of authors. But it is difficult to establish the correctness of their assertions, at least with respect to schismatics.

The general juridical status of schismatics in the past is difficult to determine. They were not considered in the same cate-

26 Wernz, *loc. cit.*

27 Bancroft, *Communication in Religious Worship with Non-Catholics,* The Catholic University of America Studies in Sacred Theology, n. 75 (Washington, D. C.: The Catholic University of America Press, 1943), p. 27.

gory as heretics, at least not inherently so, for they held no beliefs contrary to the Christian faith. The only category in which they might have been placed by law is that of the excommunicated. If it can be determined that they were held to belong to this class, then it can be concluded that the communication which was forbidden with reference to the excommunicated was likewise forbidden with reference to schismatics. The approach to the question is indirect, yet it is the only avenue open by which it can be determined what kind of communication with schismatics was permitted.

Several authors made the general statement that schismatics were *ipso facto* excommunicated, but no source of law was indicated by them in substantiation of this assertion. Hostiensis (+ 1271) stated that schismatics were under excommunication.[28] Kober (1821-1897) also stated that from the earliest times schismatics were regarded as excommunicated, even apart from any special sentence, though he too gave no references for his statement.[29] Either the fact was obvious and accordingly needed no proof, or else there was no proof to be found. Certainly in Gratian there is no clear statement that schismatics were *ipso facto* excommunicated. Certain schismatics and their supporters were excommunicated by special decrees, but from this no application can be inferred with reference to schismatics in general. It is true that by their very action schismatics cut themselves off from the communion of the faithful, but it is another question whether in the eyes of the Church they incurred excommunication and became bound by its effects.

Perhaps the status of schismatics has best been summed up by Suarez (1548-1617), who stated that schismatics were *ipso facto* excommunicated, at least in consequence of the *Bulla Coenae,* although it was not clear from the common law that they were under excommunication. Suarez cited the *Decree* of

28 "Ab hominibus (etiam) puniuntur, nam excommunicantur, et si non resipuerint, deponuntur, ut XXIII D. '*In nomine Domini.*' " — Hostiensis (Henricus de Segusio), *Summa Aurea* (Venetiis, 1570), p. 401.

29 Kober, *Der Kirchenbann nach den Grundsätzen des canonischen Rechts* (Tübingen, 1863), p. 56 (hereafter cited *Der Kirchenbann).*

Gratian, the *Decretals,* and the *Liber Sextus* in his references to the common law.[30] If these texts be examined, it will be seen that from them it is difficult to arrive at a definite and certain conclusion as to the status of schismatics.

The first reference in the *Decretum Gratiani* is made to a letter (833) of Pope Gregory IV (827-844), which concerned simply the leaders of the schismatic groups, and was not directed against schismatics in general.[31] In the second citation, which is the decree, *"In nomine Domini,"* of Pope Nicholas II (1059-1061) on the election of the Roman Pontiff, the only penalty mentioned was that of deposition, which to become effective needed to be inflicted, for it was not incurred *ipso facto.*[32] The letter of Pope Pelagius I (ca. 558) to Narses Patricius, concerning the bishops of Venetia, Istria, and Liguria, stated that if these bishops were to persist in their contumacy, Narses was to excommunicate and condemn them. This penalty was evidently not incurred *ipso facto,* but was to be inflicted by the ecclesiastical superior.[33] The *Decretum Gratiani* also treated of the excommunication of a schismatic priest, but again the penalty was a particular one, and hence was not directed against all schismatics.[34]

The Decretals of Gregory IX contain mention of an excommunication incurred *ipso facto* on the part of schismatics, but the reference is made in regard to papal elections.[35] This legislation had been enacted in canon 1 of the III General Council of the Lateran (1179). The *Liber Sextus* of Boniface VIII likewise contains mention of a like excommunication for schismatics, but

30 Suarez, *Opera Omnia* (28 vols., Parisiis, 1856-1866), disp. XII, *De schismate,* sect. 2.

31 C. 5, D. XIX; Jaffé, n. 2579; Mansi, XIV, 515.

32 C. 1, D. XXIII; Mansi, XIX, 903 (Concilium Romanum — a. 1059).

33 C. 43, C. XXIII, q. 5; Jaffé, n. 1019; Mansi, IX, 713, 715.

34 C. 5, C. XI, q. 3; II Council of Carthage (390), c. 8; Bruns, *Canones Apostolorum et Conciliorum Saeculorum IV, V, VI, VII* (2 vols., Berolini, 1839), I, 120 (hereafter cited Bruns).

35 C. 6, X, *de electione,* I, 6; Hefele-Leclercq, *Histoire des Conciles* (10 vols. in 19, Paris: Letouzey and Ané, 1907-1938), Tom. V, 2me partie, p. 1087.

reference was there made to papal elections in connection with the acceptance of a schismatic pope.[36]

In view of the above cited canons as found in the *Corpus Iuris Canonici*, it cannot be deduced with certainty that schismatics were considered excommunicated *ipso facto*. Since the consideration involved a *res odiosa*, the writer is inclined to follow the milder opinion which denies that the excommunication was incurred by the very operation of any enacted law. Schismatics were indeed subject to penalties which had to be imposed by means of a special sentence, but there is no evidence that any penalty was incurred *ipso facto*. Since the penalty had to be imposed by a special sentence, it was common only to those upon whom sentence had been passed, and consequently not all schismatics alike could be considered as falling within the category of the excommunicated.

The statement of Suarez that schismatics were excommunicated in consequence of the *Bulla Coenae* is not definite enough as to time. The early *Bullae*, in enumerating those who were excommunicated, made no explicit mention of schismatics. The reference was merely to heretics and their *fautores* and *receptatores*.[37] Even as late as 1536 there was still no mention of schismatics.[38] The earliest *Bulla* to contain an enacted excommunication against schismatics was that of Paul IV in 1559.[39] Certainly, if schismatics were under the ban of excommunication from the earliest times, as many authors contend, it seems that the Popes in their *Bullae* of excommunication would have included them prior to the year 1559. From what has been said it is evident that the status of the schismatic before the year 1559 was at most one of doubtful excommunication.

Here it is helpful to make mention of the Pamphili response

36 C. un., *de schismaticis*, V, 3, in VI° (1297); Potthast, *Regesta Pontificum Romanorum inde ab anno post Christum natum MCXCVIII ad annum MCCCIV* (2 vols., Berolini, 1874-1875), n. 24520.

37 *Bullarum Diplomatum et Privilegiorum Sanctorum Romanorum Pontificum Taurinensis Editio* (24 vols. et Appendix, Augustae Taurinorum, 1857-1872), V, 491 (Julius II, a. 1511) (hereafter cited *Bullarium*).

38 *Bullarium*, VI, 219 (Paul III).

39 *Bullarium*, VI, 552.

of June 4, 1631,[40] in regard to the penalties of the *Bulla Coenae* and their relation to the Oriental dissidents. The Pamphili response issued from the Sacred Congregation for the Propagation of the Faith in answer to a doubt presented by Capuchin missionaries working among Catholics and dissidents in the East. There arose the question whether the Oriental dissidents were liable to the penalties of the *Bulla Coenae.* The answer was in the negative, but a limitation was indicated for the following three cases:

1) if the matter touched dogmas of the faith;
2) if in his Constitutions the Pope explicitly made mention of the said subjects of the patriarchal sees, as in the case of the schismatics mentioned in the *Bullae Coenae;* and
3) if in his Constitutions he implicitly invoked legislative dispositions regarding them, as in the cases dealing with the appeal to a future council, with the bearing of arms against infidels, or with other similar matters.

Since in practice the Oriental schismatic was usually guilty of the crime of heresy, he could undoubtedly be subject to the censures of the *Bulla Coenae* imposed for errors against the faith.

As to the present status of schismatics, there are authors who consider most of the Oriental dissidents as being in good faith, and consequently as being not guilty of formal schism. This is true not only of the uncultured and illiterate Orientals, but also of the educated, for after so many years of schism they hold to many erroneous ideas about the true Church, the while they continue oblivious and unconscious of the errors they profess.[41]

Christians who were born and educated in heresy or schism, as long as they remain in good faith, are not bound by the penalties of heretics or schismatics in the internal forum in view of all lack of obstinacy on their part; however, if they are converted to the true faith after they have reached the age of fourteen years, they need absolution from the excommunication in

40 *Codicis Iuris Canonici Fontes,* cura Emi Petri Card. Gasparri Editi (9 vols., Romae [postea Civitate Vaticana]: Typis Polyglottis Vaticanis, 1923-1939 [Vols. VII-IX, ed. cura et studio Emi Iustiniani Card. Seredi]), n. 4449 (hereafter cited *Fontes).*

41 Jugie, *Theologia Dogmatica Christianorum Orientalium,* I, 23, 28.

the external forum, since in consequence of the rule expressed in canon 2200, §2, they are presumed bound by the censure.[42]

Some go even further in presuming the good faith of schismatics. The late Bishop Neveu (+ 1946), Administrator Apostolic of Moscow though at the time he resided in Paris, issued the following statement in an instruction to the Army Chaplains: "In virtue of his baptism every Orthodox becomes a member of the One and Universal Church. He therefore belongs *de jure* to the Catholic Church as long as he does not commit a formal act of schism, a mortal sin that is punished with excommunication, for excommunication is never incurred but for a mortal sin. When I am in the presence of an Orthodox Christian, I know that there are nine presumptions against one that this Christian has not committed the sin of schism. As it is morally certain that this Christian has not committed a mortal sin punishable with excommunication, and as I, as a Catholic priest, cannot affirm *a priori* that this baptized Christian is *delinquens et contumax* (can. 2241), nor that he has committed a *delictum externum, grave, consummatum, cum contumacia coniunctum* (can. 2242, §1), which alone is punished with censure, I have no right to suppose, without strong evidence, that he is severed from the communion of the faithful." [43]

C. *Notion of Communication*

Communication, as the term implies, denotes a common action, and in general may be defined as the placing of an action with another person or persons in such a way that the action, which is morally one, is participated in by both persons.[44] This notion is common to all types of communication, of which there are varying degrees and modes. In making the divisions the authors are not agreed on the terminology used to describe the

42 Beste, *Introductio in Codicem* (2. ed., Collegeville, Minn.: St. John's Abbey Press, 1944), p. 934.

43 Cf. *The Tablet*, November 11, 1939, pp. 548-549.

44 Regatillo, *Institutiones Iuris Canonici* (2 vols., Vol. I, 2. ed., 1946; Vol. II, 1942; Sal Terrae, Santander: Aldus, S. A. de Artes Graficas), II, n. 94.

various types, but the classification canonized by the Code in canon 1258 is generally followed by those who write on the subject.

Communication may occur *in profanis (in humanis)* or *in sacris (in divinis)*. These notions are expressed in English as communication in civil matters and communication in religious matters, or simply civil communication and religious communication.

The first type is that which is had in civil matters or in merely temporal affairs pertaining to social commerce, as in operations of buying and selling, at banquets, by cohabitation, in conversation, and in other similar actions.[45] The prohibition of civil communication is practically a purely historical question, for today it is not forbidden by positive ecclesiastical law except in the case of *excommunicati vitandi* (can. 2267). However, civil communication may be forbidden by virtue of the natural law when there would be danger of perversion in the faith or of scandal to others.[46] Hence, even in cases wherein it is licit, it is not always expedient, since from such communication there often arise many doubts concerning the faith, and such communication fosters indifference and is a frequent source of mixed marriages.

Religious communication is the more important and serious of the two types, for it involves a participation in the acts of religious worship. These acts may be private or public, although the present law of the Church is concerned only with acts of public religious worship which are executed in the name of a religious body by the minister of that religion.[47] *Res sacrae,* in the broad sense, are any sacred functions or prayers. Strictly considered, however, they signify functions of public worship which are properly called *res sacrae,* and hence the term *com-*

[45] Merkelbach, *Summa Theologiae Moralis ad Mentem D. Thomae et ad Normam Iuris Novi* (3. ed., 3 vols., Parisiis: Typis Desclée de Brouwer et Soc., 1938-1939), I, n. 752 (hereafter cited *Summa Theologiae Moralis).*

[46] Sipos, *Enchiridion Iuris Canonici* (4. ed., Pécs: ex typographia "Haladás R. T.," 1940), p. 699.

[47] Cf. Souarn, *Memento de Theologie Morale a L'usage des Missionaires* (Paris: Librairie Victor Lecoffre, 1907), n. 193.

municatio in sacris is in common usage.[48] By the term *sacra* is understood sacred functions such as a public sermon, religious instructions, the administration of the sacraments, any liturgical actions, rites or sacrifices, and religious burial.[49]

Religious communication is again divided into several classes, and it is herein that the authors differ in their classification and terminology. A very convenient and appropriate division into positive and negative communication is adopted by some authors.[50] This is not the terminology used by the Code, but is a more general division and thus includes the terms and divisions of canon 1258.

Positive communication is the religious communication of Catholics in the sacred functions of non-Catholics, whether the communication be formal (active participation) or material (passive presence). Negative communication, on the other hand, is the religious communication of non-Catholics in the sacred functions of Catholics. Canon 1258 is concerned merely with positive communication.

It is appropriate to note here that the present dissertation is concerned principally with positive communication, with special reference to schismatics. Its purpose is to determine the conduct of Catholics permissible at the sacred functions of schismatics. However, since negative communication does involve a true religious communication, that matter, too, will be given some treatment in the final chapter of the present work.

Positive communication, as stated, is divided into active participation and passive presence. Active participation occurs when one positively places an act of worship simultaneously

48 Vermeersch-Creusen, *Epitome Iuris Canonici*, II, n. 576; Regatillo, *Institutiones Iuris Canonici*, II, n. 94; cf. De Meester, *Juris Canonici et Juris Canonico-Civilis Compendium* (nova editio, 3 vols., Brugis: Desclée de Brouwer et Soc., 1921-1928), II, Pars I, n. 1252 (hereafter cited *Compendium)*.

49 Sipos, *loc. cit.;* Merkelbach, *Summa Theologiae Moralis*, I, n. 752.

50 Cf. Prümmer, *Manuale Theologiae Moralis* (5. ed., 3 vols., Friburgi Brisgoviae: Herder and Co., 1928), I, n. 522; *Dictionnaire de Droit Canonique* (3 vols., ed. A. Villien, E. Magnin, A. Amanieu, R. Naz, Paris: Librairie Letouzey et Ané, 1924—), III, 1091.

with a schismatic and in the rite of schismatics. It would consist in making gestures, movements, or ceremonial signs which from custom are acknowledged as implying the profession of a false sect or as signifying the practice of a false cult.[51] One would assist or communicate actively by performing such external acts as paying attention with religious decorum, or participating in those things which the other assembled persons do for the purpose of placing an act of worship.[52]

Active participation is often called formal communication, and the terms are practically synonymous.[53] The Code, in using the term *active*, connotes the same notion as that of a formal communication.[54] The division into formal and material communication introduces a distinction with which the field of Moral Theology is more properly concerned. That distinction is of relatively little importance in the present dissertation, which proposes to consider the *communicatio in sacris* from the strictly canonical viewpoint. The term *active* emphasizes the external action, whereas the term *formal* emphasizes the internal assent, which either may be explicit or at least implied in the action which is performed.

Active participation is always considered formal when one is acting freely, for it is impossible to separate the intention of assisting at a non-Catholic rite from an action that of itself at least implicitly contains a profession of a false worship. If the act which is placed signifies a false form of worship and is interpreted as an act of false worship by those who witness it, then no form of internal intention can justify that action. It is unlawful to simulate active assistance in the worship of non-Catholics, for, though the attending fact of simulation indeed precludes the internal active participation, yet the outwardly

51 Regatillo, *Institutiones Iuris Canonici*, II, n. 94.

52 Blat, *Commentarium Textus Codicis Iuris Canonici* (5 vols. in 6, Romae: ex Typographia Pontificia in Instituto Pii IX, 1921-1934, Lib. II, 2. ed., 1921; Lib. III, Partes II-VI, 2. ed., 1934), Lib. III, Partes II-VI, p. 165 (hereafter cited *Commentarium*, IV).

53 De Meester, *Compendium*, III, Pars I, n. 1252.

54 Noldin-Schmitt, *Summa Theologiae Moralis* (27. ed., 3 vols., Oeniponte Lipsiae: Sumptibus et Typis Feliciani Rauch, 1940), II, n. 34.

executed act would stand as a semblance of active assistance and participation in the function of that rite, and thus the manifestation of a profession of faith would result in consequence of the material participation in the act of worship.[55]

Active religious participation with non-Catholics is illicit, since it is opposed to the virtue of faith. By the virtue of faith one is bound to profess the true faith and never to deny it by thought, word or action. In forbidden religious communication there is contained at least an implicit denial of the true faith through the actions one performs. This is certainly true when the performed rite is non-Catholic in nature, so that it is not merely a Catholic rite exercised by a non-Catholic sect.

It is possible that some ambiguity may arise with reference to the interpretation of some actions. However, there are certain actions which either by their very nature or through their institution and use very clearly signify religious worship, such as a genuflection, the striking of the breast, an incensation, and similar actions.[56] In these actions there is no doubt that in their use an act of worship is signified. If the actions reflect a false worship, then one who communicates in these actions is formally participating in the false worship betokened by them, and hence all participation in such actions is forbidden.

There are acts which of themselves are indifferent, such as standing or sitting, but they can become vested with a religious signification. If they be vested with this signification in given circumstances, then they cannot be performed in union with others during the performance of a false rite. Thus, for example, though the act of sitting is in itself an indifferent action, yet if one took a seat among a congregation of Quakers as if meditating with them and joining in their rites, one would be taking an active part in this unlawful form of worship.[57]

Another form of positive communication is passive presence, which occurs when one is merely materially or corporally present

55 McHugh-Callan, *Moral Theology* (2 vols., New York City: Joseph F. Wagner, 1929), I, n. 965.

56 Suarez, *Opera Omnia*, Tr. I *De fide*, disp. XIV, sect. 4, n. 2.

57 McHugh-Callan, *Moral Theology*, I, n. 966.

at the sacred functions without participating or taking part in any way in the non-Catholic rites. This is called a material communication or a passive presence. It is not properly called a passive communication. Some authors apply this latter term to the act of tolerating non-Catholics at the sacred functions of Catholics.[58] However, in the present dissertation this will be referred to as negative communication. Thus all confusion between the notions of passive presence and passive communication can effectively be precluded. It is to be noted that the Code uses the term passive presence rather than passive communication.[59]

Passive presence is opposed to formal communication or active presence. It obtains when one is present for some ceremony without approving of it, or in fact disapproving of many things which take place during the ceremonies.[60] Passive presence consists in this, that a person internally preserves the true faith, and externally so conducts himself as to furnish evidence that he is in no way joining in the rite which is being celebrated.[61]

Today the Church in its laws is concerned only with the public communication of Catholics with non-Catholics. If this communication is private as, for example, between a Catholic and a non-Catholic spouse, who would recite the Lord's Prayer in common, the licitness of the action would be governed not by any ecclesiastical law, but by the divine law. Hence, the action would be licit as long as there were no danger of perversion or

58 Cf. Wernz-Vidal, *Ius Canonicum ad Codicis Normam Exactum* (7 tomes in 8 vols., Romae: apud aedes Universitatis Gregorianae, 1927-1946; Tom. IV, Vols. I-II, 1934-1935), Tom. IV, Vol. I, n. 347, n. 435, ftn. 4 (hereafter cited *Ius Canonicum);* Noldin-Schmitt, *Summa Theologiae Moralis,* II, n. 34.

59 Cf. can. 1258, §2.

60 Coronata, *Institutiones Iuris Canonici ad usum utriusque cleri et scholarum* (5 vols., Romae: Domus Editorialis Marietti, Vol. II, 2. ed., 1939), II, n. 836 (hereafter cited *Institutiones).*

61 Cocchi, *Commentarium in Codicem Iuris Canonici ad Usum Scholarum* (8 vols. in 5, Taurinorum Augustae: Ex Officina Libraria Marietti, Vol. V, 4. ed., 1938), V, n. 93 (hereafter cited *Commentarium).*

scandal.[62] Private worship in which there is no admixture of error cannot be called non-Catholic worship.

There are other words which are akin to the term *communicatio,* and which are often used interchangeably in a discussion on this matter. Two words of similar meaning are *participatio* and *cooperatio.*[63] To co-operate means to act jointly with another. It is the most general and inclusive of the three terms. *Cooperatio* is the genus of which *communicatio* is the species. All communication is a co-operation, but not all co-operation is a communication. *Cooperatio* includes the notion not only of a participation of more than one person in the same specific action, but also of more than one person in distinct actions which are morally united. To participate means to partake of, or to have in common with others a share in the same specific action. In the present connection the term *communicatio* has the same meaning as *participatio,* namely, a sharing in common. However, there is a shade of a difference, especially in the Latin. Both denote a sharing in the same specific action, but *communicatio* connotes a formal participation, while *participatio* abstracts from the formal or material character of the action.

These divisions and explanations have been made in relation to the present law of the Church. Nevertheless they will prove helpful also for gaining a clearer understanding regarding the development of the legislation which reflects the attitude of the Church with regard to religious communication.

62 Beste, *Introductio in Codicem,* p. 615; Genicot-Salsmans, *Institutiones Theologiae Moralis* (14. ed., 2 vols., Bruxellis: L'edition Universelle, S. A., 1939), I, n. 198, p. 149, ftn. 1; Jone, *Moral Theology,* translated by Adelman (Westminster, Md.: Newman Bookshop, 1945), n. 125; De Meester, *Compendium,* III, Pars I, n. 1252, p. 153, ftn. 3.

63 Cf. Bouscaren, "Co-operation with Non-Catholics" — *Theological Studies,* III (1942), 512.

Article II — Communication with Schismatics in the Early Councils and in the Decree of Gratian

A. *Communication with Schismatics in the Early Councils*

In relation to schismatics there was in the early Church little legislation which forbade a communication in religious worship with them. The Council of Laodicaea (343-381) forbade all prayer to be undertaken in common with heretics or schismatics.[64] The remaining canons which this Council devoted to the question of communication treated specifically of heretics, no mention being made of schismatics.[65] This seems to indicate that the restrictions which were placed on schismatics were less stringent than those which were placed on heretics.

In the purported IV Council of Carthage[66] one canon contained an exhortation to clerics to shun the banquets and gatherings of heretics and schismatics.[67] This canon was later included in the *Decree* of Gratian, but conjointly with canons 71 and 72 of the same purported Council of Carthage. These latter canons had referred solely to heretics, making no mention whatsoever of schismatics. However, as found in the Decree of Gratian, the laws contained in them were made to apply likewise to schismatics. Whether this be indicative of the interpretation given to them either by the commentators or as a result of the tradi-

64 Can. 33: "Quod non oportet una cum haereticis vel schismaticis orare." — Mansi, II, 569; Bruns, I, 77.

65 Mansi, II, 569 (can. XXXII); II, 565 (cans. VI, IX).

66 Mansi called this a Provincial Council and placed the date around the year 436. The canons of this purported Council are also incorporated in the *Statuta Ecclesiae Antiqua,* which may be assigned with certainty to the end of the fifth or the beginning of the sixth century. It seems equally certain that the supposed IV Council of Carthage was not the source of the various statutes which are incorporated in the *Statuta Ecclesiae Antiqua;* cf. Denzinger-Bannwart-Umberg, *Enchiridion Symbolorum, Definitionum et Declarationum de Rebus fidei et Morum* (21.-23. ed., Friburgi Brisgoviae: Herder and Co., 1937), p. 68, ftn. 1 (hereafter cited Denzinger).

67 Can. 70: "Clericus haereticorum et schismaticorum tam convivia quam sodalitates evitet aequaliter." — Bruns, I, 148; Mansi, III, 957. Note: Bruns and Mansi have "haereticorum *et* schismaticorum"; the *Decretum* of Gratian in c. 35, C. XXIV, q. 3, has "*aut.*"

tional understanding of these canons is difficult to establish.[68] Regarding this decree as found in the *Decree* of Gratian the *glossae* simply indicated that the law in its expression was but a crystallization of the general custom and usage to which the Church had traditionally adhered.

B. *Communication with Schismatics in the Decree of Gratian*

In the *Decree* of Gratian there is incorporated a text which bears directly on communication with schismatics in religious worship.[69] It is a letter of Pope Pelagius I (556-561), written during the Three Chapter Controversy in response to a plea on the part of the faithful that schismatics be not expelled and that it be acknowledged as permissible to assist at their sacrifices. The faithful had acted indifferently toward the sacrifices of Catholics and of schismatics, and they gave these reasons in support of their actions, as related in the *glossae:*

1) wrong-doers should be tolerated;
2) these schismatics had been separated from the Church for a long time; and
3) their wrong-doing was the result of their ignorance of the law or of their simplicity of mind.

Pope Pelagius replied to each of these arguments. He concluded his letter with a prohibition against communicating in religious worship with schismatics. The *glossae* were more concerned with the reasons underlying the action of Pope Pelagius than with his consequent prohibition against communicating in the sacrifices of schismatics. With reference to the first offered argument they stated that the principle there enunciated could be applied in occult cases, but not in public cases. As to the second, they maintained that Pope Pelagius contended that the duration of their schism was not a factor which decreased their guilt, but rather one which increased it, since it actually entailed

68 "Clericus haereticorum, etc. [ut supra]. Eorum conventicula non ecclesia, sed conciliabula sunt appellanda. Cum eis neque orandum est, neque psallendum." — c. 35, C. XXIV, q. 3.

69 C. 34, C. XXIV, q. 1; Jaffé, n. 994.

a greater danger of perversion when the faithful communicated with them. With regard to the third, they averred that the reasoning was likewise held to be baseless, for in their ignorance the schismatics should have been submissive, when instead they boldly resisted the Apostolic See. Consequently the Pope forbade all public communication in their sacrifices. However, it was also to be noted that no express censure was attached to the violation of this papal enactment.

In another *glossa* which dealth with a text which quoted a letter of St. Augustine (354-430) against the Donatists, it was stated that anyone who in danger of death had received baptism at the hands of a heretic could only be praised for his action, but that anyone who chose freely to receive baptism in schism or heresy was not to be deemed a Catholic, but a wicked and obstinate person.[70]

In regard to the reception of orders, Pope Urban II (1088-1099) decreed (1089) that those who in the past had been ordained by schismatic bishops who were once Catholic were to be received *misericorditer* when they returned to the Church, if their life and learning commended them, but that those who for the future would permit themselves to receive orders at the hands of schismatics were not to be considered worthy of the same concession. The Pope further declared that only inasmuch as the consideration of mercy and the strict demand of necessity had motivated his action was it to have any application in the future, for he wanted no inroads to be made against the sacred canons, and he desired that they should regain their erstwhile strength and force. Once the emergency was past, then also whatever he had done to meet that emergency would no longer have operative effect. It was the imminent threat of far-reaching harm that had compelled him to mitigate the severity of the law.[71]

70 C. 40, C. XXIV, q. 1; *De Baptismo contra Donatistas,* Lib. I, caput II — *MPL,* XLIII, 110.

71 C. 5, C. IX, q. 1; Jaffé, n. 5393; Mansi, XX, 667.

CHAPTER II

FROM THE DECREE OF GRATIAN TO THE BEGINNING OF THE XVII CENTURY

Article I — Laws Concerning Schismatics in the Decretals of Gregory IX

In the Decretals of Gregory IX (1227-1241) there appears an enactment regarding the ordination of schismatics.[1] The original source is canon 2 of the III General Council of the Lateran (1179), held under Pope Alexander III (1159-1181). In the early years of the reign of Alexander there had occurred a schism in the Church of Rome, and in consequence of it a certain Octavian had been elected Pope (Victor IV, 1159-1164), to whom in turn there succeeded a certain Guido (Paschal III, 1164-1168). These schismatics had ordained many of their adherents to the episcopate. A number of ecclesiastics had also freely taken an oath to adhere to the schism. A large-scale alienation of church property had followed, and a considerable number of benefices and dignities had been bestowed upon the schismatic ecclesiastics.

Concerning all these things the III Latern Council took action by declaring that the ordinations performed by these schismatic Popes were null and void, as also the ordinations conferred by those who had been consecrated by them. The incumbents of the conferred benefices and the recipients of the bestowed dignities were to be deprived of them. The alienation of the ecclsiastical property was without canonical effect, and all the alienated properties and goods were to be returned to the Church without any charge. Those who freely had sworn to adhere to the schism were declared to be suspended from their sacred orders and dignities.

1 C. 1, X, *de schismaticis et ordinatis ab eis,* V, 8; Hefele-Leclercq, *Histoire des Conciles,* Tom. V, 2me partie, p. 1088.

The canon used the term *"irritas"* in reference to the ordinations conferred by the schismatics. However, the term was to be understood in reference to the execution or the exercise of these orders, rather than to their validity.[2] The glossators, in commenting on this canon, were evidently more concerned with the question of the validity of the orders than with the question of the *communicatio in sacris.*

The question of communication with schismatics took on greater proportions with the separation of the Eastern Churches from the Holy See. However, legislation was still very meager with regard to the Oriental schismatics, and it was not until the close of the XVI century that general laws were instituted for the sake of regulating the relations between schismatic churches and the Church of Rome. Perhaps this was due to the fact that the Church was hesitant to cut off the Orientals entirely, lest the hoped-for attempt at reunion be made more difficult.

Two attempts were made at a reunion during the XIII and XV centuries respectively. Though on the surface the attempts seemed successful, they produced no lasting effects. The first effort was made on the part of Gregory X (1271-1276) at the II General Council of Lyons in 1274, and the second, at the General Council of Florence in 1439 under Eugene IV (1431-1447). The first reunion effected at Lyons lasted about eight years. The second reunion was repudiated formally by the Patriarch of Constantinople in 1472, and the other churches within this patriarchate followed the Patriarch's lead. In the other patriarchates, however, the reunion seemed to last about a century. Such being the circumstances, it is easy to see how there was much uncertainty among the faithful in general as to just what was the status of the Eastern Church. In view of these facts the Church was itself undoubtedly hesitant in enacting legislation concerning communication with its members. Consequently there is no evidence of any general legislation in this matter in the *Corpus Iuris Canonici.*

2 *Glossa Ordinaria* ad c. 1, X, *de schismaticis et ordinatis ab eis,* V, 8, s. v. *irritas.*

Article II — Particular Law Governing the Communication with Schismatics

In certain particular territories, however, where the question was one of major importance, there is evidence of laws which forbade communication with schismatics. A particular phase of the communication *in sacris* was reflected in the celebration of mixed marriages. While marriage was a contract, it was also a sacrament, and hence there was necessarily a communication between the contracting parties when the rite was performed. It was against such unions that the Council of Pressburg in Hungary (1309) passed a statute.[3] The decrees of this Council were confirmed by Clement VI (1342-1352) in 1346.

The fact that such legislation was passed is an indication that the practice of intermarriage between Catholics and non-Catholics had begun to assert itself. The prohibition was directed not at the party who contracted the marriage, but at those who presumed to give in marriage their daughter, their niece, or any other blood relative. The danger of the Catholic party's perversion from the faith was the reason that motivated this prohibition. The law did not imply an invalidating effect for the union which was contracted, but to its prohibition it attached an excommunication incurred *ipso facto* and the privation of Christian burial as a sanction against the violation of the law. The bishop was commanded to denounce the offender as an excommunicate with whom all association was to be shunned, and if thereupon the delinquent did not repent, the bishop could proceed against him as against one who favored heresy.

Article III — Schismatics as Included under the Laws Governing Communication with Excommunicates

Thus far the legislation that directly concerned schismatics has been considered. It has been seen that the sentence of excommunication was not applied to the general body of schis-

3 Mansi, XXV, 222. In the present, Pressburg is perhaps better identified as Bratislava in Czechoslovakia.

matics. However, in several instances, as happened in the case of papal decrees against the leaders and instigators of schism, the sentence of excommunication was passed on individual schismatics, and communication with them was to be shunned as in the case of all other excommunicates.

Some general notion of how such schismatics were considered can be gleaned from the general attitude of the Church toward communication with those who were excommunicated. In the Middle Ages the communication with those outside the Church was forbidden in almost every form. All persons under the ban of major excommunication were considered *vitandi*. They were to be shunned by the faithful not only in matters touching religion, but even in the things that fell within the sphere of daily association.[4] The question of communication *in sacris* was given little consideration, for it followed *a fortiori* as a conclusion from the fact that communication *in profanis* was so severely censured.

There was, however, a relaxation of this stern discipline under Gregory VII (1073-1085), who allowed some exceptions which favored wives, servants, and close relatives in their respective association with their husbands, masters, and near of kin.[5] But for the general body of the faithful the same restrictions continued unrelaxed until the Constitution *Ad evitanda* of Pope Martin V (1417-1431) in 1418.[6] This Constitution ushered in a marked departure from the old legislation, for it practically abolished all the previous prohibitions on the communication *in profanis*.

Just what kind of communication with excommunicates had been forbidden becomes evident from the following mnemonic:

Sí pro delíctis anáthema quís effíciátur
Ós, oráre, valé, commúnio, ménsa negátur.

This concise arrangement presented a practical summary of a

[4] Hyland, *Excommunication, Its Nature, Historical Development and Effects*, The Catholic University of America Canon Law Studies, n. 49 (Washington, D. C.: The Catholic University of America, 1928), p. 35.

[5] Cf. c. 103, C. XI, q. 3.

[6] *Fontes*, n. 45.

canon found in Gratian.[7] Still, it was not in the *glossa* on the *Decree* of Gratian, but in the *glossa* on the *Liber Sextus*, that this versified summary appeared.[8] The couplet is attributed to Hostiensis by the glossator.[9]

Communication with excommunicates has not been treated in detail, since for several reasons schismatics could not in general be properly considered as in a class with the excommunicated. If one examines the commentary on Gratian's treatment of communication with the excommunicated, one will notice that the comments of the glossators were concerned not so much with the question of communication, as with the type of excommunicated persons who were to be shunned.[10] Some canons spoke directly of the forbidden communication with excommunicates, but treated rather of the excusing causes, such as ignorance and necessity, which exempted one from the prohibition, and hence also from the consequent penalty. An example of this appears in a letter of Pope Nicholas I (858-867).[11] No mention at all was made of the nature of the forbidden communication. There is a similar silence on that point in the following canons in Gratian.

However, the canons were clear as to what type of excommunicated person was to be avoided. It was explicitly stated, both in the text itself and in the *glossae*, that only those who had been excommunicated by name were to be classed as *vitandi*.[12] Gratian himself stated that one had to be excommunicated by

7 *Epistola II Callisti Papae I ad omnes Galliarum Episcopos*, c. 2: "Excommunicatos quosque a sacerdotibus nullus recipiat ante utriusque partis examinationem iustam, nec cum eis in oratione, aut cibo, vel potu, aut osculo communicet, nec Ave eis dicat, quia quicumque in his vel aliis prohibitis scienter excommunicatis communicaverit, iuxta apostolorum institutionem et ipse simili excommunicationi subiaceant." — c. 17, C. XI, q. 3; Jaffé, n. 86; Mansi, I, 741.

8 *Glossa Ordinaria* ad c. 3, *de sententia excommunicationis, suspensionis, et interdicti*, V, 11, in VI°, s. v. *aliis*.

9 Cf. Hostiensis, *Summa Aurea*, p. 505.

10 Cf. *Glossa Ordinaria* ad C. XI, q. 3.

11 C. 102, C. XI, q. 3; Jaffé, n. 2800 (a. 865).

12 C. 20, C. XI, q. 3; Jaffé, n. 2037 (a. 625-638); Mansi, X, 584.

name to come under the ban of a *vitandus*.[13] The bishops were commanded publicly and openly to publish the names of those who were excommunicated, so that the faithful could not plead ignorance when associating with those who were under censure.[14]

Hence, even if it could be proved that schismatics were *ipso facto* excommunicated, this would not mean that they were to be classed among the *vitandi*. Certain schismatics were undoubtedly excommunicated publicly and by name, but in that event their exclusion from Christian society derived not from the simple fact that they were schismatics, but from the fact either that their excommunication had been publicly declared or that it had been imposed by public condemnatory sentence.

An added reason why one should hesitate to apply to schismatics the same principles that applied to the excommunicated is the difference of purpose inherent in the twofold prohibition against association or communication with schismatics and excommunicates. If one investigates this purpose with reference to excommunicates, one can readily see that the legislation which applied to the excommunicate could not equally apply to the schismatic. Schism simply demonstrated a spontaneous departure from the Church; but excommunication pointed to a positive exclusion authoritatively imposed by the Church.

The glossators did not treat in detail the principles underlying the prohibition against communication with excommunicates, but they at least noted that contumacy was the underlying factor in every excommunication. No one could be excommunicated except for contumacy.[15] It was precisely for the sake of breaking this contumacy that the Church forbade the faithful to communicate with the excommunicated. Suarez listed the reasons, both intrinsic and extrinsic, which motivated the Church in inflicting censures on her delinquent subjects.[16] Among them he mentioned the removal of contumacy and the observance of ecclesiastical obedience, which the Church sought to

13 Cc. 21, 24, 26, C. XI, q. 3.

14 C. 20, C. XI, q. 3; Jaffé, n. 2037; Mansi, X, 584.

15 *Glossa Ordinaria* ad c. 31, C. XI, q. 3.

16 Suarez, *Opera Omnia*, disp. VI, *de effectibus censurae*, sect. 8.

achieve in consequence of its act of depriving the delinquents of a spiritual good. Added reasons were the preservation of the honor and the safeguarding of the dignity of the Church, as also the securing of the good of the rest of the faithful — lest they too become infected.[17] With the exception, perhaps, of the protection of the faithful, and of the observance of ecclesiastical obedience, the recounted reasons were not the principal motives underlying the prohibition of the Church against communication with schismatics.

In an Instruction of the Congregation for the Propagation of the Faith for the missionaries of the Orient,[18] the reasons for prohibiting communication *in sacris* with schismatics (and heretics) were stressed as deriving from the natural and the positive divine law. These reasons were:

1) the danger of perversion from the Catholic Faith;
2) the danger of participation in a heretical or schismatical rite; and
3) the danger for the occasioning of scandal.

If the status of an excommunicated person be contrasted with that of a schismatic, it can easily be seen that the laws of the Church regarding the one group would hardly have been efficacious when applied to the other. The excommunicate was, under ordinary circumstances, an individual who lived in a community which was largely Catholic. Communication with such a one was forbidden for the sake of bringing him back to repentance. In the case of the schismatic, especially if considered in the person of the Eastern schismatic, the same prohibition of the Church would have had little if any effect, for he lived in a community that was almost exclusively schismatic. If the faithful were forbidden to associate with him, the measure was prin-

17 Smith, *Elements of Ecclesiastical Law* (3 vols., Vol. III, 3. ed., New York: Benziger Brothers, 1888), III, 276, 277.

18 S. C. de Prop. Fide, instr. (pro Mission. Orient.), a. 1729 — *Fontes*, n. 4507; *Collectanea S. Congregationis de Propaganda Fide* (2 vols., Romae: Typographia Polyglotta S. C. de Propaganda Fide, 1907), n. 311 (hereafter cited *Coll. S. C. P. F.).*

cipally a defensive one, namely, to protect the faith of the Catholic party.

Another difference to be noted is the following. Once the legislation of the Church became ineffective in its prohibition against communication with excommunicates, it had to be relaxed, for the severe penalties attached to the violation of the forbidden communication were bringing more harm to the faithful than benefit for the excommunicated. Thus Gregory VII (1079) relaxed the discipline with respect to wives, servants, and closely related persons in the matter of association respectively with their husbands, their masters, and their near relatives, for through their association the former had fallen a prey to excommunication, and had made little, if any, effort to seek absolution from that censure. But the Church's legislation which forbade communication *in sacris* with schismatics was very closely connected with the principles of the natural and the positive divine law, and accordingly could not yield to similar relaxation.

In view of these essential differences between the schismatic and the excommunicate, it was indicated that the schismatic should be considered as being in a distinct category. That there was little specific legislation regarding the question of communication with schismatics prior to the great Eastern Schism, and even for some centuries later, is quite understandable, for schism as such had not been the principal issue in those earlier centuries.

CHAPTER III

FROM THE BEGINNING OF THE XVII CENTURY TO THE CODE OF CANON LAW

ARTICLE I — THE REPLIES AND THE INSTRUCTIONS OF THE SACRED CONGREGATIONS

With reference to the matter here to be considered, the principal sources of general legislation subsequent to the completion of the *Corpus Iuris Canonici* were the responses and the instructions of the Holy Office and of the Congregation for the Propagation of the Faith. These documents cover the span of time ranging from the year 1626[1] down to the present. During this period important conciliar legislation in regard to schismatics was on the wane. It yielded its place to the decrees and the instructions of the various Roman Congregations.

In the matter of forbidden communication two Popes, Clement VIII (1592-1605) and Benedict XIV (1740-1758), issued documents containing legislation of some importance. Particular councils in the East also treated the same point. Not only were abuses condemned, but also some definite sanctions were added in aid of the enforcement of the new enactments. However, in the main it was the Sacred Congregations which, through their decrees, responses, and instructions, stressed the important principles in accordance with which the question of communication with schismatics was to be governed.

The Sacred Congregations concerned with the *communicatio in divinis* were the Holy Office and the Sacred Congregation for

1 Cf. S. C. de Prop. Fide, 1 iun. 1626 — *Codificazione Canonica Orientale, Fonti* (Serie I-III, Civitate Vaticana: Tipografia Poliglotta Vaticana, 1930—), Series I, I, 73 (hereafter cited *Fonti).* In this document the Sacred Congregation commanded the Nuncio to Poland to prevent in every possible way the joint synod of schismatics and Ruthenian Catholics, for there could be no communication between the light and the darkness, and such assemblies usually produced greater discord and enmity than peace and harmony. Note: In so far as Series I of the *Fonti* is used exclusively in the present work, no specific reference will be made to this series in the citations.

the Propagation of the Faith, since the matter was one that touched on faith and morals, or one that called for special regulation in the mission countries of the Orient. The primarily treated questions related to the *communicatio in divinis,* although occasionally instructions were given relative to the *communicatio in profanis.* The instructions furnished the general norms and directions which were to govern the question of the *communicatio in divinis* in all its usual aspects. The responses shaped the application of the norms and the directions to suit them to particular problems, principally those which arose in connection with the administration and the reception of the sacraments.

These decisions of the Sacred Congregations do not imply the enactment of positive ecclesiastical law, but interpret and apply the natural law in the matter of religious communication.[2] As interpretations they are of great value for determining the principles of operation in the relations of Catholics with schismatics. In greater part they are responses to particular questions, and so are to be applied only to the cases in question. However, with reference to similar or parallel cases the principles enunciated in these responses can be adduced as a safe norm to follow.

It is to be noted also that the present law of the Code in no way militates against the binding force of these particular responses. Since these particular replies and instructions are interpretations of the natural law, they are still cited today by the post-Code authors in interpreting the law of the Code as expressed in canon 1258.

In the historical treatment of these responses there will not be made a complete enumeration and study of them, since they would have to be cited again in the canonical commentary, and this would lead to needless repetition and cross references. Consequently, each response will be considered at the point at which its subject matter is treated in the canonical commentary. In the present chapter it will be sufficient to consider a few of the more general responses and instructions.

[2] Merkelbach, *Summa Theologiae Moralis,* I, n. 753, p. 582.

Article II — General Norms Governing Communication with Schismatics

The first Instruction presenting some of the general norms governing communication with schismatics is that of the Holy Office of May 9, 1668.[3] It is a rather lengthy Instruction, which enumerates the acts which are indifferent in themselves and also the acts which of their nature are forbidden. From this Instruction it is to be gathered that there are certain actions which, even considered in the light of attending circumstances, are indifferent relative to signifying the worship of a false religion, and hence can be permitted, e. g., to act as sponsor for a heretical child who is to be baptized according to the Catholic rite. However, there are other actions which are indeed indifferent, but nevertheless definitely signify, either of themselves or in consequence of the attendant circumstances, the worship of a false religion, and consequently are not to be permitted, e. g., to give one's child over to heretics to be educated and instructed by them. But even an indifferent action which does not signify a false worship can be permitted only where there is no contempt of the faith, no scandal, and no danger of perversion from the faith.

On April 10, 1696, the Congregation for the Propagation of the Faith in a reply to the Italo-Greeks instructed the Archbishop of Philadelphia, Miletius Typaldus, that it was not permitted for him to communicate with schismatics in rites and ceremonies which in any way involved error, schism, or the suspicion of either, or in the administration and the reception of the sacraments. In other matters, if there was neither scandal nor offense to Catholics, he could follow the counsel of theologians.[4]

A doubt was presented to the Congregation for the Propagation of the Faith, namely, whether it was licit, and in what case and under what precautions, for Catholics to communicate with schismatics and heretics, to go to their churches, and to be present at their ecclesiastical functions. The response of the Congregation was very general.[5] It stated that for a solution of

3 *Fonti,* I, 81.

4 *Fonti,* II, 81.

5 9 iul. 1723 — *Fonti,* II, 85.

these doubts the particular facts and circumstances would have to be known. However, the general principle was always applicable, namely, that Catholics must in every way abstain from acts which would approve a false sect, from acts of communication in a schismatic rite, from acts entailing the danger of perversion, and from acts which would offer the occasion of scandal. If any further doubts remained, the questioners were to resolve them by consulting the doctrine of approved theologians and of experienced missionaries.

In 1729 a similar response[6] was given for the mission countries. In a substantially similar preamble it was stated that it is morally impossible to furnish any general rule which would apply to any and every group of people, to any and every region, and to any and every period of time. This much, however, could be said, namely, that the *communicatio in divinis* with heretics and schismatics was in practice regularly to be considered illicit, either in view of the likelihood of a participation in a heretical or a schismatical rite, or on account of the danger that scandal would be taken, or the occasion for scandal would be given. These circumstances in practice regularly attended the *communicatio in divinis* with heretics and schismatics, and hence such a communication was forbidden by the natural and the positive divine law. As a consequence there was no possibility of the granting of a dispensation, nor was there any subterfuge that would excuse one in such an act of communication, as long as such circumstances prevailed in a case.

Scarcely ever could one expect among the heterodox the existence of a rite which was not tainted with some error in the matter of faith, since they venerated schismatics and observed the feasts of those who died in schism. They commemorated schismatic patriarchs and bishops in their liturgy, and commended them as preachers of the Catholic faith. There could ordinarily be no pretext in justification of even a mere material assistance; such assistance also was *ipso facto* interdicted, for it too implied under usual circumstances the presence of a moral

6 *Fontes*, n. 4507; *Fonti*, II, 85.

danger or the likely threat of scandal. The reason that was adduced as making such communication at all allowable was the persecution to which the Catholics would otherwise be subjected by schismatics or heretics. Missionaries were instructed to see just to what degree this persecution or the imminent threat of it extended, whether, namely, there was question of a real persecution, or perhaps of a mere inquiry, nettling though it might be, regarding the faith to which Catholics pledged their adherence.

Such as had communicated *in divinis* with Greek schismatics were to be refused the sacrament of penance outside of a case of extreme necessity.[7]

The unbidden, unconstrained, and voluntary attendance of Protestants at Catholic services could be tolerated, but Catholics could not positively invite them to attend, for through such an invitation they would make themselves co-operators in a forbidden *communicatio in divinis*.[8] It was permitted for Greek schismatics to be present at Catholic services and to assist materially, as long as the sacraments were not administered to them, as long as there was no active *communicatio in divinis*, and provided also that the schismatics had not been specifically invited.[9]

The Provincial Synods also passed legislation concerning *communicatio in divinis*. The Provincial Synod of the Russian province for the Greek Rite in union with the Holy See (1720) condemned the practice of going to strange pastors *(pastores extraneos)* and to their churches either for the reception of the sacraments or for the sake of satisfying a personal spiritual devotion, lest there be the appearance of taking an active part with those who were outside the fold. Ordinaries were to proceed against the delinquents as against persons suspect.[10]

[7] S. C. S. Off., 10 maii 1753 — *Fontes*, n. 804; *Fonti*, II, 97.

[8] S. C. S. Off., instr. (ad Praef. Mission. Tripol.) mense ian. 1763 — *Fontes*, n. 812; *Coll. S. C. P. F.*, n. 447; *Fonti*, II, 103.

[9] S. C. S. Off., 22 sept. 1763 — *Fontes*, n. 813; *Fonti*, II, 103.

[10] *Fonti*, XI, 155 (3); *Acta et Decreta Sacrorum Conciliorum Recentiorum, Collectio Lacensis* (7 vols., Friburgi Brisgoviae: Herder, 1870-1890), II, 22 d (hereafter cited *Coll. Lac.)*. The Synod cited here is also referred to as the Synod of Zamość.

The Provincial Syro-Maronite Synod of Mt. Lebanon (1736) stated that those who communicated *in divinis* with heretics or with schismatics, or also those who received their benedictions, which in reality were maledictions instead, made themselves alien to God. Such as received the sacraments from heretics or schismatics, or frequented their churches for services, were to be very seriously punished by the ordinary.[11]

There were also two papal documents of note concerning *communicatio in sacris*. Clement VIII (1592-1605), in his Instruction *"Sanctissimus"* of August 31, 1595,[12] stated that those who had received ordination at the hands of schismatic bishops who apart from their schismatic status were properly consecrated — the necessary form having been observed — did indeed receive orders, but not the right to exercise them.

Benedict XIV (1740-1758) confirmed this doctrine of Clement VIII in the Constitution *"Etsi pastoralis"* of May 26, 1742.[13] On the question of schismatic ordinations these two papal documents present a practically identical wording. Not only was the recognized validity of schismatic orders established, but further points were clarified. Schismatic bishops were not to be admitted for the conferring of orders or for the administration of other sacraments.

Article III — Ecclesiastical Sanctions

There is no evidence that in the universal law of the Church any censures were attached to the violation of the prohibition against the *communicatio in divinis* with schismatics prior to the present Code of Canon Law. Canon 2319 states that a *latae sententiae* excommunication reserved to the ordinary is incurred by Catholics who contract marriage before a non-Catholic minister in violation of the prohibition of canon 1063, §1. The same censure is incurred by those who knowingly presume to offer their children to non-Catholic ministers for baptism. It is

11 *Fonti*, XII, 225; *Coll. Lac.*, II, 99 d.

12 *Fontes*, n. 179.

13 §VII, n. XIII — *Fontes*, n. 328.

doubtful whether the Constitution *"Apostolicae Sedis"* (October 12, 1869) of Pius IX (1846-1878) listed in its enacted censures the act of going before a non-Catholic minister, and the declarations of the Holy Office on this point seem to vary.[14]

In particular territories, however, censures were in force against the forbidden *communicatio in sacris* before the time of the present Code of Canon Law. The III Plenary Council of Baltimore (1884) enacted a *latae sententiae* excommunication reserved to the ordinary for an attempted marriage on the part of Catholics before a non-Catholic minister.[15]

An undetermined *ferendae sententiae* penalty was enacted by the Syro-Maronite Synod of Mt. Lebanon (1736) with potential application to those who had received the sacraments from heretics and schismatics or had frequented their churches.[16] There was an obligation on the part of the ordinary or the parish priest to denounce one who communicated *in divinis* with heretics or schismatics or infidels. The denunciation was to be made to the Patriarch.[17] Those who defected from the faith into schism, schismatics, and those who withdrew from the obedience due to the Roman Pontiff and the Most Reverend Patriarch, the *"fautores, receptores, eis credentes et generaliter quilibet illorum defensores,"* those who received the sacraments from heretics, those who commemorated their leaders who had been condemned by the Church, or venerated them as saints — all these were cases reserved to the Most Reverend Patriarch.[18]

14 Schenk, *The Matrimonial Impediments of Mixed Religion and Disparity of Cult,* The Catholic University of America Canon Law Studies, n. 51 (Washington, D. C.: The Catholic University of America, 1929), p. 266; Leech, *A Comparative Study of the Constitution "Apostolicae Sedis" and the "Codex Juris Canonici,"* The Catholic University of America Canon Law Studies, n. 15 (Washington, D. C.: The Catholic University of America, 1922), pp. 91 ff.

15 *Acta et Decreta Concilii Plenarii Baltimorensis Tertii, A. D. 1884* (Baltimorae: Typis Joannis Murphy Sociorum, 1886), n. 127.

16 Pars I, cap. I, n. 4 — *Coll. Lac.*, II, 99 d; *Fonti,* XII, 225.

17 *Ibid.*, n. 6 — *Coll. Lac.*, II, 100 b; *Fonti,* XII, 349.

18 Pars. II, cap. V, *Tabella prima* — *Coll. Lac.*, II, 136; *Fonti,* XII, 1119.

In the Vicariate of Constantinople there were several reserved cases, namely, the sins committed by those who received any of the sacraments from a heretical or a schismatical minister, by those who advised recourse to such ministers for the administration of the sacraments, by those who had their marriage or *sponsalia* blessed by a heretical or a schismatical minister, by those who acted as witnesses at a marriage celebrated before a heretical minister, and, finally, by those who offered their homes as a place for the celebration of marriage in the presence of an orthodox priest.[19]

19 Souarn, *Praxis Missionarii in Oriente Servata* (Parisiis, 1911), pp. 20, 21, 170, 208 (hereafter cited *Praxis Missionarii).*

PART TWO

CANONICAL COMMENTARY

CHAPTER IV

GENERAL NORMS GOVERNING COMMUNICATION WITH SCHISMATICS

INTRODUCTION

The general norm governing the communication of Catholics with schismatics is enunciated in canon 1258 of the Code of Canon Law. This canon does not expressly mention schismatics, but uses the more general term, non-Catholic, a term which includes all those who are not of the true faith, namely, heretics, schismatics, infidels, and apostates. Consequently schismatics are comprehended in the present law, and according to the letter of the law communication with schismatics is governed in exactly the same way as communication with all other non-Catholics.

Canon 1258 is the only canon which treats directly of religious communication. It states the general principles which govern all religious communication, whether it be in regard to the sacraments or with relation to any other sacred functions. However, there are other canons which treat indirectly the matter of communication, as in the administration of the sacraments (can. 731, §2), the bestowal of blessings (can. 1149), the granting of absolution in danger of death (can. 882), and the regulation of place for the celebration of Mass (can. 823).

The Code does make a distinction between the different classes of non-Catholics (can. 1325), so that there is an essential distinction between the heretic and the schismatic. However, in the question of religious communication all non-Catholics are placed in the same category, and religious communication is equally forbidden with the one as with the other. Hence, one may wonder why the question of religious communication with schismatics is treated as a distinct topic. If one considers the literal interpretation of the law, there would seem to be no difference between the communication with heretics and the communication with schismatics.

It is true that the principles remain the same whether they be applied to heretics or to schismatics, but the difference arises in the application of these principles. In the present treatise the consideration of the circumstances and occasions attending the act of religious communication will be restricted to those factors which are common to schismatics. There are undoubtedly more occasions for religious communication with schismatics than with other non-Catholics in view of the similarity in the matter of worship of Catholics and schismatics. There is a general presumption that schismatics have valid sacraments, probably, in virtue of canon 209, even when jurisdiction is required for their valid administration,[1] which concept is something foreign in relation to most of the heretical bodies, except in the case of baptism and of matrimony. Although today one can consider schismatics as heretics, at least theoretically, they are from a practical viewpoint closer to the whole truth than any other non-Catholic body. In this respect they may be placed in a distinct category.

From another practical point of view the danger of communicating with schismatics is far greater than that with regard to other sects, because of the similarity of their rites and ceremonies to those of the Church. This is especially true in corresponding disciplines of the Oriental Catholic and "Orthodox" Churches. For this reason such communication may be more pernicious, and indifferentism may easily result. A Catholic would be more inclined and more easily persuaded to consent to communicate with schismatics than he would be were it a question of heretical worship. In view of these differences, communication with schis-

[1] Cappello, *Tractatus Canonico-Moralis De Sacramentis* (3 vols. in 6, Romae: Domus Editorialis Marietti, 1935-1945; Vol. I, 4. ed., 1945; Vol. II, pars I, 4. ed., 1944; Vol. II, pars II, 2. ed., 1942; Vol. II, pars III, 1935; Vol. III, partes I, II, 4. ed., 1939), Vol. II, pars I, n. 349 (hereafter cited *De Sacramentis).*

matics presents a distinct problem somewhat different from other types of communication.

In practice, also, there is noticeable a decided lenience in favor of the schismatic. Catholics cannot compromise with schismatics in their teachings, but there is more often manifested a more considerate attitude toward the individual schismatic than toward the heretic, who is so far from the truth. This attitude of mind has perhaps led to some abuses and practices which cannot be permitted or tolerated since they are wrong in principle, though many practices can be permitted as long as they remain short of active religious participation in schismatic rites.

Many authors today consider schismatics to be guilty also of heresy. They base their doctrine principally on the definition by the Vatican Council in 1869 of Papal infallibility. Schismatics at least by their actions imply a denial of this dogma. Many of them are in good faith, but many, too, are guilty of formal heresy. Nevertheless, this fact of the definition on Papal infallibility has not in actual practice effected a substantial change in the nature of schismatical sects. They still retain their identity, and are constituted as a group distinct from other heretical groups.

With the passing of time the gap between the Catholic Church and the Oriental schismatic churches widened, but the schismatics have retained many dogmas, traditions, and rites whereby they have much in common with Catholics at least in a practical way. Hence the problem of communication with them is still a problem distinct from that of communication with heretics, and one which accordingly is worthy of specific consideration. The Church still lives in the hope of uniting the East and the West. As long as that hope survives the Church cannot treat lightly the question of religious communication with schismatics. There are principles to be preserved, but there are also souls to be saved. The problem is a delicate one, but if it be duly understood, then souls can be saved without the sacrificing of principle in so far as human efforts can be employed to the end of securing the salvation of souls.

Article I — Active Participation
(Canon 1258, §1)

The Catholic Church is intolerant of the dogmatic errors of non-Catholics, for the opposite attitude is nothing other than indifferentism, and this is condemned by the Church.[2] Truth is one, and the Church, which has been given the commission of preserving that truth, cannot tolerate errors in faith. However, in practice the Church, with the hope of leading all people to the truth, takes a kindly attitude toward persons who are in error, and consequently it stresses the need of Christian tolerance. The Church indeed condemns error, but ever remains solicitous for the salvation of the person who is in error.[3] It exhorts its subjects to be mild in their judgment of non-Catholics, and insists that in their social obligations and ordinary human relations they perform all the duties which pertain to the law of Christian charity. However, the communication with non-Catholics cannot be carried to the point at which Catholics would expose themselves to the danger of perversion from the true faith. Hence any communication with non-Catholics which involves a danger of perversion or offers an occasion of scandal remains inherently illicit in consequence of the unchanging divine law, which cannot but disapprove of all voluntary risks for one's own true faith and of all direct occasioning of scandal for others.

Communication is forbidden in virtue of the divine law, but the Church has more clearly defined what kind of communication is forbidden and what type of participation can be permitted with non-Catholics. This law of the Church which regulates religious communication with non-Catholics is stated in canon 1258 of the Code of Canon Law. Paragraph 1 of this canon is in general a restatement, if not of the natural law itself, then certainly of the divine positive law. It reads as follows:

> *Haud licitum est fidelibus quovis modo active assistere seu partem habere in sacris acatholicorum.*

2 Sipos, *Enchiridion Iuris Canonici,* p. 699; Denzinger, nn. 1715-1718.

3 Pius IX, ex encycl. *Quanto conficiamur moerore* (ad Episcopos Italiae), 10 aug. 1863 — Denzinger, nn. 1677, 1678.

It may here again be noted that the present law of the Church is concerned with only that type of participation which is known as the *communicatio in sacris*, or religious communication. The *communicatio in profanis*, or civil communication, is forbidden by Canon Law only in the case of *vitandi*. In all other cases the licitness of civil communication must be judged in accordance with the principles of the divine law.

Schismatics as such are not *vitandi*, and hence there will be no occasion to treat of the prohibition of civil communication in regard to them. The Holy See has in the past given several responses in regard to civil communication with schismatics, but since the law of the Church today disregards the matter, the present dissertation will treat solely of religious communication. However, one should note in passing that, although civil communication is not forbidden by the ecclesiastical law, such communication is very often not expedient. Too much familiarity with non-Catholics gives rise to doubts concerning the faith, to a sense of indifferentism, and frequently leads to the contracting of mixed marriages.

Religious communication, as considered by the present law of the Church, has reference only to acts of religious worship which are public and which are exercised in a religious sect. An act is considered public when it is performed with the authorization of a non-Catholic sect. Private religious communication with individuals of a non-Catholic sect is not considered in Church law. It is governed according to the dictates of the divine law. In view of this the principal object of the present discussion will be the consideration of public religious communication with schismatics.

Active religious participation with schismatics is always intrinsically illicit.[4] The reasons for this absolute prohibition of canon 1258, §1, have their origin in the natural and positive divine law. These reasons are: 1) The Church is the only *de iure* existing true religious society in which it is licit to render to God the worship that is due Him; 2) the giving of scandal through one's quasi-approval of a false sect must be avoided; and 3) the

4 Cf. Beste, *Introductio in Codicem*, p. 614.

danger of perversion from the true faith must remain effectively neutralized.[5]

In consequence of the first reason it is illicit to assist actively or to take part in all forms of worship exercised by non-Catholics. Since Christ, our Lord, established one Church and gave it authority to teach all men, there is only one authorized way of worshipping Him.[6] Consequently, outside the true Church one cannot licitly worship the true God. Even though the rite be Catholic in form, yet when it is performed under the direction of a non-Catholic sect, then any direct participation in such a rite is illicit, except in a case of extreme necessity. It follows that the reception of the sacraments in such a rite would likewise be illicit except in a case of extreme necessity with relation to the sacraments of baptism or of penance, or also of extreme unction if the latter sacrament must supplant that of penance.[7]

The acts of religious worship performed by schismatic sects are acts of superstitious worship and hence are illicit. This follows from the nature of superstition, which denotes either the worship of a false deity or the unlawful worship of the true deity.[8] Among schismatics there is indeed a worshipping of the true deity, but the worship is paid in a manner which is unlawful. The ministers are unauthorized to perform sacred rites, and there is scarcely a sect among schismatics that is not tainted with some heretical doctrine.[9]

However, there are some authors who make the following distinction as to the intrinsic illicit nature of active religious communication.[10] They state that to perform a sacred function

5 Coronata, *Institutiones*, II, n. 835, p. 155; Blat, *Commentarium*, IV, 165.

6 Davis, *Moral and Pastoral Theology* (4. ed., 4 vols., London: Sheed and Ward, 1945), I, 282.

7 Merkelbach, *Summa Theologiae Moralis*, I, n. 755, p. 584.

8 Aertnys-Damen, *Theologia Moralis secundum doctrinam S. Alfonsi de Ligorio Doct. Ecclesiae* (13. ed., 2 vols., Romae: Marietti, 1939), I, n. 416, p. 314 (hereafter cited *Theologia Moralis*).

9 Cf. *Fontes*, n. 4507.

10 Suarez, *Opera Omnia, De fide*, disp. XXI, sect. 3, n. 5 (Suarez also cites Sancius (+ ca. 1624) and Navarrus (+ 1586) in support of his

at the same time with non-Catholics and in a non-Catholic rite is intrinsically illicit. On the other hand, to communicate with them in their sacred functions if these are administered in a Catholic rite is not illicit as such. The danger to faith and the danger of scandal which ordinarily accompany this action would, however, render the act illicit. Thus the act would be illicit even apart from the positive prohibition of the Code.

Pope Benedict XIV (1740-1758) also referred to authors in his day who considered certain types of active religious participation licit.[11] These authors did not even consider it illicit to receive the sacraments from heretics or from schismatics, although they did lay down the following conditions for such religious communication: 1) that Catholics had a very grave and urgent reason for placing such an act of religious communication; 2) that the heretical or schismatical minister who administered the sacrament be validly ordained, that he administer the sacrament in the Catholic rite, and that there be no erroneous rite added by him; 3) that this communication be not considered as an external profession of a false doctrine; and 4) that there be no scandal given. There were many who were opposed to this opinion, and it was considered not to be safe in practice. All the conditions had to be present at the same time before the religious communication could be considered as permissible, and such a situation was regarded as practically impossible of occurrence. Hence it was that the Sacred Congregations of the Holy Office and of the Propagation of the Faith always considered this kind of communication as illicit.

All types of active religious communication with non-Cath-

stand); Sporer, *Theologia Moralis* (3 vols. in 2, Venetiis: apud Nicolaum Pezzana, 1731), I, tr. 2, c. 2, sect. 3, n. 31; Vermeersch-Creusen, *Epitome Iuris Canonici*, II, n. 576; Regatillo, *Institutiones Iuris Canonici*, II, n. 94; cf. Bouscaren, "Co-operation with Non-Catholics" — *Theological Studies*, III (1942), 489.

11 Benedictus XIV, *De Synodo Dioecesana* (2. ed., 2 vols., Parmae, 1764), I, Lib. VI, c. 5, p. 134. Pope Benedict did not condemn outright the opinion of these authors, but he stated that in practice it was almost impossible to find verified all the conditions which were set by them for the lawfulness of the act in question.

olics are gravely illicit. Such assistance is intrinsically and gravely evil for a) if the worship is non-Catholic in form (as in the Mohammedan ablutions, or in the eating of the Jewish paschal lamb), it expresses a belief in a false creed symbolized in the ceremony, and b) if the worship is Catholic in form but is undertaken under the auspices of a non-Catholic body (as in the celebration of Mass by a schismatic priest), it expresses either faith in a false religious body or rebellion against the true Church.[12]

The obligation to avoid exposing oneself to the danger of perversion and to prevent giving scandal to others proceeds from the natural divine law. The positive divine law on the other hand forbids one to perform such an action which would be tantamount to at least an external denial of faith and a quasi-profession of a false sect. This prohibition is expressed in the words of our Lord: "He that shall deny me before men, I will also deny him before my Father who is in heaven."[13]

Just as one would be forbidden to profess openly his belief in a false sect, so also he is forbidden to place actions which have a religious signification and which are employed in the sacred religious functions of a false sect. Such actions imply a denial of the true faith. Even if these actions are simulated, that is, even if one has no intention of communicating formally in such a forbidden form of worship, still the actions themselves are illicit. Since they have but a single acknowledged aim, namely, to point to a form of worship, the actions will be interpreted as implying a profession of that worship. In and of themselves, then, such actions are illicit, and always and under all circumstances are forbidden.[14] If the actions were simulated, they involved an additional malice of falsehood.[15]

It had indeed been contended that it was licit to simulate false worship under certain conditions when a grave reason was

[12] McHugh-Callan, *Moral Theology,* I, p. 376, n. 964.

[13] Matthew, X, 33; Cocchi, *Commentarium,* V, n. 93, p. 179.

[14] Suarez, *De fide,* disp. XIV, sect. 1, n. 5 — *Opera Omnia,* XII, 382. (Suarez here treated of religious communication in general.)

[15] *Ibid.,* n. 6 — *Opera Omnia,* XII, 382.

present, but Suarez pointed out the fallacy of the arguments invoked in support of that doctrine.[16] When an action implied an approval and a profession of false worship, no contrary internal intention could justify the placing of such an action, no matter what the consequences might be.

Even though one should simulate an active religious participation in view of some imminent grave danger, he would be exposing himself to the danger of perversion and would be giving scandal to other Catholics. This would be especially true if the actions were repeated frequently, for such a practice would soon lead to a sense of indifferentism, to a gradual alienation from the true faith, and to a corresponding attachment to the false sect. There is question not only of a personal danger to one's own faith, but also of one's conduct as furnishing an occasion of sin to others through the scandal which is given to the weak. The latter is especially true if the one who communicates with schismatics in their form of worship is reputedly a faithful member of the Church.

Furthermore, the question is concerned not only with the fact of probable scandal for other Catholics, but also with the fact that through a Catholic's active religious communication with non-Catholics the latter are very often confirmed and strengthened in their errors.[17] There is a natural tendency on the part of non-Catholics, and especially of schismatics, to seek confirmation and support for their beliefs. They glory in affirming that they have the same sacraments, the Real Presence, the apostolic succession, and other similar marks in common with the Catholic Church. They realize wherein the difference lies, but it is a great boon to them if they see Catholics coming to their religious services and conducting themselves in a way which seems to indicate that they consider the schismatic church to be just as good as the Catholic Church. Consequently, to perform an act of religious communication would be illicit, for in so doing one would confirm the schismatic in his adherence to a false sect.

16 *Ibid.*, sect. 4, nn. 3-5 — *Opera Omnia*, XII, 391, 392.

17 Wernz-Vidal, *Ius Canonicum*, Tom. IV, Vol. I, n. 347, p. 435; Sipos, *Enchiridion Iuris Canonici*, p. 699.

His conversion to the true faith would correspondingly be made more difficult.

Active participation in any form whatsoever is forbidden, for canon 1258, §1, explicitly states *"quovis modo,"* so that to take an active part in a non-Catholic rite even by mere presence would be contrary to the ruling of the canon.[18] Thus it would be considered an active religious communication to be seated among a congregation of Quakers as if in meditation, for this action, though seemingly indifferent, would naturally have to be interpreted as an active participation in a religious rite.[19]

The phrase *partem habere,* as employed in canon 1258, §1, serves simply as a further explanation regarding the factor of active assistance. This is evident from the use of the conjunction *seu* between the word *assistere* and the phrase *partem habere.* By using the term *acatholicorum* the law of the Code comprehensively includes all those who are not of the true fold, namely, heretics, schismatics, infidels, and apostates. More precisely the *acatholici* are those who, whether baptized or unbaptized, adhere to some sect outside the Church.[20] Adherence to a sect is a necessary condition, for the law of the Church contemplates only the public religious communication. The possibility of a public religious communication with one or even a group of non-Catholics who are not members of some sect seems not admissible in fact. Prior to the law of the Code the prohibitions against religious communication contained in the numerous responses of the Holy See concerned specific sectarian groups, and principally heretical sects. But in the Code all non-Catholics are placed in the same category.

If there be some civic celebration or common cause for rejoicing in a community, Catholics must strive, in view of the prohibition of canon 1258, §1, to have separate sacred solemnities rather than join with non-Catholics in their sacred rites.[21]

18 Blat, *Commentarium,* IV, 165.

19 McHugh-Callan, *Moral Theology,* I, p. 377, n. 966.

20 De Meester, *Compendium,* III, Pars I, n. 1252, p. 153.

21 Vermeersch-Creusen, *Epitome Iuris Canonici,* II, n. 577.

Article II — Passive Participation (*Canon 1258, §2*)

Although active participation is absolutely forbidden under all circumstances, a passive participation or a material presence is permitted under certain conditions for a grave reason, as is stated in canon 1258, §2:

Tolerari potest praesentia passiva seu mere materialis, civilis officii vel honoris causa, ob gravem rationem ab Episcopo in casu dubii probandam, in acatholicorum funeribus, nuptiis similibusque solemniis, dummodo perversionis et scandali periculum absit.

As has been noted before, the Code speaks of this passive participation as a material presence, and not as a passive communication. The latter expression is more properly applied to the toleration of a non-Catholic's presence at the sacred functions of Catholics. In the present dissertation this type of communication will be referred to as a negative communication.

A passive participation or a material presence obtains when one, though corporally present, does not join in any way in the prayers and rites of the public worship of non-Catholics.[22] One exhibits a passive participation or a material presence when one is at hand as a mere spectator without giving any signs of approval. Of course a Catholic could kneel before the Blessed Sacrament in a schismatic service, but it would not be permissible for him to exhibit other signs of religious devotion which would identify him as a communicant along with the others present at the service.[23]

One who puts in but a material presence has no intention of joining in any of the acts of worship.[24] There is no intrinsic evil in such a passive presence. In and of itself the action is indifferent, but the character of its morality may become vitiated in consequence of an accompanying wrong intention. One cannot show any approval of the ceremony that is being performed, especially if it should be performed according to a non-Catholic

22 Beste, *Introductio in Codicem*, p. 614.

23 McHugh-Callan, *Moral Theology*, I, p. 379, n. 969.

24 Blat, *Commentarium*, IV, 166.

rite. One must not only preserve the true faith internally, but one must so conduct oneself that it remains evident that one in no way joins in the rite which is being observed.[25] A material presence would be impossible in relation to those ceremonies which through one's participation in them in any measure or manner necessarily imply an active participation in the sacred rites of non-Catholics.[26] Thus one could not hold a child that is being presented for baptism by a schismatic minister in accordance with his ritual. Even if one excluded the intention of assisting as sponsor and considered the action as indifferent, still the action of its very nature implies an active religious participaton.

The use of the words *tolerari potest* in canon 1258, §2, indicates that what follows is not comprehended under the prohibition enacted in paragraph 1 of the same canon. Yet the toleration of the act of passive presence is conditioned on the factor that no express approval be implied in consequence of such a presence.[27] The fact that the Church can and does tolerate a passive presence is an indication that such a participation is not inherently illicit.[28] The Church does not lend any positive approval for a passive presence; it merely tolerates such a presence, and then only under precisely indicated limitations. Hence, even this type of participation is forbidden to Catholics except under certain conditions which are expressly mentioned in the canon. The terms *civilis officii vel honoris causa* give expression to the occasion rather than to the reason or the cause which acknowledges a passive presence as permissible. These occasions, however, may very frequently if not also usually offer one a grave reason which makes a passive presence permissible.

Thus, for example, one may be an official of the state and as such be expected to be present at the funeral of a non-Catholic. The fact that he has this civil obligation occasions his presence.

25 Cocchi, *Commentarium,* V, n. 93, p. 180.

26 Coronata, *Institutiones,* II, n. 836, p. 156.

27 Blat, *Commentarium,* IV, 166.

28 Bouscaren, "Co-operation with Non-Catholics" — *Theological Studies.* III (1942), 489.

The grave cause, however, in consideration of which it becomes permissible for him to put in his presence is the fact that much harm would in all likelihood result if he absented himself from attendance at the burial service. Just reasons which could make attendance at the burial service permissible are the following:[29] 1) the bond of relationship; 2) the achievement of good will and civic co-operation through the honor bestowed in consequence of one's attendance; 3) the avoidance of enmity; 4) aversion of hostility toward the Church; 5) the preservation of social peace and tranquillity; 6) the fostering of some beneficial legislation which would greatly favor the Church; or 7) the retaining of one's position or means of employment, e. g., that of a domestic servant.

The nature of the occasion presented by the possession of civil office or the necessity of giving honor is sufficiently clear and well known in practice and customary usage among men, whether on the part of the relatives, the friends, or the associates of non-Catholics, or on the part of officials and magistrates, who must be present at non-Catholic services in consideration of the public office they hold. Because of the official position of the Catholic his presence will be interpreted as the material assistance of a civil official, and not as an act of approval for the particular form of worship in use at the ceremony.[30]

A less grave reason would suffice to make an act of attendance permissible for an unknown individual when he is present for reason of study to observe a certain rite or to hear the chant of non-Catholics. Of course, a particular law such as exists in Rome with reference to Protestant churches could prohibit even such an attendance.[31]

The more important the sacred function is, and the more closely it pertains to the non-Catholic worship, the graver also must be the reason which will suffice for making a material presence a tolerated and permissible act.[32] The functions of re-

29 Beste, *Introductio in Codicem*, p. 614; Blat, *Commentarium*, IV, 166.

30 Wernz-Vidal, *Ius Canonicum*, Tom. IV, Vol. I, n. 347, p. 435.

31 Regatillo, *Institutiones Iuris Canonici*, II, p. 56, n. 94.

32 Merkelbach, *Summa Theologiae Moralis*, I, n. 754, p. 583; De Meester, *Compendium*, III, Pars I, n. 1253, p. 154.

ligious worship can be divided into primary and secondary worship.[33] The primary acts of divine worship are sacrifice, the administration of the sacraments, and the dispensing of the sacramentals. On the other hand, prayers, processions, the profession of vows, the taking of oaths, the recitation of the divine office, the singing of hymns or also the reading of the Scriptures in common are secondary acts of divine worship. Of course, in the Protestant religion these secondary acts may constitute the central or distinctive service, and as such they would have to be judged accordingly. However, this division can be aptly applied to all schismatic sects. With relation to this division it can be stated that a greater reason would be required for a passive assistance at primary than at secondary acts of religious worship.[34]

One must also take into consideration the local customs as tolerated by the ordinary, the distinctive emphasis which socially attaches to attendance at funeral services or at other religious functions, the degree of relationship with the deceased, and the particular status and character of the person assisting.[35] Hence, if the ordinary of the place absolutely refuses to permit non-Catholics to act as witnesses at a mixed marriage, there will hardly arise a case when one could permit such a participation on their part. Also, if there were to be held a funeral in relation to which it were known in advance that open ridicule would be directed at all religious practices, one could not be permitted to assist even passively. Again, if one were only remotely related to the deceased and even this relationship were not manifest to the people in attendance, there would be little need for or expediency in tolerating a passive assistance at the funeral service. The condition and status of the person assisting must also be considered, for greater harm would result if a priest or a religious assisted than if a layman who was hardly known to the bystanders assisted at the service.

If there is any doubt as to the gravity of the reason, the

33 McHugh-Callan, *Moral Theology,* I, p. 376, n. 963.

34 McHugh-Callan, *Moral Theology,* I, p. 378, n. 966.

35 Cocchi, *Commentarium,* V, n. 93, p. 180.

approval of the bishop must be given. Under the term bishop there is also understood here the abbot or prelate *nullius* (can. 215, §2) and the vicar or prefect apostolic in his own territory (can. 294, §1).[36] But if there were no time for recourse to the bishop or if the delay occasioned by the recourse would entail some risk or danger, one would have to resort to the use of *epikeia.* However, all necessary precautions would have to be taken against any probable danger of perversion or scandal.

This tolerance does not avail in all cases. Its exercise should be restricted to such services as 1) funeral services accompanied with religious rites; 2) weddings celebrated in a religious atmosphere; and 3) other similar ceremonies, e. g., the ritual bestowal of baptism, the holding of thanksgiving services for some civil cause, etc.[37] It would not be illicit in satisfaction simply of one's curiosity to go to the churches of non-Catholics outside the time of sacred functions, since the restriction pertains only to those times when sacred functions or rites are taking place.[38]

Even in consequence of the above mentioned circumstances the practice of participating passively or materially in non-Catholic religious ceremonies will never be licit if there is present any probable danger of perversion to oneself or of scandal for others. The absence of these two factors is a necessary condition set by the divine law itself for any licit communication in religious worship with non-Catholics. Much good can be accomplished through association with non-Catholics, but before any Catholic may permit himself any participation with them in religious worship, the non-emergence of the four following evils must be duly assured:

1) the danger of perversion; 2) the danger of scandal; 3) the confirmation of a non-Catholic sect; and 4) the favoring of indifference. Any of these evils, if present, would affect any good that might be accomplished, and, even if any good could result, the evil could never serve as a permissible means for reaching that result.

36 Blat, *Commentarium,* IV, 166.
37 *Loc. cit.*
38 *Loc. cit.*

CHAPTER V

COMMUNICATION IN THE RECEPTION OF THE SACRAMENTS

Article I — General Observations

For a proper understanding of what is to follow it is essential to keep clear in one's mind that the present treatment touches simply the positive communication of Catholics in schismatic rites. In the present chapter there will be no consideration of the administration of the sacraments to schismatics. This points rather to a negative communication, to which some study will be given in the final chapter. For the present there will be considered simply the activity of the Catholic in the sacramental rites of schismatics.

The general principles to be applied here are those which have already been outlined in the previous chapter. Active religious communication with schismatics is absolutely forbidden, whereas a passive presence at the celebration of schismatical rites can be tolerated under certain postulated conditions. It will be seen here how these general principles are to be applied to particular cases. In determining the solution of each case, one must attach great importance to the decisions and responses handed down by the Holy Office and the Sacred Congregation for the Propagation of the Faith in reference to particular questions. Most of the canonical authors in treating the matter of religious communication rely almost exclusively on these responses in formulating their opinions.

These decisions do not enact a positive ecclesiastical law; they simply interpret and apply the natural and positive divine law in this matter.[1] It is also to be duly noted that certain things which are stated to be licit by some particular response may have

[1] Merkelbach, *Summa Theologiae Moralis*, I, n. 753, p. 582.

to be designated as illicit by some other particular response in view of the altered circumstances attending the case under consideration.[2] Hence these responses and decrees must be considered with careful advertence and accurate approach, lest they be understood to permit more than they actually allow, or lest they be interpreted to forbid something which is not intended as a prohibition. Some of the decrees declare an absolute prohibition; others by their very tenor condition or temper their directives; still others are concerned with circumstances which can vary from case to case, and hence can reflect divergent regulations.[3]

In referring to the last mentioned type of responses one must pay preponderant heed to the most recent ones, since in several instances a later response with reference to some variable factor has reversed a former one in view of the changed circumstances confronting the Church. These changes in the responses always, of course, concern matters which are not intrinsically illicit. The Code itself has relaxed some of the severity expressed in former decisions of the Holy Office.[4]

In determining the lawfulness of action in a given case, one must carefully ponder and accurately weigh all the circumstances that attend the case, for example, the customs of the place, the proximity of relationship, the status and social standing of the person assisting, and other similar factors through which scandal could probably be occasioned, or in consequence of which the danger of perversion could probably arise.[5]

Although the responses of the Holy See do not enact any positive ecclesiastical law, nevertheless they can be cited as a safe norm to be followed in the question of religious communication. There have been handed down so many responses, adapted for so many varied situations, that they cover the greater number of possible and likely eventualities. The fact that few, if indeed any, instructions or responses have been issued since the promul-

2 Wernz-Vidal, *Ius Canonicum*, Tom. IV, Vol. I, n. 347, p. 437.

3 Vermeersch-Creusen, *Epitome Iuris Canonici*, II, n. 577.

4 Augustine, *A Commentary on Canon Law*, IV, 144.

5 Beste, *Introductio in Codicem*, p. 614.

gation of the Code is a fair indication that the matter has been sufficiently defined and clarified. Of course, circumstances change with the times, and if new cases arise, then a satisfactory solution seems available if one can draw an analogy with similar cases and circumstances in the past. The mind of the Church has been very well expressed in the responses that have been given, and this expression of its mind can be used as a norm of interpretation in the particular case.

When in the historical consideration of religious communication with schismatics references were made to the decrees and responses of the Holy See, an attempt was made by the writer to treat only of those responses which directly concerned schismatics. Many other responses which dealt exclusively with heretics or infidels were duly inspected by the writer, but they were passed over as irrelevant. It was the purpose of the writer to treat the question of religious communication, not indeed with all non-Catholics, but simply with those who were members of schismatical sects. Today, however, the distinction between heretics and schismatics is in actual practice not very great. Consequently, the responses issued by the Holy See with reference to heretics can with safety be applied also with reference to schismatics if the circumstances are the same in character. These responses are based fundamentally on the principles that govern the matter of religious communication whether with schismatics or with any other non-Catholic body.

Article II — The Sacraments in General

It is nowhere stated as a general principle in the Code of Canon Law that the sacraments are not to be received from a heretical or a schismatical minister, but this principle is logically deduced from canon 1258, §1. To receive the sacraments or to request their reception from a schismatical minister, or to present someone to a schismatical minister for the reception of a sacrament, involves a forbidden *communicatio in sacris*. The sacraments are classed among the primary *res sacrae,* so that whenever one speaks of religious communication one is principally considering the communication in the reception of the sacraments. In fact, the sacraments are considered as the bond of unity among Christians. Even those who essay a very liberal interpretation of the Church's legislation on religious communication acknowledge without equivocation the complete unlawfulness of taking an active part in the dispensing of the sacraments when conferred by ministers of schismatical sects.

It can be stated as a general principle that it is illicit to ask for the reception of the sacraments from a schismatical minister.[6] Such a request implies a recognition of the authority of the minister of the sect, when in fact it is known that he acts without the authorization of the Church.

To petition the reception of the sacraments from schismatics, or to assist actively in their administration, would involve a forbidden communication in the dispensing of these sacraments.[7] The sacraments are not only something sacred, but they are also signs and symbols in the acts of public worship. The public nature of the sacraments is bound up in their very essence. They are external signs of grace which Christ has given to His Church to be used as a means of salvation. In administering these sacraments the Church always proceeds with a certain solemnity and chooses a public place, such as a church, whenever that is possible. The sacraments are also to be administered by the Church's official ministers, or at least in their presence, as is the case with matrimony. Only in a case of necessity are the sacraments administered privately, as in private baptism, and even then the Church desires that this sacrament be administered by her official minister when that is possible, and that at least one witness be present when it is being administered. Hence, when the sacraments are administered in the Catholic Church, they are administered as something sacred and as an act which is public in its nature. The same characteristic elements attend

6 Merkelbach, *Summa Theologiae Moralis,* I, n. 755, p. 584; Noldin-Schmitt, *Summa Theologiae Moralis,* III, n. 43, p. 42; Cappello, *De Sacramentis,* I, n. 78, p. 69; Genicot-Salsmans, *Institutiones Theologiae Moralis,* I, n. 199, p. 149; II, n. 130, p. 116.

7 Merkelbach, *Summa Theologiae Moralis,* III, n. 79, p. 72.

the administration of the sacraments when they are conferred in a schismatical sect. Inasmuch, then, as schismatics administer the sacraments in the nature of a sacred and public act, it remains illicit to participate in the dispensing of the sacraments when they are administered by a schismatic minister.

Since to the exclusion of others the present treatment contemplates only schismatical ministers, there exists in their favor the presumption for the validity of the sacraments which they administer. This presumption is certainly present in regard to baptism.[8] Their ministers are commonly considered as validly ordained, and hence they administer validly all the sacraments which do not require a simultaneous possession of jurisdiction for their valid administration. This fact follows logically from the nature of a schismatic sect, since in theory schismatics profess no dogmatic error, and in practice they are very close to the complete truth taught by the Catholic Church.

When the possession of jurisdiction is necessary on the part of the minister, then the question of the validity of the sacrament administered by schismatic priests is a disputed one. The absolution which they confer under ordinary circumstances would be invalid, for they lack the necessary jurisdiction. This is particularly true of public and notorious schismatics, and it is they who are now being considered. However, Cappello thinks that it must be admitted that a common error regarding the non-possession of jurisdiction can easily occur in many cases.[9] Consequently the prescriptions of canon 209 can be applied to these cases for the good of souls, so that schismatic ministers, as long as they are validly ordained, could absolve validly. Cappello asserts that some authors hold the contrary opinion, but that in his judgment their opinion is without foundation. The Church by its very purpose must look to the salvation of souls, and hence is bound to grant, to that end, all things that depend on its power. He states also that Pope Pius XI openly declared and

[8] Waldron, *The Minister of Baptism,* The Catholic University of America Canon Law Studies, n. 170 (Washington, D. C.: The Catholic University of America Press, 1942), p. 153, ftn. 72.

[9] Cappello, *De Sacramentis,* II, n. 349, p. 316; cf. canon 209.

wished it to be expressly known that the Roman Pontiff supplied jurisdiction, if there be need for it, to whatever extent it was required.[10]

However, the question here is rather one of licit administration. From the standpoint of the schismatic minister it is illicit for him to administer the sacraments, for he is certainly an unworthy minister. As such he may be considered under a threefold possible aspect: 1) as being in the state of mortal sin, though not being bound by a censure; 2) as being bound by a censure; or 3) as being the minister of a schismatical sect.[11] Mortal sin is a matter of the internal forum, though it is possible that one could be morally certain that a particular schismatical minister is in bad faith and in the state of mortal sin. However, if one considered a schismatic merely as being in the state of mortal sin, one could receive the sacraments from him for a just cause. Even if the schismatic is considered as bound by a censure, the faithful could receive the sacraments from him for any just cause as long as he were not a *vitandus* or under censure upon a condemnatory or declaratory sentence.[12] But the schismatic minister cannot be considered merely as one in the state of mortal sin or as one bound by a censure. He is more than that. He is the minister of an unauthorized sect. Only a person in danger of death could licitly receive the sacraments from him.

Fagnanus (1598-1678), in commenting on the Decretal law, offered a treatise on the title *"De schismaticis et ordinatis ab eis."* Therein he stated that it was not licit to seek or to receive the sacraments from a minister no matter how he had been excommunicated. A transgression of this nature which connoted the presence of a spiritual danger could not be derogated by a contrary custom.[13]

The act of seeking or receiving the sacraments from a schismatical minister is forbidden in virtue not only of the divine law

10 *Loc. cit.*

11 Cf. Cappello, *De Sacramentis,* I, n. 78, pp. 68-70.

12 Cf. cc. 2261; 2275, 2°; 2284.

13 Fagnanus, *Commentaria in Decretales Gregorii IX* (Venetiis: apud Paulum Balleonium, 1708), V, 108.

but also of the law enacted in canon 1258, §1. There also have been responses of the Holy Office which have forbidden positive religious communication with schismatics in the dispensing of the sacraments. It is never licit to request the reception of the sacraments from one who would administer them in a way different from the Catholic rite and thus would differentiate the administration from the one employed by the Church. This would be an immediate participation in an illicit form of worship, and an implicit profession of a false sect. Such a request is likewise illicit if the sacrament be administered by a schismatic minister in a Catholic rite, except in extreme necessity and then only in the cases of baptism and penance. Even in these cases the circumstances would have to make it manifest that the request did not imply the recognition of a false sect.[14]

The prohibition against the communicating with non-Catholics in the dispensing of the sacraments has existed since the earliest times. There is a reference to this in the *Decree* of Gratian.[15] The *glossa* to the text in question cited a letter of St. Augustine against the Donatists. It was there stated that only in danger of death should one seek baptism from a heretic or a schismatic, and that it would be gravely illicit to do so outside any such necessity.[16]

Even when a schismatic minister confers a sacrament according to the Catholic rite, he acts illicitly. In order that the minister of the sacraments may confer them licitly, he must have the authorization of the Church. Since the Church alone is given the power of administering the sacraments, it remains within the exclusive province of the Church to depute its ministers.[17] This authorization is certainly lacking in the case of a schismatic minister, except when the Church allows of exceptions in order to

14 Merkelbach, *Summa Theologiae Moralis*, I, n. 755, p. 584.

15 C. 40, C. XXIV, q. 1.

16 *De Baptismo contra Donatistas*, lib. I, caput II — *MPL, XLIII*, 110.

17 Noldin-Schmitt, *Summa Theologiae Moralis*, II, n. 32, p. 27; Cappello, *De Sacramentis*, I, n. 45, p. 43; Prümmer, *Manuale Theologiae Moralis*, III, n. 60, p. 49; Aertnys-Damen, *Theologia Moralis*, II, nn. 9, 36; Davis, *Moral and Pastoral Theology*, III, 23.

provide a safeguard for souls, as, e. g., in canon 209, or in consideration of the extant danger of death or of some similar extreme necessity. General authorization is given by the law with relation to private baptism and also the contracting of marriage in cases of necessity. In all other cases special authority as conferred either by the law or by the properly accredited minister is necessary.[18]

Since schismatic priests are without the necessary authorization except in extraordinary cases, they administer the sacraments illicitly, and one could not request or receive the sacraments from such ministers. To do so would be to co-operate in their illicit administration, which in the absence of a just cause is forbidden. But since the ministers are schismatics, there is also involved a religious communication which is forbidden outside the case of danger of death.

There are other requirements for the licit administration of the sacraments, such as the proper intention and the necessary attention, but these are more the concern of moral theologians than of canonists.[19] These conditions are of no particular concern in the present discussion. However, the obligation to observe the rites of the Church has a canonical foundation in canon 733. As a rule these rites of the Church, at least those which are of an accessory character, will not be observed by schismatic ministers.

In the administration of the sacraments the rites and ceremonies which are prescribed in the approved rituals of the Church are accurately to be observed.[20] Of these sacramental rites some are essential while others are merely accessory. They are essential rites in so far as they regard the matter and form necessary for the valid administration of the sacraments. They are accessory rites when they have been instituted by the Church

18 Davis, *Moral and Pastoral Theology,* III, 23.

19 Cf. Noldin-Schmitt, *Summa Theologiae Moralis,* III, nn. 28-33, pp. 25-28.

20 Can. 733, §1: Cf. Conc. Trident., sess. VII, *de sacramentis in genere,* can. 13 — Schroeder, *Canons and Decrees of the Council of Trent* (St. Louis: B. Herder, 1941), p. 53.

to serve the purpose of a more worthy and appropriate administration of the sacraments. It is evident that the observance of the essential rites is a serious obligation, for they involve the validity of the sacraments. Of the accessory rites some are preceptive and some merely directive. With relation to these it is the performance of only the preceptive rites that binds under pain of sin. The moral gravity of the omission remains to be determined according to the measure of importance attaching to the matter concerned.[21]

The foregoing discussion on the rites to be observed in the administration of the sacraments has a bearing on the present subject. There are times when the Church does permit the faithful to receive the sacraments from a schismatical minister, but when such a permission is granted a necessary condition is set, namely, that the sacrament be administered according to the rite of the Church.[22] It is not very likely that the schismatical minister will administer the sacraments in exactly the same rite as would be observed by a Catholic priest. However, before the faithful could receive the sacraments from a schismatical minister, there would have to be some certainty that the substantial or essential rites necessary for the validity would be observed by him when he confers the sacrament. As for the accessory rites, be they preceptive or directive, one could tolerate an omission or change in them. Suarez (1548-1617) held that if the non-Catholic minister employed other accessory rites which were of a superstitious character or foreign to the customs of the Roman Church, one could not co-operate in them. However, he admitted that one could sometimes tolerate them if there were no scandal or contempt of religion, and if at the same time one could not exclude the use of them.[23]

For the present it suffices to have indicated the principles involved in the dispensing of the sacraments in general. The application of these principles will become more clearly illus-

21 Cappello, *De Sacramentis*, I, n. 50, pp. 46, 47.

22 S.C.S. Off., 7 iul. 1864 — *Fontes*, n. 978.

23 Suarez, *Defensio fidei*, Lib. VI, cap. IX, n. 29 — *Opera Omnia*, XXIV, 713.

trated when the sacraments are considered each in turn. It is then that the review of specific cases with relation to the individual sacraments will furnish examples of how these principles apply in practice.

Article III — Baptism and Confirmation

Baptism and confirmation are here treated under one heading, for the problems which arise concerning these two sacraments are very similar. There is also the reason that among most of the Oriental schismatics it is the practice for the schismatic priest to administer both sacraments together. Hence, to participate in the ceremony of a schismatical baptism will usually involve a similar participation with reference to the sacrament of confirmation. In both of these sacraments sponsors are employed, and the same principles govern the use of sponsors, whether these be used in baptism or in confirmation. In prohibiting Catholics to act as sponsors for schismatics, the Holy See frequently considered these sacraments conjointly. As a result there will be no need to devote separate articles to each sacrament.

A. *The Minister of Baptism*

In speaking of the minister of baptism the Code does not positively and explicitly prohibit the non-Catholic minister from acting as the licit minister of solemn baptism. However, canons 738 to 741 determine the licit minister of solemn baptism, and since in these canons schismatic ministers are left unmentioned, they are thereby excluded from acting as licit ministers in the solemn rite of baptism. If the ordained Catholic priest who has no jurisdiction and is without any parochial rights *(sacerdos simplex)* is excluded from acting licitly as the minister of solemn baptism under ordinary circumstances, then certainly a schismatic minister is excluded for a more compelling reason.

The silence of the Code and the absence of any positive prohibition in canons 738 to 741 must, therefore, be interpreted as an implicit prohibition against the admissibility of a non-Catholic minister. This is supported by the fact that disabilities and penalties are enacted against those who permit a schismatic or a non-Catholic minister to baptize them. One who permits himself to be baptized in any manner by a non-Catholic priest, except in a case of extreme necessity, incurs a delictual irregularity.[24] Also, those Catholics who knowingly presume to offer their children to non-Catholic ministers for baptism incur *ipso facto* an excommunication reserved to the ordinary.[25]

Here, as in the administration of all the sacraments, the schismatic minister is without authorization, and he cannot in ordinary circumstances licitly administer any sacrament. Since it is illicit for him to administer solemn baptism, so also is it illicit for a Catholic to request him to confer the sacrament solemnly. Outside the danger of death or of some similar extreme necessity, one would not be permitted to request solemn baptism from a schismatic minister even though he were to administer the sacrament in exactly the same way as Catholics do.[26]

Prior to the pronouncements of the Holy See there was some difference of opinion on the question of the lawful seeking of baptism at the hands of a schismatical minister. Authors did not consider the practice illicit in all cases. Schmalzgrueber (1663-1735) stated that it was illicit for Catholics to receive the sacraments from heretical pastors or bishops if there was scandal, the danger of perversion, and if the sacrament were administered in a heretical rite.[27] He seemed to infer from this that, if the sacrament were administered according to the Catholic rite and if there were no scandal or danger of perversion, the practice could be permitted for a grave reason.

De Lugo (1583-1660) stated that it was licit for parents to permit their children to be baptized by a heretical minister when they could not prevent it without grave inconvenience.[28] Accord-

24 Canon 985, 2°.

25 Canon 2319, §1, 3°.

26 Merkelbach, *Summa Theologiae Moralis*, I, n. 755, p. 584.

27 *Jus Ecclesiasticum*, Lib. V, tit. 7, n. 218.

28 *Disptationes Scholasticae et Moralis* (editio nova, 8 vols., Parisiis: apud Ludovicum Vivès, 1868-1869), *De Virtute Fidei Divinae*, disp. XIV, sect. 5 — Tom. I, 557 (hereafter cited *Disputationes*).

ing to De Lugo a father was not bound to prevent such a baptism by the use of armed force. However, the father had to remain passive in his attitude, for it was not allowable for him to manifest any approval of the action. It was a grave offense to seek baptism from a heretic outside of necessity, and some authors contended that the necessity had to be an extreme one. De Lugo concluded that only in the case of necessity was one permitted to request baptism from a heretic. This necessity had to be at least such as proved sufficient to allow one to request the baptism from a lay person.[29]

According to St. Alphonsus (1696-1787) it was stated by Pignatelli († after 1700) that outside of extreme necessity it was illicit to request the sacraments from schismatics.[30] Pignatelli[31] supported his statement with the words of Clement VIII (1592-1605) in his Instruction *Sanctissimus*.[32]

In the question at hand there is, in general, a possibility of four different ministers: 1) the official Catholic minister, namely, any one of those specified in canons 738 to 741; 2) the Catholic lay minister; 3) the official schismatic minister, i. e., the schismatic priest or deacon; and 4) the schismatic lay minister. It is not always clear in the writings of those who take up this problem which minister they precisely consider. Among the older writers a distinction is not always made between the official schismatic ministers and the Catholic lay ministers, or at least no preference is indicated for one or for the other class. Pignatelli stated that the children of Catholics could be baptized by schismatics if the Catholic pastor was absent, if no other

29 *Ibid.*, p. 558.

30 St. Alphonsus, *Theologia Moralis* (ed. L. Gaudé, 4 vols., Romae, 1905-1912), lib. VI, n. 117 — Tom. III, 105.

31 *Consultationes Canonicae* (6 vols., Coloniae Allobrogum, 1700), IV, 237.

32 31 aug. 1595, §4: "Non sunt admittendi Episcopi Schismatici, sive pro ordinibus, sive pro aliis sacramentis conferendis, sed detinendi, quoad Sancta Sedes Apostolica desuper consulatur, et responsum habeatur." — *Fontes*, n. 179.

Catholic minister was present,[33] and if the Catholics were forced to permit such a baptism in consideration of some just and grave necessity. He placed the usual conditions under which such a *communicatio in sacris* was permitted. But the point at issue here is the precise meaning of the statement: *"Si . . . non adesset alius minister."*

It is not definite whether with this expression Pignatelli referred to an official minister of the Church or to a lay minister. However, the difficulty was clarified through a reply of the Holy Office.[34] In this response the Holy Office stated that schismatic monks, even with the consent of the parish priest in the Latin diocese of Trau in Dalmatia, were not to be permitted to administer the sacrament of baptism, except in the case of necessity, and then only when no Catholic person was available. In a later response the Holy Office used the words "extreme necessity."[35]

In the Austrian Empire under Joseph II (1780-1790) an executive order was issued concerning the rights of Orthodox priests in administering the sacraments to Catholics. This was a Governmental Instruction under date of September 9, 1788, which ruled, upon the request of the Orthodox Consistory of Czernovitz for normative instructions, that Greek Orthodox priests could in case of an emergency administer the sacrament of baptism to newly born children of Greek-Catholic inhabitants, but were not permitted either to administer the sacrament of confirmation or to observe and employ the usual ceremonies of their ritual for the conferring of baptism. They were permitted to administer the sacrament of penance to the dying, but in no case could they administer Holy Viaticum and extreme unction, since these sacraments, like that of confirmation, were held not to be indispensable for the attainment of the salvation of the

33 "Si tamen abesset Parochus catholicus, et non adesset alius minister." — *Consultationes Canonicae*, IV, 237.

34 20 aug. 1671 — *Fontes*, n. 746.

35 5 iul. 1853: "Sedulo autem curet idem Episcopus Vicarius Apostolicus admonere catholicos sibi subditos licitum ipsis non esse extra casum extremae necessitatis petere pro filiis suis Baptismum a schismaticis vel haereticis." — *Coll. S.C.P.F.*, n. 1095

soul.[36] This decree was entirely in harmony with Catholic principles, and accordingly could be followed with safety.

An interesting response of the Sacred Congregation for the Propagation of the Faith concerned those Oriental Catholics who lived in a place where schismatics and heretics had the favor of the civil authorities.[37] Under fear of persecution these Catholics felt compelled to have their children baptized by a heretical priest. Though such a baptism could not be permitted for the children of Catholic parents, a solution for the difficulty was offered. Since the pressure which was placed on Catholics was motivated principally by the desire for the stipend which attended the administration of the sacrament, Catholic parents were advised to pay that stipend if they could hope thus to become relieved of the obligation of submitting their children to heretical or schismatical ministers for baptism. But the parents could not submit their children to heretical baptism merely for the purpose of avoiding the payment of a fine. This had been made clear in an earlier response.[38]

In the present law of the Code the only licit minister of solemn baptism is the Catholic pastor or some other Catholic priest or deacon who acts with the express or at least legitimately presumed permission of the proper pastor or ordinary.[39] If anyone else baptizes, the sacrament is to be conferred privately. Consequently, the schismatic priest can never be considered as the licit minister of solemn baptism. If one were forced to have his child baptized by an official schismatic minister, a Catholic parent could allow, though he could not actively request, such a baptism for the child. It is permitted for the Catholic parent to

36 Willibald Ploechl, "The Church Laws for Orientals of the Austrian Monarchy in the Age of Enlightenment" — (Reprinted from the *Quarterly Bulletin of the Polish Institute of Arts and Sciences in America*, April, 1944), p. 43.

37 6 aug. 1764 — *Fontes*, n. 4544; *Fonti*, II, 105.

38 S.C.S. Off., 26 sept. 1668 — *Fontes*, n. 736.

39 Cf. cans. 738 to 741.

remain passive when the effort at resistance has been found to be useless.[40]

In regard to non-solemn or private baptism the Code does not absolutely except anyone from being a licit minister, for it uses the words *"potest a quovis ministrari."* [41] This idea is contained in the Decree for the Armenians of Eugene IV.[42] Neither in this decree nor in the Code is any distinction made between a Catholic and a non-Catholic minister. Hence, from the literal wording of the law, it could seem that no preference was to be given to the Catholic minister, and that the schismatic minister might very well baptize licitly even in the presence of a Catholic who was able to baptize. However, the authors logically point out that a Catholic must be preferred to a non-Catholic.[43] An order of preference is indicated in canon 742, §2, and this is to be understood only of Catholic ministers.[44] This opinion is based on the response of the Holy Office which stated that a schismatic is permitted to baptize only if there is no Catholic present.[45]

The usual condition under which baptism may be administered privately is danger of death, as stated in canon 759, §1. In territories where the Church is well established and organized, the danger of death would ordinarily be the only reason which would permit one to baptize privately. When a priest is readily available, solemn baptism can usually be administered within a reasonable time after the child's birth or the adult is prepared to receive the sacrament. However, other reasons are

40 Davis, *Moral and Pastoral Theology*, I, 283; Genicot-Salsmans, *Institutiones Theologiae Moralis*, I, n. 199, p. 150.

41 Cf. Can. 742, §1.

42 Bull *Exultate Deo* (22 nov. 1439), §10, *de Baptismo:* "In casu autem necessitatis, non solum sacerdos, vel diaconus, sed etiam laicus, vel mulier, imo etiam paganus et haereticus, baptizare potest." — *Bullarium*, V, 49; Denzinger. n. 696.

43 Vermeersch-Creusen, *Epitome Iuris Canonici*, II, n. 25; Regatillo, *Ius Sacramentarium* (2 vols., Sal Terrae, Santander: Talleres Tipograficos J. Martinez, 1945-1946), I, n. 40, p. 32; Cappello, *De Sacramentis*, I, n. 139, p. 118.

44 Regatillo, *loc. cit.;* Cappello, *loc. cit.*

45 20 aug. 1671 — *Fontes*, n. 746.

sufficient for the conferring of private baptism, such as scarcity of priests and difficulty in travel.[46] The practice of conferring private baptism under these conditions was commended by the Holy See.[47]

Even in danger of death a schismatic minister may not be called to baptize, unless there is nobody else who knows how to baptize and is willing to do so.[48] If no Catholics who can baptize are present, then a lay schismatic would be preferred to a schismatic priest, since there would be less danger of scandal or perversion. The schismatic priest would be preferred to the lay schismatic only if there were a prudent doubt that the layman would be unable to baptize validly.

When a schismatic minister baptizes, he must baptize privately. If he should insist on using the solemn form of baptism and on employing certain schismatic rites which are accessory to the rite of baptism, such ceremonies may be tolerated.[49]

According to De Lugo it was licit to permit a child to be "rebaptized" in a heretical rite if the refusal of "rebaptism" would have resulted in grave danger or injury. One could not act positively; accordingly one had to remain passive in one's attitude when "rebaptism" could not be foregone without the consequence of a very grave injury.[50] This opinion of De Lugo

46 Cappello, *De Sacramentis,* I, n. 138, p. 116; Vermeersch-Creusen, *Epitome Iuris Canonici,* II, n. 25.

47 S. C. de Prop. Fide (C. P. pro Sin.), 21 ian. 1788, ad 1 — *Fontes,* n. 4618; *Coll. S.C.P.F.,* n. 593; S. C. de Prop. Fide (C. P. pro Sin. — Cochinchin.), 16 ian. 1804, ad 2 — *Fontes,* n. 4677; *Coll. S.C.P.F.,* n. 674.

48 Woywod, *A Practical Commentary on the Code of Canon Law* (9. printing, 2 vols., New York: Joseph F. Wagner, 1945), I, 330 (hereafter cited *Practical Commentary*): S. C. S. Off., 20 aug. 1671: "Non permittat (Episcopus) schismaticis administrare sacramentum Baptismatis nisi in casu necessitatis, et deficiente quacumque alia persona catholica."—*Fontes,* n. 746; *Coll. S.C.P.F.,* n. 198.

49 Suarez, *Defensio Fidei,* Lib. VI, Cap. IX, n. 29 — *Opera Omnia,* Tom. XXIV, p. 713.

50 De Lugo, *De Virtute Fidei Divinae,* disp. XIV, sect. 5 — *Disputationes,* Tom. I, 558.

was supported by a response of the Holy Office.[51] If it was foreseen that "rebaptism" would take place, then De Lugo thought it preferable to omit baptism in the Catholic rite, and to let the child be baptized in the heretical rite, since this mode of procedure seemed to give place to the lesser of the two evils.[52] However, if it was prudently feared that the heretic or the schismatic would confer baptism invalidly, then it was preferable to have the child baptized previously in the Catholic rite.[53]

B. *Sponsors at Baptism and Confirmation*

In the latter part of the seventeenth century the Holy Office forbade Catholics to act as sponsors at the baptism of schismatics.[54] Regularly it was not permitted for Catholics even to be present at the baptisms of schismatics. But Catholics were absolutely forbidden, either themselves or through others, to exercise the office of sponsor in the baptism of the children of heretics when it was administered by a heretical minister.[55]

A similar prohibition was contained in a response of the Sacred Congregation for the Propagation of the Faith for the Island of Paros on March 12, 1789,[56] and again of the same Congregation on August 2, 1803.[57]

The Holy Office in the past century[58] expressly forbade a

51 S. C. S. Off., 19 sept. 1765: "Non esse prohibendos sacerdotes catholicos ne baptizent privatim infantes natos a parentibus catholicis, tametsi certo praevideant eosdem infantes fore iterum per ministros schismaticos sacrilege baptizandos; quantum tamen christiana prudentia permittere potest, monendos et instruendos eosdem infantium parentes de illicita eorum cooperatione ad iterationem praedicti baptismi." — *Fonti,* II, 109.

52 De Lugo, *loc. cit.*

53 Bancroft, *Communication in Religious Worship with Non-Catholics,* p. 96.

54 S. C. S. Off., 14 oct. 1676, ad 1 — *Fontes,* n. 753; *Coll. S. C. P. F.,* n. 211.

55 S. C. S. Off. (Smyrnen.), 10 maii 1770 — *Fontes,* n. 828; *Fonti,* II, 109.

56 Ad 1 — *Fontes,* n. 4626; *Fonti,* II, 111.

57 Ad 2 — *Fontes,* n. 4675; *Fonti,* II, 113.

58 (Smyrnen.), 30 iun., 7 iul. 1864, ad 4 — *Fontes,* n. 978.

Catholic to hold the child of a heretical schismatic at the sacred font, when the sacrament was administered by a heretical minister, and drew attention to the earlier decree of May 10, 1770.[59] Finally, in 1871, the Holy Office in still another Instruction repeated the same prohibition.[60]

Even after the Holy Office had forbidden the practice, there were authors who held that a Catholic could act as sponsor at the baptism of non-Catholics when conferred by a non-Catholic minister. Evidently referring to the practice in Germany, Schmalzgrueber stated that it was licit for a Catholic in some places to receive the child of a heretic from the font at baptism, i. e., to act as sponsor, if the child were baptized properly in the Catholic rite, and not in a heretical or schismatical rite.[61] He based his assertion on the fact that there was not in existence any universal law which prohibited the practice. Regarding the non-existence of any universal law he was correct, for there had not been enacted any universal law, although the Holy Office had forbidden the practice in particular cases.

La Croix (1652-1714) stated that according to Laymann (1574-1635) this practice was permitted, but that the majority of the authors held the contrary opinion.[62] Laymann held that this custom in Germany could not be disapproved. In his stand he argued from the Constitution *Ad evitanda* of Pope Martin V (1417-1431).[63] He claimed that this papal constitution applied not only to civil communication but also to religious communication. He added that it was better to have a Catholic sponsor than a heretical sponsor, for inasmuch as the baptized person became a member of the Church, he needed instruction in the faith.[64]

59 *Fontes*, n. 828.

60 Instr. (ad Archiep. Corcyren.) 3 ian. 1871, ad 1 — *Fontes*, n. 1013.

61 *Jus Ecclesiasticum*, lib. V, tit. 7, n. 216.

62 La Croix, *Theologia Moralis* (2 tomes in 1 vol., Coloniae: ex officina Noetheniana, 1729), I, p. 131, n. 65.

63 Cf. Const. *Ad evitanda*, a. 1418 — *Fontes*, n. 45.

64 Laymann, *Theologia Moralis* (2 vols. in 1, Patavii: sumptibus Remondinianis, 1760; in epitomen redacta a Joanne Dominico Mansi), lib. V, tit. 2, c. 9, n. 6.

De Lugo stated that some authors considered it licit for a Catholic to act as sponsor at the baptism of heretics if the sacrament were administered in a Catholic rite and there were no offense or scandal to Catholics.[65] But he considered the opinion impractical, for in his day such baptisms were administered regularly in a heretical or schismatical rite.

Prümmer (1866-1931) indicated various reasons for the prohibition of Catholics to act as sponsor at heretical baptisms. He stated that the sponsor presents the one to be baptized to a heretical minister, and consequently the action is illicit. Also, the sponsor has the obligation of educating the baptized person in the faith, and this is practically impossible when the person baptized is a child of a heretic baptized by a heretical minister.[66] In acting as sponsor at a non-Catholic baptism, a Catholic would be assuming a responsibility which would be impossible for him to fulfill. Although the authors speak principally of heretical baptisms, the situation is analogous when one considers the present case with reference to a schismatic minister and schismatic baptism.

There seem to be some good arguments in support of the opinion which these authors held, but the practice of having a Catholic act as sponsor at the baptism of non-Catholics is wrong in principle, and the good which might follow does not render the act licit. When one acts as sponsor, he thereby requests the sacrament from a minister of a schismatical sect and thus co-operates in an illicit action. The schismatical minister is not authorized to confer the sacrament. Hence, when he confers the sacrament outside of extreme necessity, he does so illicitly, and when one acting as sponsor requests the sacrament from the schismatic minister, he co-operates in an illicit action. Furthermore, inasmuch as the schismatic minister is acting as the official minister of his sect, there is implied the fact of a religious communication in a false sect.

All doubt concerning this practice was removed by the re-

65 *De Virtute Fidei Divinae*, disp. XIV, sect. 5 — *Disputationes*, Tom. I, 558.

66 Prümmer, *Manuale Theologiae Moralis*, I, n. 526.

peated prohibitions of the Holy Office. Its responses have already been cited in the opening paragraphs. There were at least six replies from the Sacred Congregation of the Holy Office and from the Sacred Congregation for the Propagation of the Faith. In every case the practice was forbidden. It seems rather strange that the same question was presented so many times, but the Sacred Congregations evidently considered the question each time because of its great importance. However, in several instances reference was made to earlier replies which had already decided the question.

In view of these responses it is evident that a Catholic cannot be permitted to act as sponsor at the baptism or confirmation of a schismatic by a schismatical minister. The Catholic cannot perform the office himself, nor can he do so through a proxy. In considering this problem the present-day authors have nothing more to add; they are satisfied with making a reference to one or the other of the responses of the Holy Office. Since under the contemplated circumstances there is involved an active religious communication with schismatics, the practice cannot in any way be tolerated. The solemn conferring of baptism by a schismatic minister is a schismatic rite, and one who acts as sponsor at such a baptism actively participates in the rite and implicitly approves it. One's material presence in the role of a spectator could be permitted for a grave reason, but one would not be permitted to take an active part by acting as sponsor. However, even the practice of being materially present is not to be encouraged, and any such practice should not be allowed to continue as a regular usage anywhere.[67]

67 Davis, *Moral and Pastoral Theology,* I, 284. S. C. S. Off. (Smyrnen.), 10 maii 1770: "Catholicis regulariter non licere haereticorum aut schismaticorum concionibus, baptismis et matrimoniis interesse." — *Fontes,* n. 828; *Coll. S. C. P. F.*, n. 478.

Article IV — The Holy Eucharist

A. *Sacrifice of the Mass*

1. *Place of Sacrifice*

(Canon 823, §1)[68]

As a general rule promiscuity between Catholics and non-Catholics in the use of churches was not allowed at any time in the Church's history. The Holy Sacrifice of the Mass was to be offered only in a Catholic church. However, particular circumstances very often modified the application of this principle, as is evident from the following responses of the Holy See.

The Sacred Congregation for the Propagation of the Faith on August 13, 1627,[69] instructed the Archbishop of Zara to see to it that in the church of St. John of Cartolla, in the diocese of Cattaro, Catholics would not offer up Mass *(divina celebrent)* with Greek schismatics. Although different altars had been used, yet the Masses had been offered in the same church, and thus there was exercised a forbidden religious communication with schismatics.

Capuchin missionaries asked the same Sacred Congregation whether they could celebrate Mass in schismatic churches and use the vestments and the chalices belonging to the latter. The answer was in the negative. The missionaries were told to use the privilege of the portable altar and to bless their own vestments.[70]

It was likewise forbidden for schismatics to celebrate Mass in the churches of Catholics.[71] The question was raised whether it could be permitted, for the avoidance of scandal, that schismatic Armenians celebrate Mass in the church of the Capuchins, after the altar stone had first been removed. The answer was

68 Canon 823, §1, treats of a particular phase of religious communication, namely, that of the simultaneous use of churches by both Catholics and non-Catholics, and in this respect is related to the more general principle expressed in canon 1258.

69 *Fonti*, II, 73; *Coll. S. C. P. F.*, n. 36.

70 7 maii 1631, ad 2 — *Fontes*, n. 4447; *Fonti*, II, 77.

71 26 sept. 1695 — *Fonti*, II, 79.

simply that this had never been permitted, and that likewise it was not to be permitted in the future.

In a similar prohibition of the Holy Office on May 10, 1753,[72] it was added that such a practice implied a *communicatio in sacris*, or that at least it gave occasion to Catholics to communicate with schismatics *in divinis*, and thus certainly offered an occasion of scandal.

A missionary in Albania presented his case to the Sacred Congregation for the Propagation of the Faith, which in turn referred the matter to the Holy Office. In a certain village there was but one church, where according to an ancient usage schismatics and Catholics promiscuously officiated, for there existed a long-standing but unsettled dispute over the ownership of the church. The missionary suspended the services for Catholics until the Sacred Congregation would issue a definite instruction in the matter.

The Sacred Congregation called into doubt the missionary's manner of action, for it noted that if everyone did so in similar cases in the territories where heretics and schismatics performed their sacred functions in Catholic churches even through the use of violence, Catholics would very quickly be deprived of practically all the churches which at one time had been Catholic churches before the advent of the Turkish tyrannical rule. The Holy Office indicated that the missionary had acted wrongly in forbidding Catholics to avail themselves of attendance at divine services in churches of their own, for they could well have continued with their usage as long as they did not join in the ceremonies of the schismatics.[73]

An exception to the general principle was allowed by Pope Clement XI (1700-1721).[74] For the purpose of facilitating the conversion of schismatics and infidels through the use of the sacred ceremonies as an incentive, Clement XI allowed the Prefect or the Vice-Prefect of missionaries in Ethiopia, according to their judgment and conscience, to grant the faculty of celebrat-

72 Ad 1 — *Fontes,* n. 804; *Fonti,* II, 95.

73 S. C. S. Off., 27 oct. 1632 — *Fonti,* I, 75.

74 S. C. S. Off., 12 apr. 1704 — *Coll. S. C. P. F.,* n. 265; *Fonti,* II, 81.

ing the Mass of the Roman Catholic Rite on the altars in the temples of heretics and schismatics in Ethiopia. However, these altars were not to be used except as tables, and were to be set up with altar stone, linens, crucifix, candles, and the other necessary accessories according to the Catholic practice. The use of the indult was not to be pressed for a general application; it was to obtain only in particular cases, when a better arrangement could not be made, and when it was thought necessary as a means for facilitating conversion to the Church. The sufficiency and the urgency of the reason were to be weighed by the Prefect or the Vice-Prefect.

On April 30, 1753, the Sacred Congregation for the Propagation of the Faith forbade priests, whether regulars or seculars, to celebrate Mass in private houses where schismatic and heretical officials resided. Mass could be celebrated in private homes during a plague, but not in the homes of schismatics or heretics.[75]

The general principle was further clarified by means of a response of the Holy Office on December 1, 1757.[76] It was asked whether there could be tolerated the practice of celebrating Mass in Catholic churches which had been usurped by the Greek schismatics, or in the churches which were purely schismatic. The Holy Office replied that the generally accepted rule could admit of some exceptions. If in the same church there were separate chapels and altars, some exclusively for the use of Catholics and others for the use of schismatics, or if there was a separation of parts in the church so that the Catholics celebrated Mass in the one part, and the schismatics in the other, then the combined use of the church could be tolerated. But if these conditions were not fully verified, then the privilege of the portable altar was to be called into use.

A response, not directly concerned with the Sacrifice of the Mass, but adverting to an analogous matter, was issued by the Sacred Congregation for the Propagation of the Faith on March

[75] Ad 1 — *Fontes*, n. 4517; *Coll. S. C. P. F.*, n. 388; *Fonti*, II, 93.
[76] *Fontes*, n. 809; *Fonti*, II, 97.

7, 1805. It regarded the reservation of the Blessed Sacrament.[77] The answer was directed to Switzerland. It did not directly mention schismatics, but its wording was sufficiently general to apply to similar situations in other countries. It was asked whether it could be tolerated for Catholics to reserve the Blessed Sacrament in a sacristy which was shared in common by the Protestants and the Catholics. The answer was that the Blessed Sacrament was to be reserved in a place not shared in common with non-Catholics, and, if any other place was wanting, then in the parish house.

The present law of the Church concerning this matter is stated in canon 823, §1: Mass may not be said in the churches of heretics or schismatics even though they were in the past properly consecrated or blessed. Canon 823 indicates the general principle to be applied, but it does not revoke the provisions made in previous particular responses of the Holy See. Blat states that the prohibition of canon 823, §1, is absolute, but that by virtue of the norm of canon 6, 2°, the provisions of the responses of the Holy Office of December 1, 1757,[78] and of June 5, 1889,[79] are still in effect.[80]

[77] *Fontes,* n. 4681; *Coll. S. C. P. F.,* n. 681; *Fonti,* II, 115.

[78] S. C. S. Off. (Archiep. Antibaren.), 1 dec. 1757: "An toleranda sit praxis quam habent parochi catholici castri Lastruae S. Missae sacrificium celebrandi in ecclesiis catholicis, a graecis schismaticis usurpatis atque ab iisdem officiatis, seu etiam in illis quae ad ipsos schismaticos pertinent.

R. Haberi pro regula universe accepta et servata, non licere catholicis communicare in divinis cum haereticis et schismaticis; verum in quibusdam casibus particularibus regula haec aliquas patitur exceptiones, nempe si in eadem ecclesia habeantur cappellae et altaria separata, quorum aliqua tantum catholicis, alia schismaticis inserviant; si eiusdem ecclesie partes sint separatae, et in una celebrent solum catholici, in altera tantum schismatici: tum promiscuus ecclesiae usus tolerari poterit. Quatenus vero haec deficiant, R. P. D. Archiepiscopus mandare poterit suae dioecesis parochis ut altaribus portatilibus utantur iuxta facultates illis in Formula impertitas, quasque Sanctitas Sua rursus dare et renovare intendit." — *Fontes,* n. 809.

[79] S. C. S. Off. (ad Vic. Ap. Malacen.), 5 iun. 1889: "Per i soldati della guarnigione inglese il governo britannico ha già da lungo tempo edificato una cappella unica, ove alternativamente ad ore diverse hanno luogo nella Domenica le funzioni religiose per i soldati cattolici e protestanti. Esistono alle due estremita della cappella due altari, destinato ciascuno esclusiva-

If a heretical or a schismatical church has not been consecrated or blessed, Mass cannot be celebrated in it, because it is not a sacred place. But if it was consecrated by a heretical or a schismatical priest or by a heretical bishop, or also if the church was formerly Catholic and later occupied by non-Catholics, the consecration would still be valid. The fact that the church was occupied by non-Catholics does not destroy the consecration. But the celebration of Mass in such a church is illicit, because it implies a religious communication with non-Catholics.[81] If a church that has always in its past belonged to heretics or schismatics comes into the possession of Catholics, Mass cannot be celebrated in it until it is consecrated or blessed.[82]

According to Vermeersch (1858-1936) -Creusen, canon 823, §1, refutes the opinion of some authors who held that Mass could be celebrated in churches of Oriental schismatics if formerly they were Catholic churches.[83] However, it is more readily admitted that Catholic priests may celebrate Mass in churches which were validly and licitly consecrated by the Catholics themselves and later occupied by heretics.[84]

In a case of necessity Catholic soldiers were permitted to use the same chapel which was used by Protestant soldiers, as long

mente ad un culto; e durante il servizio religioso o cattolico o protestante, rimane celato da una cortina l'altare dell'altro culto. Il Vicario Ap. attesa la difficolta di ottenere dal governo la erezione di un' altra cappella, domanda se può tollerarsi l'uso attuale.

R. Attentis expositis, usum, de quo quaeritur, tolerare posse, dummodo scandalum absit, et nulla alia habeatur ecclesia in qua catholici milites religionis officiis satisfacere valeant; et ad mentem. Mens est ut Vicarius Ap. sollicite curet et a gubernio britannico erectionem cappellae obtineat, quae soli catholicorum usui sit destinata; et si quidem gubernium recuset, studeat cappellam huiusmodi, quo citius fieri potest, aedificari, conrogatis undecumque eleemosynis." — *Fontes*, n. 1119.

80 *Commentarium*, IV, n. 135, p. 146.

81 Coronata, *Institutiones*, I, n. 255, p. 225; Cappello, *De Sacramentis*, I, n. 713.

82 Cappello, *De Sacramentis*, I, n. 713.

83 *Epitome Iuris Canonici*, II, n. 102.

84 Coronata, *Institutiones*, I, n. 255, p. 225; cf. S. C. S. Off., 13 iun. 1634 —*Coll. S. C. P. F.*, n. 75.

as a Catholic chapel could not be erected, provided of course that there was no emergence of scandal.[85] In this particular case there were altars at both ends of the chapel. One was used by the Catholics and the other by the Protestants. Each group held its services at different times, and while one group had its services, the altar at the opposite end of the chapel was covered. The Vicar Apostolic was to make every effort to obtain from the government a chapel for the exclusive use of the Catholic soldiers. If this could not be obtained, then he was to try to erect the chapel from funds obtained through an appeal for alms for this purpose.[86]

In the military faculties granted to chaplains in World War II there was included the faculty to celebrate all the divine offices and ecclesiastical functions in chapels assigned to the armed forces, whether or not these chapels had been reserved exclusively to Catholics, unless the rubrics stood in the way of the use of the faculty.[87] The rubrics there mentioned were those which governed the celebration of divine services in semi-public oratories.[88]

Noldin (1838-1922) -Schmitt state that even if Catholics and heretics were to offer up the Sacrifice of the Mass at the same time in the same church, the action would not of its nature be a religious communication in a forbidden form of worship. Consequently for a most grave reason the Church does permit such simultaneous celebration of Mass. As a matter of fact, in the Church of the Holy Sepulchre at Jerusalem all sects perform their own rites.[89]

However, the practice of the Church is to disapprove such promiscuity in the offering of the divine services, and hence the principle of canon 823, §1, is to be followed as a general norm. Although the Church does not favor the promiscuous use of

85 Coronata, *Institutiones*, I, n. 255, p. 226; S. C. S. Off., 5 iun. 1889 — *Fontes*, n. 1119.

86 *Fontes*, n. 1119.

87 "Military Faculties" — *The Ecclesiastical Review*, CVII (1942), 30.

88 Cf. can. 1193.

89 *Summa Theologiae Moralis*, II, n. 39.

churches by heretics and Catholics, it has been forced by necessity in certain localities to tolerate certain practices contrary to its wishes. However, in any case there must be no forbidden religious communication, and the occasion of scandal must be ruled out.

Although the law makes no exception to the general principle, the authors hold that in a case of necessity which is unaccompanied with any occasion of scandal it would be licit to celebrate Mass in a heretical or a schismatical church.[90] They base their opinion on the decision of the Holy Office of June 5, 1889, in reference to army chapels.[91]

The occasion for such a promiscuous use of churches was of rather rare occurrence, for, as the Holy Office frequently indicated in its responses, when a Catholic church was not available, one could resort to the use of the privilege of the portable altar. Of course, it could be that the use of this privilege did not always adequately answer to the particular need of the time. If Mass could not be celebrated in the open air, and if a schismatical church was the only available building when a large number of people had to be accommodated in their obligation to hear Mass, then such a case of necessity would certainly lend itself as a reason for allowing the celebration of Mass in such a church. All necessary precautions would have to be taken against the emergence of scandal. Efforts should likewise be made to secure some other non-sectarian building for the celebration of Mass whenever such efforts prove feasible.

If Mass were to be celebrated under such circumstances, then one should follow the instructions given to the Ethiopian missionaries under similar circumstances.[92] The schismatic altar should be used merely as a table, and should be set up with altar stone, linens, crucifix, candles, and the other necessary accessories according to the Catholic practice.

90 Wernz-Vidal, *Ius Canonicum*, IV, n. 96, p. 117; Regatillo, *Ius Sacramentarium*, I, n. 214, p. 123; Cappello, *De Sacramentis*, I, n. 713.

91 *Fontes*, n. 1119.

92 S. C. S. Off., 12 apr. 1704 — *Coll. S. C. P. F.*, n. 265.

In a recent issue of *The Eastern Churches Quarterly*[93] the Orthodox Bishop Polycarp is cited as stating in his *Missionarul* that the Uniate and Orthodox Rumanians maintain a church between themselves at Gray, Indiana. There is evidently a misprint in regard to the name of the place, since the writer has been unable to find any evidence of the existence of a town called Gray in the State of Indiana. However, there is a Rumanian Catholic Church in Gary, Indiana,[94] and it is evidently to this community of Orientals that Bishop Polycarp is referring. The writer made an attempt to discover whether the circumstances as represented by Bishop Polycarp were actually true. He corresponded with the pastor of the Rumanian Catholic Parish in Gary and discovered that there was no evidence of any simultaneous use of churches or of a *communicatio in sacris* between the Catholic and the Orthodox Rumanians. In some instances it may have appeared that there was a forbidden religious communication, but what happened in reality was that some of the Rumanian Catholics defected from the faith and joined the schismatic sect. In any event there was no ecclesiastical approval of any intercommunication between Catholics and Orthodox that might have occurred.

2. *Assistance at Mass*

Numerous responses of the Sacred Congregations forbade active religious communication in the Masses celebrated by schismatics. On December 5, 1668, the Holy Office instructed the Bishop of Trebinje[95] to order the Catholics subject to him not to go to Mass or to other divine offices in the churches of schismatics, and to warn them that they were not bound by the precept of hearing Mass when there was no celebration of a Catholic Mass.

93 "Uniates and Latinization" — VI, n. 8 (October-December, 1946), p. 434.

94 Cf. Marbach, *Marriage Legislation for the Catholics of the Oriental Rites in the United States and Canada*, page 272.

95 *Fontes*, n. 738; *Fonti*, II, 79. The former diocese of Trebinje (Jugoslavia) became united with the diocese of Mastar in the year 1881.

A more particular response concerning a matter which entailed more than the mere attendance at Mass was given by the Holy Office on April 10, 1704.[96] Definitely present in the case was the question of an active participation in the schismatic rites. In this response Pope Clement XI (1700-1721) decreed that it was not licit on the principal feasts of the year for converts, in order to avoid persecution, to go to the churches of schismatics, especially during divine services, and there to kiss the door of the church, to make the three adorations to the Blessed Trinity, to venerate the sacred images, or to recite privately some psalms, a *Pater*, an *Ave*, or other similar prayers.

On August 7, 1704, the Holy Office stated that the decree which prohibited Catholics from being present at the Masses and prayers of schismatics applied also in those places where there were no Catholic priests and with reference to such prayers as contained nothing contrary to faith and the Catholic rite.[97] In the same response the Holy Office considered the case of an Armenian schismatic priest who had been converted to Catholicism. He wished to be dispensed from pouring water into the chalice publicly at Mass. Instead he expressed his desire to perform this action secretly in the sacristy before the Mass. The Holy Office forbade him to make use of the contemplated dissimulation.[98]

The prohibition of assisting at the Mass of schismatics was further clarified by a response of the Holy Office on May 10, 1753.[99] An answer was sought for the question whether it could be permitted for Catholics of the Greek rite who did not have a church of the same rite to communicate with Greek schismatics and heretics. The practice was condemned, for from the circumstances presented in the case it was evident that they could attend a church of the Latin rite, so that, while they lacked a priest of their own rite, they could receive the sacraments from a priest of the Latin rite.

96 *Fontes*, n. 769; *Fonti*, II, 81.

97 Ad 1 — *Fontes*, n. 770; *Fonti*, II, 83.

98 Ad 2 — *loc. cit.*

99 Ad 1, 2 — *Fontes*, n. 804; *Fonti*, II, 95.

A similar prohibition of such religious communication was stressed by the Sacred Congregation for the Propagation of the Faith on April 17, 1758, and attention was called to the former decrees concerning this matter.[100]

In the Acts of the Sacred Congregation for the Propagation of the Faith of 1769 certain priests were called to task for joining in the celebration of Mass with schismatics. The ignorance was inexcusable, and the act was a sacrilege which violated the true faith.[101] As far as could be ascertained, this was the latest decree to be issued concerning the assistance of Catholics at the Mass of schismatics.

When the Holy See forbade the attendance of Catholics at the Mass of schismatics, it was always a question of active participation. This active participation at the sacred functions of schismatics is forbidden by the general law of the Code (canon 1258, §1) as well as by the particular decisions of the Sacred Congregations. If any function is sacred and symbolical of Christian unity, certainly the Eucharist has this characteristic. Consequently to participate actively in the sacrifice of the Mass of schismatics is to perform an act of forbidden religious communication.

It is absolutely forbidden to assist formally at the Mass of heretics or schismatics. However, a material presence at the Mass of schismatics is permitted under the usual circumstances stated in canon 1258, §2. Since the sacrifice of the Mass is connected with most solemn occasions, such as funerals, marriages, and the like, the principal problem confronting Catholics will be the manner in which they are to conduct themselves when they are present in a schismatic church on these occasions.

A Catholic of the Oriental church will feel more at ease in a schismatic church, for there is a great similarity of rite and ceremony, and he will not feel too conspicuous among the schismatic congregation. For a Catholic of the Latin rite there is not only the difference in religious tenets but also the difference in rite. Consequently he will feel very much a total stranger. However,

100 *Fonti,* II, 99.
101 *Fonti,* XII, 227.

in either case, since neither the Oriental nor the Latin Catholic can participate actively in the the schismatic form of worship, their actions will single them out as not being members of the schismatic church.

With reference to Oriental schismatics there is a general presumption in favor of the validity of their priesthood and consequently in favor of the validity of their sacraments, especially that of the Eucharist. However, due to recent developments among Oriental schismatics much doubt has been cast upon the validity of the orders of certain schismatic priests, and consequently the individual case has to be judged on its own merits. However, the general presumption in favor of the validity of Oriental schismatic orders remains, and when it is known that a schismatic priest is validly ordained, it must be concluded that he consecrates validly at Mass. As a result, when such priests reserve the Blessed Sacrament in their tabernacles, one must recognize the fact that Christ is truly present there, and one must manifest that belief in one's external actions. Upon entering a schismatic church one must make the usual act of reverence toward the Blessed Sacrament according to the rite to which one belongs, whether it be a genuflection or a profound reverence. One does not participate in a non-Catholic rite when one genuflects before the tabernacle where true consecrated hosts are reserved.[102]

While in the presence of the Blessed Sacrament, one should say some of the prayers that one is accustomed to recite upon entering a Catholic church. When the services begin, one should not take an active part in the ceremonies. Certainly one would not be allowed to join in any of the prayers with the priest or the congregation, even though there were nothing contrary to faith or morals in these prayers. It seems advisable to remain seated during the Mass. By this action one would not reflect any irreverent conduct, and at the same time one would be giving some indication to those in attendance that one has no intention

102 Vermeersch-Creusen, *Epitome Iuris Canonici*, II, n. 577; Genicot-Salsmans, *Institutiones Theologiae Moralis*, I, n. 200, p. 150; S. C. de Prop. Fide, 15 dec. 1764, ad 1 — *Fontes*, n. 4545.

of participating in the sacrifice. However, at the time of the Consecration of the Mass, one should kneel down and remain kneeling until the Communion. One should take care that with respect to the remaining actions there is no common link between them and the acts of the officiating minister.[103] If the service is one that heretics have in common with Catholics, then the active participation, even if no scandal should derive from such a participation, is forbidden at least by Church Law.[104]

Reverence may be shown also to the images of the Blessed Mother and of the saints. However, one should not become demonstrative in his acts of reverence toward the sacred images. The circumstances of the place determine to a great extent the practice to be followed. In this matter there are some very surprising practices which evidently have the sanction of ecclesiastical authority. The following statement which gives evidence of such practices is an excerpt from a current publication:

"In Rome (before the war) the students of the Russicum were allowed to go with their rector's permission to the liturgical services at the little Russian Orthodox church. While there they assisted at the liturgy with due reverence, kissing the eikons on entering the church and during the liturgy, kneeling with the congregation during the consecration and the Lord's Prayer, kissing the cross at the end of the service. The same practice was adhered to by Catholic religious in Belgium who accompanied groups of Orthodox boys (pupils of a Catholic school) when they went to make their Easter duties."[105]

According to the author of the article it would be licit under certain circumstances to bow at the blessing given with the book of the Gospels, to make a sign of the cross at the priest's benediction, to accept a candle when one is offered, and to kiss the

103 Vermeersch-Creusen, *loc. cit.;* Cocchi, *Commentarium,* V, n. 93, p. 180.

104 Jone, *Moral Theology,* n. 125.

105 "On Conducting Oneself in an Orthodox Church" (taken from *Stoudion,* August-October, 1926) — *The Voice of the Church,* December, 1944, p. 16; cf. also *Eastern Churches Quarterly,* V (1944), July-September, 351 ff.

cross and the hand of the priest if he presents it. He justifies these actions on the score that they do not imply a profession of a false dogma and for the reason that there is no danger of personal perversion or likelihood of scandal to others present. The schismatic priest has no intention of obliging the participant to acknowledge to him the trueness of his church any more than the latter recognizes it by his actions. One simply gives honor to those things which are holy both in the priest and in the object itself. One testifies to the priest his respect for the person of a servant of God. However, if the Orthodox religious authority claimed that by such actions one positively took part in their worship as the only true one, one would be obliged to remain passive.[106]

The author of course considered the case of a practicing Catholic who is well grounded in his faith. Otherwise there would be a danger of perversion. Ill-instructed Catholics who are inclined to indifferentism are advised not to go into Orthodox churches until they are better informed. The author concludes his article with the admonition that the individual Catholic consult a well-informed priest or his confessor before assisting at such services. Consequently these actions are to be considered as exceptions to the general principle which forbids all active religious communication.

The article which has just been cited contains some rather startling statements, and it is difficult to see how they can be reconciled with the general law of the Church as contained in canon 1258. The author of the article seems to prescind entirely from Church law, and appears to consider the question merely from the standpoint of the divine law. In the examples he proposes there may be no danger of scandal or perversion in the light of the specific circumstances of time and place, but the actions definitely imply an active participation in schismatic worship, and hence appear to offend against the law enacted in canon 1258, §1. One is obliged to manifest a reverent attitude toward the Blessed Sacrament even in a schismatic church, for that kind of behavior and conduct is warranted on the authority

106 "Art. cit." — *The Voice of the Church*, December, 1944, p. 14.

of the Holy Office. But it is difficult to see how the same can be said of such actions as making the sign of the cross at the priest's benediction, accepting a candle when it is offered, and kissing the cross and the hand of the priest when he presents it. In the given circumstances such actions may not constitute any profession of a false dogma or furnish any occasion for perversion or scandal. Moreover, the fact that these actions have been accepted as part of the liturgical ceremony by both Catholics and Orthodox alike may mitigate the culpability of the performance of them under schismatic auspices, but it does not entirely justify the performance of these acts. Such a performance still constitutes an active participation in an illicit form of worship, and as such is forbidden.

However, the author of the article does admit that there can be no participation in the schismatical dispensing of the sacraments. This is one matter in which Catholics may not have part, for from the earliest times the sharing in the reception of the sacraments has been regarded as the visible token of unity and communion among the faithful. To receive the sacraments from a schismatic priest one must have an authorization or a dispensation from the visible Head of the Church, or from one of his delegates empowered to grant it. Such a dispensation is rare, but not unknown. The most common example is the general authorization to receive from a schismatic priest certain sacraments when one is in danger of death.[107]

Although the law has consistently provided that one is ordinarily not permitted to enter a schismatic church when sacred services are in progress, some concessions were made in regard to visiting the Blessed Sacrament outside these times. On December 15, 1764, the Sacred Congregation for the Propagation of the Faith issued a response to the Island of Chios in regard to this matter. According to the response Catholics were allowed to enter the church of schismatics out of mere curiosity, but outside of those times when services were being held, and provided that no scandal resulted. Catholics could also visit and adore the Blessed Sacrament reserved by the schismatics, and pray

107 "Art. cit." — *The Voice of the Church*, December, 1944, pp. 14, 15.

before the images of the Saints, even in the presence of the schismatics themselves, as long as they did not join in prayer with the schismatics.[108]

Another difficulty was answered with reference to the case in which the Blessed Sacrament was being carried to the sick by a schismatic priest. Catholics were not only permitted to adore the Blessed Sacrament on such an occasion, but they were obliged to do so. However, in making their adoration, they were to refrain from associating with the schismatics.[109]

B. *Holy Communion*

Since it is ordinarily illicit to receive the sacraments from a schismatic, then accordingly as the Eucharist is to be considered as a sacrament, the reception of Holy Communion in a schismatic rite by a Catholic will always be illicit outside the danger of death. There is little doubt concerning this matter, and the question of receiving Holy Communion from the hands of schismatics was seldom presented to the Holy See for consideration. On June 17, 1839, the Sacred Congregation for the Propagation of the Faith forbade the reception of Holy Communion from a heretical priest.[110] There was also the general prohibition to receive any of the sacraments from the schismatics, which prohibition was contained in a response to the Italo-Greeks.[111] Clement VIII (1592-1605)[112] and Benedict XIV (1740-1758)[113] also forbade the use of the services given by schismatics for the conferring of the sacraments. The reception of Holy Communion from schismatics is an act of formal religious communication, and hence is forbidden.

In danger of death the circumstances are changed. However, Holy Communion cannot be placed in the same class as baptism, penance, and extreme unction when there is danger of death.

108 Ad 1 — *Fontes*, n. 4545; *Coll. S. C. P. F.*, n. 458; *Fonti*, II, 107.
109 Ad 4 — *loc. cit.*
110 *Fonti*, I, 93; V, 73.
111 S. C. de Prop. Fide, 10 apr. 1696 — *Fonti*, II, 81.
112 Instr. *Sanctissimus*, 31 aug. 1595, §4 — *Fontes*, n. 179.
113 Const. *Etsi pastoralis*, 26 maii 1742, §VIII, n. XI — *Fontes*, n. 328.

These three sacramnts are of greater necessity for salvation than is the reception of Holy Communion. Hence, one is not given the same freedom in receiving Holy Communion from schismatics, as in the reception of these other three sacraments, when one is in danger of death. However, there is an opinion which holds that in danger of death Holy Communion can be received from schismatics. Noldin-Schmitt state that if one would die without the sacrament unless he were to request it of a schismatic, he could request not only baptism and absolution, but even extreme unction and Holy Viaticum.[114]

These authors seem to be alone in their view, but their opinion should be considered in the light of what they have to say in the following paragraph. Although they state that it is permissible for a dying Catholic to receive Holy Viaticum from a schismatic priest when there is no Catholic priest present, these authors nevertheless state that ordinarily because of the accompanying danger of perversion one should not call a schismatic minister to administer the sacrament even when one is in the proximate danger of death. This danger of perversion is usually present because a heretical minister will seldom administer the sacraments to the dying, unless the dying person professes a belief in the sect of the minister.[115] However, when the danger of perversion is absent, it would be licit to receive the sacraments, at least those of penance and extreme unction, from a schismatic minister when no Catholic priest is present.

In regard to the reception of Holy Viaticum from a schismatic minister, there is here present an apparent conflict between two divine precepts, the precept of avoiding forbidden religious communication and the precept of receiving Holy Viaticum. The problem is to determine which of the two precepts takes precedence over the other. In the present case the basis for prohibiting the reception of Holy Viaticum from a schismatic priest is the danger of perversion. This is a serious danger, and in view of this danger one would not be bound by the divine precept of receiving Holy Viaticum. In fact, a dying Catholic

114 *Summa Theologiae Moralis,* III, n. 43, p. 42.

115 *Loc. cit.*

would be bound not to receive Holy Viaticum from a schismatic minister, if there were no Catholic minister present.

It should be added also that from the nature of the responses which the Holy Office gave to questions concerning the reception of absolution and extreme unction from schismatics on the part of persons who are in danger of death, it seems to be the mind of the Church that Viaticum should not be received from schismatics under any conditions.

Noldin-Schmitt do not present any arguments in support of their opinion that Holy Viaticum may be received from a schismatic minister when no Catholic minister is present. In view of this fact and by virtue of the positive arguments for the contrary opinion, it is to be concluded that Holy Viaticum must not be received by a dying Catholic from the hands of a schismatic minister.

ARTICLE V — PENANCE

A. *Outside the Danger of Death*

As early as 1631 there arose the question to whom Catholic priests were to apply for permission to use their faculties. The nature of these faculties is not evident from the response, but they had been granted by the Holy Office, and the permission of the bishop was needed for the use of them. In reply to this matter the Sacred Congregation for the Propagation of the Faith stated[116] that priests could seek permission for the use of their faculties from bishops who were regarded to be Catholic, provided that the priests had that degree of certitude regarding the orthodoxy of the bishops which excluded all suspicion of the schism or the error current in that region as attaching to them. In answer to further doubts proposed by the Capuchin missionaries, the same Congregation replied[117] that it was not permissible to seek the permission for the use of even one of the faculties from schismatic bishops. It insisted that the clause which had stated that permission was to be sought must be

116 7 maii 1631, ad 1 — *Fontes*, n. 4447; *Coll. S. C. P. F.*, n. 69; *Fonti*, II, 75.

117 S. C. de Prop. Fide, 7 maii 1631, n. 1 — *Fonti*, II, 75.

understood in regard to bishops who were in communion with the Church of Rome. There was asked the further question whether this permission could be obtained from schismatic pastors, but the reply of the Congregation was the same as that in regard to schismatic bishops.[118]

On May 15, 1709, the Holy Office forbade Catholics to hear the confessions of schismatics or to confess to them.[119] Under no circumstances, not even in the case of necessity, according to a response of the Sacred Congregation for the Propagation of the Faith on February 17, 1761,[120] was it permissible for a Catholic to confess his sins to a schismatic priest in order to obtain absolution from him. In this response no mention was made of the extreme case of a penitent in danger of death, but there was an express advertence to this eventuality in a later reply of the Holy Office.[121]

To a question presented to the Sacred Congregation for the Propagation of the Faith in 1839,[122] the following reply was made. Ethiopian converts were not to receive the sacrament of penance from a heretical priest. Upon the further question whether it was permissible for an Ethiopian missionary to confess to a heretical priest in a case of necessity, the Sacred Congregation furnished the ironical, if not also indignant, reply: "*Nihil esse respondendum.*" The answer to the question appeared so manifest and evident, that to raise the question at all branded the questioner's action as foolhardy, and consequently as deserving no reply.

Here as in every other sacrament the general principle is that it is gravely illicit to request or receive the sacrament of penance from a schismatic minister outside the danger of death. The ordinary necessity which a person senses when he is in the state of mortal sin is not sufficient to allow him to confess to a schismatic priest and to receive absolution. Such a person would be

118 S. C. de Prop. Fide, 1 maii 1631 — *Fonti,* II, 77.
119 *Fontes,* n. 773; *Fonti,* II, 83.
120 *Fontes,* n. 4538; *Fonti,* II, 103.
121 7 iul. 1864 — *Fontes,* n. 978.
122 *Fonti,* I, 93; V, 73.

obliged to make an act of perfect contrition as best he could, and then to await the opportunity to confess his sins to a Catholic priest. He would have to be in extreme necessity, namely, in danger of death, before he would be permitted to confess his sins to a schismatic priest.

However, there is an opinion according to which one could confess his sins to a schismatic priest in circumstances other than when one is in danger of death. There is a practical difficulty current in the Orient where Catholics live in sections which are predominantly schismatic. It is very probable that a Catholic may find himself in a situation which implies the guilt of a mortal sin in his soul and will not have the opportunity of going to confession to a Catholic priest for two or three months. He is in the state of mortal sin, and his conscience is troubled. He tries to make an act of perfect contrition, but he cannot satisfy his conscience in this matter. In this case, if there were no scandal or danger of perversion, such a person could probably confess his sins to a schismatic priest and receive absolution in order that he would no longer remain in the state of mortal sin.[123] Because of the doubt concerning the jurisdiction of the confessor there may arise the question of the validity of such a granted absolution, but if the conditions of common error according to canon 209 are verified, there should be no doubt that such an absolution is valid.[124]

This opinion of Souarn enjoys some probability in so far as there is here involved no violation of the divine law, and under the circumstances as presented, because of the very grave inconvenience, the ecclesiastical law forbidding such religious communication would cease. However, in practice it is unlikely that all the necessary conditions would be present in order to permit such a religious communication. It is difficult to see how the danger of perversion and of scandal could efficaciously be removed.

123 Souarn, *Praxis Missionarii*, pp. 125, 126.

124 Cf. *supra*, page 58.

B. *In Danger of Death*

The case is much different when one is in danger of death. In danger of death all priests, though not approved for confessions, can validly and licitly absolve any penitent from any sins and censures, though reserved and notorious, even if an approved priest is present. However, the prescriptions of canons 884 and 2252 must be observed.[125] The use of the words "all priests" makes the canon very general, and according to the literal sense no one who has the sacerdotal character is excluded. This refers not only to priests of the Catholic Church but also to heretical and schismatical priests.[126]

According to a reply of the Holy Office under date of July 7, 1864,[127] it was stated that one could lawfully seek absolution from a schismatical priest, as long as no scandal was given to the other faithful, provided of course that no Catholic priest was available, provided also that there was no danger of the Catholic's perversion by the heretic, and provided finally that there was a probable belief that the heretical priest would administer the sacrament according to the rites of the Church. This, of course, was but a clarification of the practice that had long been generally accepted in the Church, and that had been expressly sanctioned, at least implicitly, by the Council of Trent.[128]

When a person as a penitent in confession is in danger of death, the Church supplies jurisdiction to all priests for this particular case. Consequently, any priest can give valid absolution when he is face to face with a person who is in danger of death. According to canon 882 no preference is given to a priest of the Catholic Church. Whoever has been validly ordained to the priesthood, no matter how unbecomingly he may have subse-

125 Canon 882.

126 Cappello, *De Sacramentis*, II, n. 298, p. 266; Noldin-Schmitt, *Summa Theologiae Moralis*, III, n. 346, p. 351; Genicot-Salsmans, *Institiones Theologiae Moralis*, II, n. 332, p. 293; Merkelbach, *Summa Theologiae Moralis*, III, n. 585, p. 541.

127 Ad 6 — *Fontes*, n. 978.

128 Conc. Trident., sess. XIV, c. 7 — Schroeder, *Canons and Decrees of the Council of Trent*, p. 96.

quently fulfilled his sacred office, can validly and licitly grant absolution in danger of death, with the single exception of the restriction made in canon 884 regarding licitness.[129] However, the Holy Office has given a particular response in this matter.[130] A schismatic priest can absolve licitly in danger of death only if there is no Catholic priest present. The decision given in this response of the Holy Office is repeated by the authors.[131]

The force of this particular response is still in effect in so far as it is an application of the divine law to a particular situation. Although canon 882 states that in danger of death all priests, though not approved for confessions, can validly and *licitly* absolve any penitent from any and all sins and censures, although reserved and notorious, *even if an approved priest is present,* nevertheless the danger of scandal and of perversion must be avoided. The absence of the danger of scandal and of perversion are conditions of the divine law and take precedence over the prescriptions of canon 882. These dangers will be precluded if a Catholic priest is preferred to the schismatic or the heretic. Consequently this preference is of obligation.

The authors qualify the response of the Holy Office in some respects. Some authors attempt to establish some order or degree of preference among those priests who can be called to absolve the dying, and they list them as follows: 1) One who is approved and who has the faculties of the place; 2) one who is approved in any other diocese; 3) the priest in good standing

129 Moriarty, *The Extraordinary Absolution from Censures,* The Catholic University of America Canon Law Studies, n. 113 (Washington, D. C.: The Catholic University of America, 1938), p. 73. Canon 884 states that a priest cannot validly absolve his accomplice *in peccato turpi* except in danger of death, and that even in danger of death it is illicit for him to do so outside the case of necessity.

130 S. C. S. Off., 7 iul. 1864 — *Fontes,* n. 978.

131 Cappello, *De Sacramentis,* II, n. 298, p. 267; Genicot-Salsmans, *Institutiones Theologiae Moralis,* II, n. 332, p. 293; Regatillo, *Ius Sacramentarium,* I, n. 354, p. 194; Coronata, *Institutiones Iuris Canonici ad usum utriusque cleri et scholarum "De Sacramentis"* (3 vols., Romae: Domus Editorialis Marietti, 1943-1945), I, n. 359, p. 359 (hereafter cited *De Sacramentis).*

who is merely ordained but has no faculties; 4) a priest who is suspended or under interdict; 5) a priest who is irregular; 6) the *excommunicatus vitandus;* 7) the degraded priest; and 8) the heretical and schismatic priest.[132] This gradation, of course, has no preceptive value except for the preference of the Catholic over the heretic or the schismatic.

All other priests are to be preferred to the schismatic or the heretic because religious communication with schismatics or heretics is forbidden, and this is a more serious matter than the reception of the sacraments from an unworthy priest. However, if one is dying and there is no other priest present to whom he can confess without too great difficulty or repugnance, he can licitly call a priest who is publicly a schismatic, and this priest can absolve him validly and licitly from all sins and censures whatever they may be. Although the authors do not mention it, it seems that if the Catholic priest did not understand the language of the penitent, it would be licit for the penitent to prefer a schismatic priest for the administration of the sacrament, especially if this would give him greater peace of conscience.[133] However, the danger of scandal and of perversion would have to be removed.

Absolution given by a schismatic priest to a dying person is ordinarily given licitly, but because of attending circumstances such an absolution could become illicit. The danger of scandal and of perversion must be prevented. Genicot (1856-1900)-Salsmans (1873-1944) considered a dying person to be unworthy of absolution *(incapax absolutionis)* if he should wish to confess to a schismatic priest when there was present another priest to whom he could confess his sins without too great repugnance.[134] When a Catholic chooses a non-Catholic priest in the presence of a suitable Catholic priest he chooses an unauthorized minister and subjects himself to the dangers involved. In fact, the danger of scandal to others, and possibly also to the non-Catholic

132 Coronata, *De Sacramentis*, I, n. 359, p. 359.

133 Cf. Cappello, *De Sacramentis*, II, Pars I, n. 298, p. 266; Regatillo, *Ius Sacramentarium*, I, n. 354, p. 194.

134 *Institutiones Theologiae Moralis*, II, n. 332, p. 293.

minister, will be all the greater when the latter is chosen in the presence of a Catholic priest. In case the penitent would have a justifiable repugnance to making his confession to a Catholic priest, and in consequence thereof made his confession to a non-Catholic priest, precautions would have to be taken to remove whatever dangers are present.[135]

The circumstance under which a schismatic may absolve licitly is the danger of death. This danger arises from a hazardous condition or situation from which as a result it is truly and seriously probable that a person may either survive or die.[136] For a danger of death to exist it is sufficient that the danger be truly probable; and it is not necessary that the danger be certainly imminent or even imminently certain. A real probability of peril constitutes the person in a condition which is to be acknowledged as a danger of death for him.[137] This danger may proceed from either an extrinsic cause, such as war, a dangerous voyage, or from an intrinsic cause, such as sickness, old age, or serious injury. One who is in danger of becoming perpetually insane is to be accounted as in the same condition as one who is in danger of death.[138]

The presence of a danger of death is sufficiently verified if the danger is morally and subjectively judged to be present. Serving as an explanation in this matter are the faculties granted by a decree of the Sacred Penitentiary,[139] which permitted approved confessors who were acting as army chaplains to grant absolution from all sins and censures, *iniunctis de iure iniungendis*, to all those who were engaged in battle and also to all those

[135] Bancroft, *Communication in Religious Worship with Non-Catholics*, p. 106.

[136] Moriarty, *op. cit.*, p. 70; Regatillo, *Ius Sacramentarium*, I, n. 354, p. 194.

[137] Moriarty, *loc. cit.*; Cappello, *Tractatus Canonico-Moralis De Censuris iuxta Codicem Iuris Canonici* (3. ed. Taurinorum Augustae: Marietti, 1933), n. 114, p. 107 (hereafter cited *De Censuris*); Woywod, *Practical Commentary*, I, 430.

[138] Regatillo, *Ius Sacramentarium*, I, p. 194, n. 354; Woywod, *op. cit.*, I, 431; Coronata, *De Sacramentis*, I, n. 359, p. 357.

[139] 25 maii 1915 — *AAS*, VII (1915), 281.

who were attached to the army in any capacity by being assigned to an army camp. There was also a response of the Sacred Penitentiary[140] which declared that every soldier in a state of mobilization could *ipso facto* be regarded as in danger of death, so that he could be absolved by any priest.[141] This seems to refer, however, only to those cases of mobilization in which war is actually being waged or at least is imminent.[142]

It is to be noted that, to describe the case justifying absolution of Catholics by non-Catholic priests, the Council of Trent used the phrase *"articulus mortis,"* whereas canon 882 employs the phrase *"periculum mortis."* There is a difference in these terms, for *in articulo mortis* death is morally certain, whereas *in periculo mortis* there is merely a prudent fear that death will follow shortly.[143] Coronata and Cappello state that the two phrases may be considered as synonymous.[144] Moriarty writes that in the laws on absolution given to a person in danger of death the phrase *articulus mortis* has constantly been interpreted in a broad sense as equivalent to the phrase *periculum mortis.*[145] However, there is now no need for concern over the distinction, since canon 882 uses the more comprehensive phrase of *periculum mortis.*

Although it may be licit in a given case to confess one's sins to a schismatic and to receive absolution from him, there are authors who recommend that a dying person should rather elicit an act of perfect contrition and thus commit himself to the divine mercy.[146] However, if one were not satisfied in conscience that

140 18 martii 1912; 29 maii 1915 — *AAS,* VII (1915), 282; cf. Bouscaren, *The Canon Law Digest* (2 vols., Milwaukee, Wis.: The Bruce Publishing Co., 1934-1943), I, 411.

141 Moriarty, *op. cit.*, p. 71.

142 Aertnys-Damen, *Theologia Moralis,* II, n. 361, p. 253.

143 Genicot-Salsmans, *Institutiones Theologiae Moralis,* II, n. 332, p. 293.

144 Coronata, *De Sacramentis,* I, n. 359, p. 358; Cappello, *De Sacramentis,* I, n. 432, p. 398.

145 *Op. cit.*, p. 69.

146 De Lugo, *De Virtute Fidei Divinae,* disp. XIV, sect. 5 — *Disputationes,* Tom. I, 558; Noldin-Schmitt, *Summa Theologiae Moralis,* II, n. 43, p. 42; Cappello, *De Sacramentis,* I, n. 78, p. 70; II, Pars I, n. 298, p. 267.

he had sufficient sorrow for his sins, it would be better for him under such circumstances to seek absolution from a schismatic priest, as long as there was no danger of perversion or of scandal.

Article VI — Extreme Unction

Religious communication with non-Catholics in regard to the sacrament of extreme unction is given little or no consideration by the authors. As far as can be ascertained, there is also no record of a response having been given by the Holy See specifically in reference to *communicatio in sacris* through this sacrament. The administration of this sacrament apparently presented no particular problem of this kind to those who labored among schismatics. Consequently general principles affecting *communicatio in sacris* will have to be applied by the writer in his consideration of their relation to this sacrament.

The sacrament of extreme unction can be validly administered only by a priest.[147] The laity have no power to administer this sacrament. Canon 938, §2, determines the ordinary minister of the sacrament, who is the pastor of the parish in which the sick person resides. However, exceptions to this rule are contained in canons 397, 3°, 514 and 1368, which refer respectively to the specified dignitary's right of anointing the diocesan bishop, to the right of the superior in a clerical religious communty, and to the right of the seminary rector in the seminary. In what has been said there is no provision which would allow a non-Catholic minister to administer the sacrament.

However, canon 938 continues with the concession that in a case of necessity, or with at least the reasonably presumed permission of the pastor or of the local ordinary, any other priest may administer the sacrament. The problem here is to determine what necessity, if any, would allow a schismatic priest to administer the sacrament.

There is no doubt that a validly ordained schismatic priest can administer the sacrament validly. He has the power of Orders necessary for the administration of the sacrament, and

147 Canon 938, §1.

he needs no jurisdiction for the valid administration.. When he uses oil blessed by his bishop for the anointing of the sick, he uses valid matter. Hence, there is no reason to doubt the validity of his anointing.

There is the custom among Orientals of employing more than one priest for the administration of the sacrament. Kilker (1901-1944) cited Denziger as stating that among the Orientals seven priests regularly perform the rite. If seven are not present then five or three take part in the ceremony and in a case of necessity even one may administer the sacrament.[148] Among the Latins the practice is different. The Roman Ritual leaves place for but a single minister. In any case it is sufficient for the validity of the sacrament that one priest anoint the sick person.[149]

Canon 938, §1, uses the words *"omnis et solus sacerdos."* The scope of *omnis* is in no way circumscribed or qualified, and hence can be understood to include schismatic priests. In stating this point Kilker made no explicit mention of the non-Catholic minister.[150] However, there seems to be no reason for excluding him.

In a case of necessity any priest may lawfully administer the sacrament. The Code itself grants the necessary faculty for the licit administration of the sacrament in such circumstances. Necessity exists when the ordinary minister or his delegate is unavailable and there is danger in any delay occasioned by the quest of another priest.[151] This necessity may be physical or moral.[152] The necessity is physical if the pastor absolutely cannot be called in view of his absence or in consequence of his incapacity through illness. A moral necessity exists when the pastor has incurred some censure which would prevent him from administering the sacrament licitly. Tantamount to a moral

148 Kilker, *Extreme Unction* (St. Louis: B. Herder, 1927), p. 88.

149 Kilker, *op. cit.,* p. 89; Cappello, *De Sacramentis,* Vol. II, pars II, n. 367.

150 *Op. cit.,* p. 84.

151 Regatillo, *Ius Sacramentarium,* I, n. 788.

152 Coronata, *De Sacramentis,* I, n. 548, p. 593; Kilker, *Extreme Unction,* p. 99.

necessity is the case wherein the pastor is asked to grant permission to another priest to confer the sacrament and thereupon unreasonably refuses to do so.[153] However, these distinctions are made by authors to be applied to cases in which the minister is always a Catholic priest. The situation involving the necessity to permit a schismatic priest to act is somewhat different.

The sacrament can be administered by a schismatic priest only when the sick person is in danger of death, and hence this circumstance will always have to be verified. But the necessity which would warrant the reception of the sacrament from a schismatic minister is further dependent on an additional factor. One must consider whether the sacrament of extreme unction is necessary for the salvation of the individual in the given case. Only then is the schismatic priest allowed to confer it on him.

In and of itself the sacrament of extreme unction is not necessary as an essential means for salvation. This denotes that it is not so necessary that, even if a person were to omit receiving it through no fault of his own, his salvation could not be attained. However, extreme unction can in view of particular attendant circumstances be necessary for salvation to certain dying persons. There are cases in which this sacrament is the only and consequently the necessary means of salvation. Such a case would be verified when a man in the state of mortal sin for which he is habitually attrite is deprived of the use of reason.[154] Heaven lies open to him only through the sacrament of extreme unction. Such a condition of soul follows upon circumstances quite incidental, however, for the primary end of extreme unction is not the forgiveness of sins.[155]

Extreme unction can supply a need which a conditional absolution cannot meet. In fact, when one is bereft of his senses, greater security of salvation is given to the dying person through the sacrament of extreme unction than through absolution, for internal attrition is sufficient for the administration of extreme

153 Coronata, *loc. cit.*

154 Regatillo, *Ius Sacramentarium,* I, n. 799; Kilker, *Extreme Unction,* p. 271; Blat, *Commentarium,* IV, n. 288.

155 Kilker, *op. cit.,* p. 271.

unction whereas an attrition externally manifested is very probably required for the sacrament of penance.[156] In the sacrament of extreme unction attrition is required not as an essential part of the sacrament as in penance but as a necessary disposition without which God does not remit sin.[157] The value of extreme unction over absolution lies in the fact that attrition may follow the conferring of the sacrament. In this case the absolution would be valueless, but the grace of extreme unction would revive.

If the penitent were able to confess his sins and receive absolution, it would not be necessary for him to receive extreme unction in order to gain his salvation. Under these latter circumstances he would not be permitted to request the sacrament from a schismatic minister.

Noldin-Schmitt state that it would be licit for one to request the sacrament of extreme unction from a schismatic minister if one would die without the sacrament unless he were to make such a request.[158] This is a rather broad statement which seems to need considerable qualification. Merkelbach (1871-1942) permitted a dying person to receive extreme unction from a schismatic minister if the reception of the sacrament of penance was no longer possible.[159] It would be impossible to receive the grace of the sacrament of penance if attrition were not present at the time absolution was granted. The circumstances must be such that the request for the sacrament will not be considered as a recognition of a false sect. Hence, there would have to be verified the same conditions which were set by the Holy Office in regard to the sacrament of penance.[160]

156 Tanquerey, *Synopsis Theologiae Dogmaticae* (24. ed., 3 vols., Parisiis: Typis Societatis Sancti Joannis Evangelistae, Desclée et Socii, 1933-1938), III, n. 974.

157 Schmitz, *De Effectibus Sacramenti Extremae Unctionis* (Friburgi Brisgoviae: Sumptibus Herder, 1893), p. 73.

158 *Summa Theologiae Moralis*, III, n. 43, p. 42.

159 *Summa Theologiae Moralis*, I, n. 755, p. 584.

160 7 iul. 1864, ad 6: "Licere [i. e., exquirere absolutionem a sacerdote schismatico], dummodo tamen et aliis fidelibus non praebeatur scandalum, nec sit alius sacerdos catholicus, nec sit periculum ut fidelis ab haeretico

Since a person can be constituted in extreme necessity relative to the need of receiving the sacrament of extreme unction, there can arise the situation in which it would be licit for a schismatic minister to administer the sacrament to him. When it is possible for the penitent to confess his sins and to receive absolution he must do so, and there will then be no real necessity for him to receive extreme unction from a schismatic minister. However, when he has lapsed into a state of unconsciousness and is unable to confess his sins or manifest any sorrow for them, it will be licit for a schismatic priest to anoint him as long as no Catholic priest is available. In this case the schismatic minister should first give conditional absolution to prevent a violation of the divine law which requires a person in mortal sin to receive the sacrament of penance when in danger of death.[161] Non-Catholic priests, when administering extreme unction in the name of the Church, should observe its positive dispositions, but it is not presupposed that they will have the knowledge to guide them.[162]

When the schismatic priest anoints a dying Catholic under the conditions and circumstances postulated in authorization of this act, it seems inconceivable that his act could give rise to any danger of perversion for the dying person, but there remains always the question of possible and probable scandal to the bystanders and to the schismatic minister himself. This must be guarded against, and it seems that scandal can effectively be precluded when explanation is made that the Church permits such an action whenever a Catholic is in such great spiritual need.

In reference to this sacrament one should mention that just as it is forbidden to reserve the Blessed Sacrament in a place that is simultaneously used by Protestants, so also the holy oils cannot be kept in a place shared in common by non-Catholics and

pervertatur, et tandem probabiliter credatur sacerdotem haereticum administraturum hoc sacramentum secundum ritus Ecclesiae." — *Fontes,* n. 978. Cf. *supra,* p. 93.

161 Bancroft, *op. cit.,* p. 112.

162 Bancroft, *op. cit.,* p. 110.

Catholics. In lieu of any better place the oils are to be reserved in the parish rectory.[163] Furthermore, in the Constitution *Etsi pastoralis* of Benedict XIV, issued on May 26, 1742,[164] it was forbidden to receive the holy oils from Greek schismatic bishops.

Article VII — Holy Orders

The question of ordination by a schismatic bishop had already been considered in the *Decree* of Gratian[165] and in the Decretals of Gregory IX.[166] The concern of the glossators was not the licitness of the action, but the validity of the orders conferred. In the legislation which followed, the question of licitness was of greater importance, for there was then no doubt about the validity of the orders, if the minister had been validly consecrated and had used the proper matter and form. The question of the validity of orders conferred by schismatics is rather a dogmatic than a juridic consideration. However, it should be affirmed at this point that the ordinations of the Oriental dissidents are generally considered as valid.[167] The same is to be said for the ordinations of the Jansensists in Holland and of the Old Catholics in Germany and Holland.[168] However, because of recent developments among the Oriental dissidents and among schismatics in general, much doubt has been cast upon the validity of the orders of certain schismatic priests, and consequently each individual case should be judged on its own merits.

Clement VIII in his Instruction *Sanctissimus* of August 31, 1595,[169] stated that those who had received ordination at the hands of schismatic bishops who apart from their schismatic status were properly consecrated — the necessary form having

163 S. C. de Prop. Fide (C.G. — Helvetiae), 7 mart. 1805 — *Fontes,* n. 4681; *Fonti,* II, 115.

164 §IV, n. II — *Fontes,* n. 328.

165 C. 5, C. XI, q. 1.

166 C. 1, X, *de schismaticis et ordinatis ab eis,* V, 8.

167 Cappello, *De Sacramentis,* II, Pars III, n. 283, p. 235.

168 Algermissen, *Christian Denominations,* p. 357.

169 *Fontes,* n. 179.

been observed — did indeed receive orders, but not the right to exercise them. In this he repeated the doctrine of the glossators.[170]

Benedict XIV in the Constitution *Etsi pastoralis* of May 26, 1742,[171] confirmed this doctrine of Clement VIII. On the question of schismatic ordinations these two papal documents present a practically identical wording. Not only was the recognized validity of schismatic orders established, but further points were clarified. Schismatic bishops were not to be admitted for the conferring of orders or for the administration of any of the other sacraments. Persons ordained by schismatic bishops were, upon a proper rectification or amendment in their status, to be reconciled and absolved. An appropriate penance was to be imposed on them. If they had embraced any errors, they had previously to abjure them; if they had not embraced any errors, they had nevertheless to renounce the schism of their ordaining prelate. The abjuration was to be made either publicly or secretly, as the facts in the case directed. Before the ordained persons could exercise their Orders, it was necessary for them to receive from the Holy See a dispensation from the irregularity which they had incurred.[172]

In spite of the teaching set forth in the Instruction *Sanctissimus* of Clement VIII, the Holy Office seemed to take a rather lenient view toward permitting ordinations by schismatics in its response of June 7, 1639.[173] It was asked how one should act toward those who when coming to confession had the intention of presenting themselves to a Greek Bishop for the reception of sacred orders, and in particular to a bishop who was a schismatic or a heretic, or who was involved in simony inasmuch as his consecration had been accompanied with a payment of money. The answer was given that those who *for a just cause* wished to approach a schismatic bishop who, if excommunicated, was nevertheless not a *vitandus,* could be absolved, since the desire,

170 Ad c. 1, X, *de schismaticis et ordinatis ab eis, V,* 8.

171 §VII, n. XIII — *Fontes,* n. 328.

172 *Ibid.,* nn. XI, XIV, XV — *Fontes,* n. 328.

173 *Fonti,* I, 79.

motivated by a just cause, did not entail a sin. However, it was not permissible for one to entertain the arbitrary desire to approach a simoniacal bishop for the reception of Orders.[174] At the same time it was asked whether it was licit to absolve those who approached the confessor in good faith, thinking namely that they had not sinned and that they had not incurred any censure or any penalty by having received sacred Orders from dissidents and simoniacal bishops, and, further, whether they should be left in good faith. The Holy Office stated that they could be absolved, in so far as they needed absolution, by one who had the requisite authority, and that they were to be given a warning or an admonition in the same sense in which it was called for in relation to other sins.

On this same matter there was still another response of the Holy Office on November 21, 1709.[175] No Armenian Catholic bishops were available for ordaining priests who were needed in Ispahan, and so it was asked whether sacred Orders could be received from schismatical or heretical bishops. The Holy Office replied that in no way could that be allowed, and that those who had been ordained by such bishops were irregular and suspended from the exercise of their Orders.

The reception of holy Orders from the hands of schismatic bishops has practically always been forbidden by the Church. Rarely has the Holy See ever considered it necessary to receive Orders from a schismatic bishop.

The prohibition to receive holy Orders at the hands of a schismatic bishop is contained in the general prohibition against active religious communication as expressed in canon 1258, §1. There is also an implicit prohibition contained in canon 2372, wherein it is stated that those who presume to receive Orders from a notorious schismatic automatically incur a suspension *a divinis* reserved to the Apostolic See. Any person who has

174 "Posse absolvi volentes ex iusta causa accedere ad Episcopos schismaticos excommunicatos toleratos, cum taliter volendo non peccent; volentes accedere ad simoniacos communicando cum ipsis in crimine non posse." — *Fonti*, I, 79.

175 *Fontes*, n. 774; *Fonti*, II, 115.

been ordained in good faith by such men forfeits the right to exercise the Order thus received until he obtains a dispensation from the prohibition. Sipos remarks that any Orders which a cleric had prior to the reception of Orders in good faith from a schismatic would not fall under the penalty, and the cleric could exercise such Orders. His argument is based on the wording of the canon, *ordines sic recepti.*[176]

Canon 2372 adequately provides a solution for any case in which holy Orders have been received from schismatics, for it distinguishes between the reception of Orders in good faith and the reception of Orders in bad faith. In the present it is impossible to imagine a situation in which necessity would warrant the reception of Orders from the hands of a schismatic contrary to the prescriptions of the Church.

Article VIII — Matrimony

When a mixed marriage is contracted, whether the contract be made before a priest of the Catholic Church or in the presence of a non-Catholic minister, there is necessarily involved a religious communication between the parties contracting the marriage. In a valid marriage the sacred character of the ceremony is evident. Since a valid marriage between baptized persons is at the same time a sacramental bond, and since the parties themselves are the ministers of the sacrament, the *communicatio in sacris* becomes apparent.[177] The *communicatio in sacris* is much more apparent in mixed than in disparate marriages, since in a disparate marriage at least the unbaptized party cannot receive the sacrament.[178] However, for the present the religious communication which takes place between the parties contracting a valid mixed marriage *coram Ecclesia* is not the principal concern. This religious communication belongs to the category of negative communication, which will be given some consideration

176 Sipos, *Enchiridion Iuris Canonici,* p. 462.

177 Schenk, *The Matrimonial Impediments of Mixed Religion and Disparity of Cult,* pp. 74, 75; cf. Blat, *Commentarium,* III, 561.

178 Schenk, *op. cit.,* p. 75, ftn. 6.

in the latter part of this dissertation. The concern here is rather with the religious ceremony which takes place in the presence of a schismatic minister.

A. *Marriages of Catholics Before a Schismatic Minister Acting in His Official Religious Capacity*

Marriages between Catholics and schismatics are forbidden by the prohibitive impediment of mixed religion.[179] If there is a danger of perversion for the Catholic spouse and for the offspring, such a marriage is prohibited also by the divine law. But even the Church's own prohibition is a very severe one, and a dispensation is not granted unless: 1) there be just and grave causes; 2) the non-Catholic party give guarantees that the danger of perversion for the Catholic party will be removed, and both parties promise that the children will be baptized and brought up only in the Catholic faith; and 3) there be a moral certainty that the promises will be fulfilled.[180]

It is not the purpose here to discuss the nature of this impediment, and hence for further information the reader is referred to authors who treat this question specifically.[181] It is sufficient for the purposes of this study to recall that the impediment exists. From the days of St. John and St. Paul, who forbade association with heretics, the Church has traditionally forbidden mixed marriages.[182] When the Holy See in later centuries repeated the constant prohibition of the Church in regard to mixed marriages it emphasized as the reason the disgraceful communion in sacred things involved in such marriages.[183]

Even when the Church dispenses from the impediment, the

179 Cf. can. 1060.

180 Can. 1061, §1.

181 Schenk, *op. cit.;* Ayrinhac-Lydon, *Marriage Legislation in the New Code of Canon Law* (new revised edition, New York: Benziger Bros., 1940), pp. 98-117.

182 Ayrinhac-Lydon, *op. cit.*, p. 99; Schenk, *op. cit.*, p. 73; Petrovits, *The New Church Law on Matrimony* (2. ed., Philadelphia: J. J. McVey, 1926), n. 188.

183 Schenk, *op. cit.*, p. 74.

marriage must take place in the Catholic Church. In this case there is nevertheless a religious communication between the spouses. The schismatic actively participates in the Catholic religious ceremony, for he is at once the minister and the recipient of the sacrament. Active participation of schismatics with Catholics is ordinarily forbidden, but the action in this instance is licit. This can be proved from the universal practice of the faithful and of the Church, which has always permitted it for a grave reason.[184] Some danger of perversion is always present when one contracts marriage with a schismatic, but for very serious reasons it is sometimes licit to expose oneself to such danger if proper measures are taken to forestall it.[185]

Although the Church dispenses from the impediment of mixed religion, it most seriously forbids the marriage to take place before a schismatic minister. As early as 1672 the question of going before a heretical minister to exchange marriage consent was presented to the Holy Office.[186] It was asked whether one could appear before a heretical minister for this purpose in order to evade more serious evil consequences, even after marriage had been duly contracted *in facie Ecclesiae.* The Holy Office replied that, if the minister acted in the capacity of a *minister politicus,* the action was licit. But if he acted as a minister *addictus sacris,*[187] then it was illicit to appear before him, and

184 De Lugo, *De Sacramentis in Genere,* disp. VIII, sect. 14 — Disputationes, Tom. III, 428-431.

185 De Lugo, *De Virtute Fidei Divinae,* disp. XXII, sect. 2 — *Disputationes,* Tom. III, 90.

186 *Fontes,* n. 751.

187 A non-Catholic minister acts in the capacity of a minister *"uti sacris addictus"* if he assists at the marriage by virtue of the fact that he is a minister of religion, not as a civil official deputed by the State to assist at marriages. If he is at the same time deputed by the civil authority to witness marriages he acts in his ministerial capacity if he uses any vestment of his office, namely, such vestments as are worn at religious functions and not the ordinary ministerial apparel worn on the street or about the house, such as a roman collar or the equivalent of a cassock or a habit, or if he employs any religious rites or ceremonies. Presumably he acts also in this capacity by the mere fact that he witnesses the marriage in a non-Catholic place of worship. Cf. Schenk, *op. cit.,* pp. 258, 259.

those guilty of such an action sinned mortally and were to be admonished of their guilt. This same distinction was made in a reply of the Sacred Congregation for the Propagation of the Faith on August 6, 1764.[188] Even in order to evade or escape from a most grave persecution, Catholics could not contract marriage before a heretical priest. However, since the act of contracting in his presence was forced upon Catholics principally for the sake of reaping the stipend attached to the service, then, if a person by paying the stipend could free himself from all further obligation, he was not only allowed, but even advised, to do so.

It was illicit for a Catholic to ask for or to receive the nuptial blessing from a non-Catholic minister. This was stated in a response of the Holy Office on January 29, 1817.[189]

In 1858 the Sacred Congregation for the Propagation of the Faith in an Instruction[190] ordered the Greek Rumanian Bishops diligently to acquaint the faithful and to warn them concerning the sin which they would commit if they approached a schismatic priest for the celebration of the marriage or the reception of the nuptial blessing. So doing the faithful transgressed the law of the Church which forbade a *communicatio in sacris*, and they likewise gave scandal to others and exposed themselves to the danger of perversion.

The legislation of the Church regarding the manner of the celebration of mixed marriages was finally summarized in an Instruction of the Holy Office on December 12, 1888.[191] This Instruction was directed to all bishops of the Oriental rite, and

188 *Fontes*, n. 4544; *Fonti*, II, 105.

189 *Fontes*, n. 852; *Fonti*, II, 117.

190 *Fontes*, n. 4843; *Fonti*, X, 245.

191 N. 7: "Illicitum porro ac sacrilegium est se sistere coram haeretico seu schismatico ministro ante vel post contractas mixtas nuptias, quoties ipse ut minister sacris addictus adsistat, et quasi parochi munere fungens; nam pars catholica ritui haeretico aut schismatico se consociaret, ex quo vetita omnibus haberetur cum haereticis in eorum sacris communicatio. Quare ita contrahentes mortaliter peccarent, ac monendi sunt. Si vero, ut in nonnullis locis evenit, haereticus seu schismaticus personam agat magistratus mere civilis, et quidquid ipse praestat, civilis dumtaxat et politicus

in it were enunciated the principles which were to form the basis of the future legislation concerning the manner of contracting mixed marriages.

The content of this Instruction was summarized in canon 1063 of the Code of Canon Law. The prohibition of canon 1063 refers only to those cases wherein one appears before a non-Catholic minister in his official religious capacity. Among schismatics there is no doubt that the marriage ceremony is a religious ceremony when the schismatic priest performs the marriage as the official minister of the schismatic church. For one to contract marriage before a schismatic minister acting in this capacity would be to participate actively in a forbidden religious rite. This is contrary to the general principles of canon 1258, and the practice has been repeatedly condemned by the decisions of the Holy See. Even when an Oriental Catholic could contract a valid marriage before a schismatic minister,[192] he would be forbidden to contract marriage in the presence of such a minister because of the forbidden religious communication implied in such an act.

The only case in which one would be permitted to appear before a schismatic minister would occur when the schismatic minister acts merely as a civic official, and the parties, in order to comply with the civil law and to obtain civil recognition for their marriage, appear before him.[193] If the minister were to make the act a religious ceremony by using sacred vestments or rites, it would be forbidden to appear before him.

The Church has always taken this stand in regard to the contracting of marriages before a non-Catholic minister. Those Catholics who violate the prescriptions of canon 1063, §1, automatically incur an excommunication reserved to the ordinary.[194]

actus sit, ac civiles effectus respiciat, et nulla prorsus acatholici ritus professio habeatur, aut inde colligi possit, non improbatur quod pars catholica, urgentibus schismaticis seu haereticis, aut civili lege imperante, eumdem ante vel post initum matrimonium adeat." — *Fontes*, n. 1112.

192 Marbach, *Marriage Legislation for the Catholics of the Oriental Rites in the United States and Canada*, p. 202.

193 Can. 1063, §3.

194 Can. 2319, §1, 1°.

Since this is a penal canon, it is to be interpreted strictly, but because of the precise wording of canon 1063, there are many divergent opinions as to the conditions under which the excommunication is incurred.

Canon 1063 envisions a double ceremony, although the authors generally hold that the double ceremony is not postulated as a condition for the incurring of the censure. The canon is concerned primarily with the *communicatio in sacris* with non-Catholic ministers through the parties' appearing before them to give or to renew matrimonial consent. It is the violation of this prohibition, quite independently of any condition of a *doubleness* of the ceremony, that entails the censure enacted in canon 2319, §1, 1°.[195]

It is disputed also whether the censure is incurred if both parties are Catholic. Cappello[196] holds that in this case the censure would not be incurred, but there are authors who hold the opposite view.[197]

In conjunction with the penalty enacted in the common law of the Church in canon 2319, §1, 1°, consideration must be given to the particular law of the III Plenary Council of Baltimore (1884). The Council of Baltimore enacted an excommunication reserved to the ordinary for an attempted marriage before a non-Catholic minister.[198] The wording of this law is more general than that of canon 2319, §1, 1°, and certainly does not restrict the application of the censure to a double ceremony, or to a mixed marriage. In virtue of canon 6, 5°, the authors con-

195 Schenk, *op. cit.*, pp. 263, 264; cf. Ayrinhac-Lydon, *Marriage Legislation in the New Code of Canon Law*, p. 114.

196 *De Censuris*, n. 369, p. 320.

197 Petrovits, *op. cit.*, n. 270; Schenk, *op. cit.*, p. 265; cf. Ayrinhac-Lydon, *op. cit.*, p. 114.

198 N. 127: "Item decernimus Catholicos, qui coram ministro cujuscumque sectae acatholicae matrimonium contraxerint vel attentaverint, extra propriam dioecesim, in quolibet statu vel territorio sub ditione praesulum qui huic concilio adsunt vel adesse debent, excommunicationem incurrere Episcopo reservatam, a qua tamen quilibet dictorum Ordinariorum sive per se, sive per sacerdotem ad hoc delegatum absolvere poterit." — *Acta et Decreta Concilii Plenarii Baltimorensis Tertii* A. D. 1884.

sider this legislation of the Baltimore Council to be still in effect.[199]

B. *The Presence of Catholics at Schismatic Marriages*

When speaking specifically of schismatic marriages, the Holy See always has forbidden Catholics to act as the official witnesses in a schismatic marriage ceremony. Catholics were forbidden to assist in an active way *(per compari nel matrimonio)* according to a response for the Isle of Paros on March 2, 1789.[200] Later, in another response of the Sacred Congregation for the Propagation of the Faith on August 2, 1803,[201] it was again forbidden for Catholics to act as witnesses at the marriages of schismatics.

Authors do not treat this phase of religious communication under the specific consideration of a schismatic ceremony. They rather consider it from the viewpoint of non-Catholic marriages in general. Many have in mind the Protestant marriage ceremony which has few characteristics of a religious ceremony. Consequently the statements and opinions of authors are not always applicable to the question at hand.

Under the laws of Oriental schismatic churches, a schismatic marriage is in general always a religious ceremony. The marriage of schismatics is to take place in the presence of witnesses, and furthermore the priest must be present and there must be a religious rite, since clandestine marriages are forbidden.[202] There is some dispute among the authors as to what, in the eyes of schismatics, precisely constitutes the essence of a valid marriage contract, but there is no disagreement as to the religious nature of the ceremony.

Merkelbach stated that it is never licit to act as a witness for a marriage which takes place in the presence of a heretical

199 Cf. Beste, *Introductio in Codicem*, pp. 58, 939; Ayrinhac-Lydon, *op. cit.*, p. 114.

200 *Fontes*, n. 4626; *Fonti*, II, 111.

201 *Fontes*, n. 4675; *Fonti*, II, 113.

202 Jugie, *Theologia Dogmatica Christianorum Orientalium*, III, 448, 449.

minister.[203] It is also illicit, he stated, to act as a *paranymphus* who leads the bride, not to the groom, but to the altar or to the minister. The reason for this prohibition is that by participating in this ceremony the witness or the *paranymphus* implicitly recognizes the authority of the minister. The term *paranymphus* was used by De Lugo in his description of the same functionary,[204] and his opinion was substantially that which more recently was espoused by Merkelbach.

Noldin-Schmitt express a similar opinion in stating that it is illicit to perform any function in the marriage of heretics which is necessary for the validity of the marriage, such as to act as a witness, or to do that which constitutes a part of the sacred rite, since it connotes a tacit approval of a false sect.[205] However, in a note to the paragraph these authors add that the office of the first bride's maid is commonly considered here in America as a mere civil function.[206]

Prümmer holds a similar position in regard to this matter, stating that it can be tolerated for a Catholic, by reason of civil duty, to perform the office of bridesmaid *(munus domicellae honorariae)* or of best man at the marriage ceremony of heretics and even at mixed marriages contracted in the presence of a non-Catholic minister, as long as there is no scandal or danger of perversion or any contempt of ecclesiastical authority.[207] He bases his opinion on the response of the Holy Office of January 14, 1874.[208]

203 *Summa Theologiae Moralis,* I, n. 756, p. 585.

204 *De Virtute Fidei Divinae,* disp. XIV, sect. 5 — *Disputationes,* Tom. I, 556; De Lugo stated that the *paranymphus* was also referred to as the *Pronubus* or *Auspex.*

205 *Summa Theologiae Moralis,* II, n. 39, p. 39.

206 "Puellae, quae ut in America septentrionali principalem assistentiam sponsae agunt (first bride's maid), ex communi aestimatione solum civile officium praestare censentur." — *Summa Theologiae Moralis,* II, n. 39, p. 40.

207 *Manuale Theologiae Moralis,* I, n. 526, ftn. 3.

208 Ad 2: "Possuntne catholici interesse quovis modo nuptiis haereticorum, schismaticorum, et infidelium; vel etiam iis nuptiis quae illicite contrahuntur, valide aut invalide, ab uno ex istis cum parte catholica? — Ad 2. "De regula, Negative. Tolerari tamen posse ut catholici huiusmodi

McHugh-Callan hold a similar opinion when they give as an example of passive participation in a non-Catholic service the act of officiating as bridesmaid or best man at a wedding.[209] Davis states that in Protestant marriages Catholics in general should not act as witnesses, although in some places this act is tolerated when no scandal is given.[210] However, he adds that little good comes from the participation of Catholics in non-Catholic services.

In spite of the rather lenient opinions of the above-cited authors, it cannot be stated as a general principle that one is permitted to act as the maid of honor or first bridesmaid or as the best man at a non-Catholic marriage ceremony. This office is commonly considered as an active participation in the non-Catholic ceremony and as contrary to the prohibition of canon 1258, §1. It is possible that in certain localities this office may be considered as a mere civil function, but this fact should not be determined by private authority. The procedure which is to be followed should be determined by the ordinary of the place. Consequently, in a practical difficulty the ordinary should be consulted before one is permitted to act as the maid of honor or first bridesmaid or as the best man at a non-Catholic marriage ceremony.

Although Prümmer draws his conclusion from a response of the Holy Office,[211] his opinion is not expressly supported in the response. The response merely permits passive participation in a non-Catholic marriage ceremony, whereas Prümmer concludes that to act as bridesmaid or as best man would be a passive participation.

Genicot-Salsmans forbid a Catholic to act as the official witness in a non-Catholic marriage ceremony for the reason that it

nuptiis civilis officii causa tantum adsint, semoto scandalo, et quovis perversionis periculo, et ecclesiasticae auctoritatis contemptu." — *Fontes,* n. 1028.

209 *Moral Theology,* I, n. 974, p. 382.

210 *Moral and Pastoral Theology,* I, 285.

211 14 ian. 1874, ad 2 — *Fontes,* n. 1028; cf. *supra,* page 113.

involves a recognition of the sect.[212] Vermeersch, although referring specifically to a mixed marriage contracted in the presence of a non-Catholic minister, stated that a Catholic could not act as a witness in the strict sense of the term.[213]

In practice the official witnesses of the marriage are the maid of honor or first bridesmaid and the best man. However, even when the maid of honor or first bridesmaid or the best man do not act as official witnesses, or when their office is not necessary for the validity of the marriage contract, it would still be illicit for a Catholic to perform this office in a non-Catholic marriage ceremony, since it regularly constitutes an active participation in a non-Catholic rite.

In consideration of the factors of civil duty and civic honor, it will be licit, if there is no danger of scandal or perversion, for a Catholic to act as one of the attendants, ushers, or bridesmaids as long as this office does not entail any active religious participation or imply an approval of the schismatic sect. One could give the bride away to the groom, but not to the schismatic minister. However, it is difficult to envision a case in which one would be justified in performing this function. If there is any serious doubt in the matter, the ordinary should be consulted.

Provision for the material presence of a Catholic at a schismatic marriage is made in canon 1258, §2. When there is no danger of scandal or of perversion, a Catholic may assist materially at the marriage ceremony for the purpose of showing respect to a person, if he has a grave reason for so doing. This type of communication has been permitted in the replies of the Sacred Congregations, although in general the replies tend to discourage such practices.

Catholics were ordinarily forbidden to be present at the celebration of marriages on the part of heretics or schismatics. This was stated in a response of the Holy Office on May 10,

212 *Institutiones Theologiae Moralis*, I, n. 201, p. 151.

213 *Theologiae Moralis Principia, Responsa, Consilia* (4 vols. in 3, ed. altera auctior et emendatior, Brugis — Firme Charles Beyaert: Parisiis, 1926-1928), II, n. 52.

1770.[214] The wording of the prohibition was such as evidently to allow exceptions, but no direct indication was given in explanation of what constituted such exceptions. However, at a later date the Holy Office was asked whether Catholics were in any way allowed to be present at the wedding ceremony of heretics, of schismatics, and of infidels, or at marriages which were being illicitly contracted, validly or invalidly, by one of the above-mentioned with a Catholic person.[215] As a rule, so the answer stated, their presence was not allowed, but it could be tolerated in consideration of the fulfillment of a civil duty, provided, always, that scandal was duly obviated, that no danger of perversion was present, and that no contempt of ecclesiastical authority was implied in the act of their presence.

The authors likewise permit such a material presence of Catholics at schismatic marriages. De Lugo stated that it is licit to be present at the marriages of heretics which take place before a heretical minister as long as Catholics do not join in the rites or prayers, but look upon the rite as a profane ceremony.[216] Genicot-Salsmans asserted that precaution must be taken lest one's passive assistance be considered as an approval of an illicit action. This is especially true if close relatives are present at a wedding ceremony in which a Catholic contracts marriage before a Protestant minister contrary to the prohibition of the Church.[217] Since this same prohibition exists in the case of a schismatic minister, the opinion of these authors can be applied also to it.

Noldin-Schmitt restate the provisions of canon 1258, §2, which permit a material presence at non-Catholic marriages.[218] Merkelbach stated that it is regularly illicit to assist at non-Catholic marriages even in a material way, unless the presence at the ceremony is warranted in consideration of the factors of

214 *Fontes,* n. 828; *Fonti,* II, 109.

215 14 ian. 1874 — *Fontes,* n. 1028; cf. *supra,* page 113.

216 *De Virtute Fidei Divinae,* disp. XIV, sect. 5 — *Disputationes,* Tom. I, 556.

217 *Institutiones Theologiae Moralis,* I, n. 201, p. 151.

218 *Summa Theologiae Moralis,* II, n. 39, p. 39.

civil duty or civic honor, provided always that the act of presence does not occasion any scandal or reflect any contempt of ecclesiastical authority.[219]

From what has been said in regard to mere presence at marriages contracted before non-Catholic ministers, the following conclusions can be made. It can be stated as a general principle that it is regularly illicit to be present at marriages which take place in the presence of a schismatic minister. Consequently one could not be present for such a ceremony merely out of curiosity. However, if the marriage is contracted between two non-Catholics, even though it takes place in a schismatic church, one could be materially present for this ceremony if he had a grave reason in view of the considerations of civil duty and civic honor, as long as there was no occasion for the emergence of scandal.

If one of the parties of the marriage is a Catholic, and consequently is contracting marriage contrary to the prescriptions of the Church, a more serious reason is necessary to allow one to assist at such a marriage. It would be better for one not to be present at all, for in this case one's presence is all too readily interpreted as an approval of the illicit action. This would offer a cause for scandal, for it would confirm the person in his evil action. A parent would have the obligation of disapproving such an action on the part of his or her son or daughter. A parent's presence at the wedding ceremony would almost inevitably imply an approval for the very action against which a disapproval must in duty be registered. The material presence of a close relative at a marriage attempted by a Catholic contrary to the laws of the Church is to be discouraged, although it cannot altogether be declared illicit, for the Holy Office declared that it can be tolerated under the particular conditions which warrant a material presence.[220]

219 *Summa Theologiae Moralis,* I, n. 756, p. 585.

220 14 ian. 1874 — *Fontes,* n. 1028; cf. *supra,* *page* 113.

CHAPTER VI

COMMUNICATION IN REGARD TO THE SACRAMENTALS

ARTICLE I — THE SACRAMENTALS IN GENERAL

Sacramentals are sacred things, although they do not compare with the sacraments either in their dignity or in their effects. There is likewise no similar strict obligation of receiving them. The consideration here is the sacramentals not of the Catholic Church but of the schismatic churches. Since the sacramentals are of ecclesiastical institution, their use could be restricted by the Church, which could under pain of nullity forbid schismatics to confer or administer the sacramentals. However, there is no such general prohibition which forbids schismatics to administer the sacramentals. Consequently, water blessed by a schismatic priest for the use of his subjects can have a salutary effect according to the mind of the Church if the ubject is properly disposed. Only blessings which are expressly reserved to the Apostolic See would be invalid if administered by a priest without a special faculty.[1]

Whether the sacramental be validly or invalidly administered by a schismatic, since it is a *res sacra* which is administered in a schismatic rite, Catholics are forbidden to participate in its administration. This follows in virtue of the prohibition of canon 1258, §1.

Since this canon does not distinguish between the various types of *res sacrae* in non-Catholic sects, it is forbidden to participate actively in the use of the sacramentals of schismatics as well as in the use of their sacraments. Exceptions are granted in regard to the sacraments in circumstances of extreme necessity. Since there cannot exist an extreme necessity in regard to the sacramentals, it will never be licit to receive them or actively to

1 Cf. can. 1147, §3.

participate in the use of them at the hands of a schismatic priest. This principle has been borne out by the responses of the Holy See in this matter.

On March 12, 1789, the Sacred Congregation for the Propagation of the Faith forbade a Catholic who had schismatic parents to observe a year of mourning by burning lamps in a Greek schismatic church according to the practice of the Greeks.[2]

In an Instruction of the Holy Office for the United States[3] it was declared to be wrong to invite heretics to the choir for sacred functions, to sing the psalms alternately with them, to give them the *pax,* blessed ashes, candles, blessed palms, and other like things which form part of the external worship, all of which are properly considered as indications of an interior bond and of the union of mind and heart among the worshippers, either in the active, or in the passive sense. Not only were Catholics forbidden to give these sacramentals to heretics, but they were likewise forbidden to receive similar objects from heretics in their sacred functions. In either case such actions would be tantamount to welcoming them and to communicating in their evil *(malignis)* works.

It was also illicit for a Catholic to ask for or to receive the nuptial blessing from a non-Catholic minister.[4]

Toward the close of the nineteenth century the Holy See had on several occasions received word that in the provinces of Imperial Russia Catholic students in the public schools and in the gymnasia were repeatedly in the course of the year forced to go to non-Catholic places of worship, to join with non-Catholics in their sacred functions, and to participate in non-Catholic rites. They had to kiss a cross offered by a non-Catholic minister, genuflect, take blessed bread, and perform other ceremonies. In consideration of the attendant dangers and disquieting anxieties, and with a view to setting at rest the disturbed minds of the

2 *Fontes,* n. 4626; *Fonti,* II, 113.

3 22 iun. 1859 — *Fontes,* n. 952; *Fonti,* II, 133.

4 S.C.S.Off. (Saxoniae), 29 ian. 1817 — *Fontes,* n. 852; *Fonti,* II, 117.

authorities responsible for the faithful, the Holy Office on April 26, 1894,[5] decreed the following:

1) The indicated circumstances could not be considered as implying merely civil ceremonies, but entailed the absolutely forbidden *communicatio in sacris* with non-Catholics, and hence it was absolutely illicit for the Catholic students to take an intimate part in such ceremonies.
2) Teachers of religion in the said schools were bound, if they were asked by the students or their parents, to issue a warning that such a communication could not be tolerated, since it was contrary to the divine and the ecclesiastical laws.
3) But if upon being asked they had warned the students, or had objected in vain to the enforced communication, they were not bound to repeat the protestations or warnings, unless there was a founded hope that the repeated protestation would turn out to be useful and efficacious. They could also refrain from repeating the warning whenever greater evils were to be feared as superseding the already current evil.
4) But if the instructors of religion were not asked by the students, then in view of the very grave situation, and with the factor of scandal duly obviated, they could remain silent, if the students were in good faith. In this matter the said teachers could stand by the judgment of the bishop.
5) Confessors concerned with this matter were bound diligently to instruct, to correct, and to exhort those students who, although not ignorant that such communication was gravely illicit, nevertheless practiced it because of the fear of imminent evils; they were similarly to correct and warn the parents who were the authors of the wrong committed by their children. They accordingly had to deny absolution in the absence of a serious promise on the part of the children and the parents to abstain in the future from committing or commanding the forbidden communication. But if the children or the parents were in good faith, then in view of the very delicate and serious situation, the confessors could dissimulate the issue, leave the penitents in good faith, and abstain from warning them.

[5] *Fontes*, n. 1169; *Fonti*, XI, 885, 887; *Analecta Ecclesiastica*, III (1895), 147.

6) But whenever it was the custom that not all the students were charged to be present at the sacred functions of non-Catholics, but only a part, as chosen from the rest, assisted in the name of all, the Sacred Congregation declared that any participation, whether in the election or in the representation of the group, was illicit. However, if the students were in good faith, one could remain silent as long as such action did not give rise to scandal.

On this matter of communication in regard to the sacramentals the authors have nothing to say, or at most they refer to the decisions of the Sacred Congregations. Recently, however, some views have been expressed in a current publication, and the opinions of the author are rather extreme.[6] According to the author of the article it would seem to be licit to participate actively in the sacramentals of Oriental schismatics as long as there is no danger of perversion or scandal, and provided that one has no intention of professing a false worship. He states that when one is present in a schismatic church, it is licit for him to make the sign of the cross at the priest's benediction, to accept a candle offered to him, or to kiss the cross or the hand of the schismatic priest. In the case as it is explained the author states that there is no profession of the tenets of a false sect, since one is simply giving honor to those things which are held as holy both by the schismatic priest and by the Catholic who is participating. Furthermore, he argues that there is no danger of scandal or perversion under the circumstances as they are presented, and because of these facts he justifies the action. An important factor is the locality in which such communication is represented, namely, in sections of Europe where Catholics and schismatics live in close contact, and where in many instances the schismatics predominate.

However, the view just presented is difficult to reconcile with the present law of the Code which prohibits without qualification active communication in the sacred rites of non-Catholics. This

6 Cf. "On Conducting Oneself in an Orthodox Church," *The Voice of the Church*, December, 1944, pp. 14-17; also *Eastern Churches Quarterly*, V (1944), 351 ff.

opinion likewise finds no support in the responses of the Holy Office on these matters.[7]

A frequent source of communication with schismatics in the sacramentals is the burial service of schismatics. Apart from the funeral Mass there are the transportation and the deportation of the body, the carrying of lighted candles, the recitation of various prayers, and similar actions which occasion a religious communication of Catholics with schismatics. On this particular point the Holy Office has issued numerous instructions and responses, and has designated specifically what is permitted and what is forbidden when Catholics are present at schismatic funeral services. Because of the particular nature of the funeral service and the frequency with which it occurs, the treatment of it as a specific problem seems indicated here.

Article II — Funerals and Burials

The principles governing assistance of Catholics at the funeral services of schismatics are similar to those which regulate assistance at weddings. Both occasions are specifically mentioned in canon 1258, §2, and the same conditions must be present for a licit assistance in either case. Out of respect for the dead by reason of one's relationship, in view of one's civil duty, or in honor of the deceased, one would be permitted to be present at the complete funeral service of a schismatic, but his presence would have to be passive.

By an analogy with the complete Catholic funeral service, there are three principal parts in the schismatic service: 1) the transfer of the body; 2) the funeral services in the church; and 3) the burial or interment of the body. In showing respect for the dead it is not always necessary to be present for all three of these rites, and when it is possible to absent oneself from one or the other without giving offense, one should do so. The principal service is the one which takes place in church, and if one has a duty of any kind to be present for the funeral, he will certainly

[7] Cf. S.C.S.Off. instr. 22 iun. 1859 — *Fontes,* n. 952; S.C.S.Off. 26 apr. 1894 — *Fontes,* n. 1169.

be expected to be present for the church service. One might readily omit attendance at the other parts of the funeral service without giving any offense, though, under the law of the Code, there is no strict obligation to do so.

The customs of the place will determine to a great extent what is to be expected of the one who attends a schismatic funeral. However, no Catholic is permitted to assist actively in any way. Since Mass for the dead will be the principal part of the service, the one who is present for it will have to conduct himself according to the principles regulating passive assistance at Mass.[8]

The Holy See has given responses in regard to particular practices which take place during a funeral rite. The answers all follow the general principles. When the action constitutes an active participation, such as the carrying of a lighted candle or the joining with others in their prayers, the Holy See forbids the action. A mere material presence is tolerated, although in general all attendance at such functions is discouraged.

On April 4, 1658, the Holy Office was questioned concerning the licitness of a bishop's presence at the funeral services of heretics.[9] The recently-converted bishop of the Jacobites had asked whether he could attend the funerals of his priests, also recently converted, even if some of them had lapsed and died in heresy. The answer was in the negative.

On December 9, 1745, the Holy Office forbade Catholics together with the missionaries to accompany the corpses of heretics to their churches and to be present there with lighted candles.[10]

A few years later the Holy Office replied that Catholics were permitted to accompany the corpse of a heretic to the cemetery, and to be present while the exequies were performed in the heretical rite.[11] However, in a reply of the Sacred Congregation for the Propagation of the Faith on August 2, 1803, it was for-

8 Cf. *supra*, pp. 81 ff.

9 *Fonti*, I, 81.

10 *Fontes*, n. 797; *Fonti*, II, 87.

11 21 ian. 1751 — *Fontes*, n. 803; *Fonti*, II, 87.

bidden for Catholics to hold a candle while accompanying the corpse of a schismatic to the sepulcher.[12]

Although it treats specifically of heretics, the decree of the Holy Office as issued to the Bishop of Bardstown, Kentucky, could well be applied as a norm for analogous situations in which schismatics are involved.[13] The presence of Catholics at the funerals and burials of heretics was to be shunned, but such a presence could be permitted for the sake of preventing graver harm to Catholics, provided that the following conditions were fulfilled:

1) The presence could not be one which evinced a formal religious character. It had to be one of a purely material nature, as was demonstrated, for instance, in the act of one whose presence answered the fulfillment of a civic duty. The act of presence had to stand unidentified with any intention to perform an act of religion, to partake in divine worship, or to join in a religious rite.
2) The harm or the injury, or also the imminent danger thereof, which followed upon non-attendance had to threaten as an evil of more far-reaching import than the evil which might be inherent in the act of attendance. The toleration of a lesser evil was justified as a lawful means of escape from a greater evil.
3) The presence had to be such as not to imply a *communicatio in sacris* with the heretics. Hence there could be no praying in common with them, no joining in their rites, no carrying of candles, no offering of prayers for the soul of the dead.

These same principles were again enumerated, at least substantially, in a response of the Holy Office in 1864.[14] However,

[12] *Fontes*, n. 4675; *Fonti*, II, 113.

[13] 13 ian. 1818 — *Fontes*, n. 856; *Fonti*, II, 117.

[14] S. C. S. Off. (Smyrnen.), 30 iun. 1864, ad 1: "Si può permettere a cattolici di accompagnare i funerali degli eretici sino all parta della chiesa?" — Ad 1. "Dummodo catholici comitantes funera haereticorum aut schismaticorum usque ad ianuam coemeterii, meram praesentiam materialem exhibeant, civilis honoris causa erga defunctos, nec se immisceant ritibus haereticorum, nec luminaria deferant, nec pro defuncti anima suffragia persolvant, tolerari posse." — *Fontes*, n. 978.

in the case considered there was merely question of accompanying the funeral cortège to the portal of the church. No mention was made of the factor of grave injury or of the imminent danger of harm, and the practice was permitted if the other conditions were realized. But in a later Instruction of the Holy Office,[15] with reference to assistance at funerals in general, the factor of the graver harm consequent upon non-attendance was again enunciated as a condition requisite for rendering of the attendance permissible.

On January 14, 1874, the Holy Office applied the decree of January 13, 1818, in relation to the funerals of all non-Catholics.[16] However, the Holy Office added a further condition for lawful attendance, namely, that the exclusion from the funeral exequies of every sacred rite and ministration be not intended as a manifestation of unbelief and as a demonstration of contempt for religion.

In regard to clerics the Holy Office stated[17] that a pastor, as pastor, should not be present at the funerals of non-Catholics. However, it was permissible for him to be present if he assisted in a merely civil manner, that is, by not wearing any sacred vestments and by not communicating with the heretics in the sacred rites. The bond of relationship or of friendship between the pastor and the deceased non-Catholic should be commonly known in justification of his presence.

"Mere civility" or "tolerance" is by no means an all-sufficient blanket with which to cover what has the appearance of *communicatio in sacris*. The practice of attending non-Catholic fu-

15 S.C.S.Off., instr. (ad Archiep. Corcyren.), 3 ian. 1871, ad 2: "Si quando necessitas cogat catholicos ad acatholicorum funera comitanda, sedulo advertendum est id solum licere, quotiescumque agatur de praesentia materiali praestanda civilis officii causa, a qua eximi nequeunt catholici sine gravi damno vel periculo, et dummodo nullo modo communicent in eorum ritibus ac sacris caeremoniis quibuscumque. Hisce itaque adhibitis conditionibus, consuetudo adsistendi acatholicorum funeribus et sepulturis, si quando nec facile tolli posset, quin exinde oriantur odia et inimicitiae catholicos inter et acatholicos, tolerari potest."—*Fontes*, n. 1013.

16 *Fontes*, n. 1028.

17 8 maii 1889 — *Fontes*, n. 1117.

nerals is to be eradicated unless it cannot be done without grave danger to Catholics.[18] One does not have a serious reason merely because he wishes to be present, when one's presence is not necessitated in consideration of a civil duty or of a grave inconvenience consequent upon non-attendance.[19]

In a place where Catholics are well known they should attend such services as little as possible because of the danger that by their attendance a spirit of indifferentism would be fostered. In evaluating the case one should consider not only the proximity of the relationship with the deceased, but the status, condition, and character of the person attending. One should also consider the implications involved in the act of attendance, for sometimes the funeral ceremony is not vitiated by any latent malice, whereas in other cases it is infected with manifestations of hostility to the Church.[20]

A common difficulty is the question of acting as pall-bearer at a schismatic funeral. Here in America it seems to be regarded as a merely civil action.[21] Consequently there will be little danger of scandal or perversion. However, the action in itself appears to be an active participation in the funeral service, since the *translatio cadaveris* to the church and again from the church to the cemetery is an integral part of the burial service. Hence, if strictly considered, the action could be regarded as being forbidden.

On the other hand, a contrary custom here in America may be invoked in favor of permitting the practice. McHugh-Callan state that Catholic laymen may act as pall-bearers at ordinary non-Catholic funerals for a proportionate reason, all scandal and danger of perversion being averted.[22] The authors in general do not consider the problem.

There also arises the question concerning the place of burial.

18 Bouscaren, "Co-operation with Non-Catholics" — *Theological Studies,* III (1942), 491.

19 Genicot-Salsmans, *Institutiones Theologiae Moralis,* I, n. 201.

20 Vermeersch-Creusen, *Epitome Iuris Canonici,* II, n. 578.

21 Bancroft, *op. cit.*, p. 138.

22 *Moral Theology,* I, 382.

It is the right of the Church to have its own blessed cemeteries for the burial of its deceased members.[23] The Sacred Congregation for the Propagation of the Faith stated that only in a case of necessity, and not otherwise, is it to be tolerated that Catholics have cemeteries in common with schismatics.[24]

At a later date the Holy Office stated in an Instruction[25] that where Catholics and heretics had cemeteries in common, and it was impossible for Catholics to have their own separate cemetery, then part of the cemetery was to be blessed for the burial of Catholics and another part was to be used for the burial of heretics.

A more detailed Instruction was issued by the Holy Office on February 12, 1862.[26] In it the Holy Office stated that bishops were to take care that Catholic cemeteries be distinct from the non-Catholic cemeteries. If this could not be achieved, then an attempt was to be made to have a section reserved for Catholics. However, if even this objective could not be gained, then until such time as a separate blessed plot of ground could be obtained the grave was to be blessed at each burial of a Catholic.

The content of this Instruction is substantially repeated in the present law of the Code.[27] However, canon 1206 adds a new provision. In some countries the state disregards the rights of the Church and claims ownership of all cemeteries, in which it permits the burial of all classes of people, believers and infidels alike.[28] When these conditions exist, and there is no hope of changing them, the ordinaries should see to it that the cemeteries belonging to the state are blessed, if those who are buried there are in larger number Catholics. The Church seems to accept this inconvenience rather than to have the cemetery divided, and in

23 Canon 1206, §1.

24 29 aug. 1763, ad 4—*Fontes*, n. 4541.

25 (Ad Ep. Scepusien.), 16 aug. 1781—*Fontes*, n. 843.

26 *Fontes*, n. 969; *Fonti*, II, 135.

27 Cf. canon 1206.

28 Cf. Ayrinhac, *Administrative Legislation in the New Code of Canon Law* (New York: Longmans, Green and Co., 1930), p. 63 (hereafter cited *Administrative Legislation*).

consequence to have only one part of it assigned to Catholics. In any event, at least this much should be demanded, that the Catholics have in the cemetery a separate blessed portion which is to be used by them exclusively. If even this cannot be obtained, then the individual graves may be blessed, according to the rite prescribed in the Ritual,[29] as often as a Catholic is buried there.[30]

29 *Rituale Romanum*, tit. VI, c. 3, n. 12.
30 Cf. can. 1206.

CHAPTER VII

MISCELLANEOUS QUESTIONS

Article I — Entering a Schismatic Church

From the nature of the terms used in canon 1258 it is evident that the Church wishes to discourage anything which savors of a *communicatio in sacris*. Active religious communication in the rites of non-Catholics is absolutely forbidden, while a material presence is merely tolerated for serious reasons when there is no danger of scandal or perversion. Any type of presence at non-Catholic rites is discouraged, but at the same time there are some actions, apart from presence at such rites, which cannot inherently be declared illicit.

One must have a serious reason to attend a non-Catholic religious function, even to assist at it only materially. A less grave reason would certainly excuse one who as an unknown person once or twice uses the occasion to observe the manner in which a rite is performed, or to hear the chant of non-Catholics, as long as the danger of scandal is removed, and provided of course that there be no particular prohibition such as exists in Rome in respect to Protestant Churches.[1] Jone states that it is sometimes lawful to attend a non-Catholic service through mere curiosity, if the sect has long been established in the place.[2]

The Holy See has issued some responses in this matter. It was acknowledged as permissible for a Catholic to enter the church of schismatics out of mere curiosity if he made his visit outside those times when their divine offices were being celebrated. Also, if a Catholic were invited by a schismatic to see his church, his oratory, or his chapel, the Catholic could accept the invitation in order not to offer any displeasure, as long as no

1 Vermeersch-Creusen, *Epitome Iuris Canonici,* II, n. 578; cf. *Acta Sanctae Sedis* (41 vols., Romae, 1865-1908), XI (1878), 173-175 (hereafter cited *ASS).*

2 *Moral Theology,* n. 126.

scandal threatened and provided, of course, that he did not join in prayer with the schismatic.[3]

According to a response of the Holy Office as given on January 13, 1818,[4] it was declared licit for one to enter the churches of heretics whenever one entered them after the fashion of entering a profane edifice. The act of entering was in and of itself something indifferent, but its neutral character could become vitiated through the presence of sinister and suspicious circumstances, or as the result of one's wrongful intention. The act of entering became evil:

1) if one entered with the intention of assisting at heretical rites;
2) if one's entry actually implied or even seemingly involved a *communicatio in divinis* with heretics, and hence offered an occasion of scandal;
3) if such entry was commanded by a heretical government as an act of the profession of the same faith and religion between Catholics and non-Catholics alike; and
4) if the very act of entering was commonly considered as a token of one and the same communion of faith between Catholics and non-Catholics.

In all such cases it was invariably illicit for Catholics to enter the churches of heretics. Though this response did not treat specifically of schismatics, still its doctrine is applicable as a norm of action with reference to schismatics.

The Code considers only the case which involves one's presence at sacred rites. If at the time no religious services were in progress, and one wished to enter a schismatic church merely out of curiosity, and consequently there was no danger of scandal or perversion, then there would be nothing to prevent one from entering the church. The entering of a church is an indifferent action, and hence such an action will be licit as long as there are no vitiating circumstances or evil intentions. Prümmer stated that for a sufficient reason one could enter a heretical church to

[3] S. C. de Prop. Fide, 15 dec. 1764 — *Fontes*, n. 4545; *Fonti*, II, 107.
[4] S. C. S. Off. (Kentucky), 13 ian. 1818 — *Fontes*, n. 856; *Fonti*, II, 119.

see the pictures, or to hear the music or the sermon, if there was no danger of perversion or scandal.[5]

Generally considered, the entering of a church is something altogether indifferent in itself. The act can be licit in many cases, when there is no scandal, no injury to the true faith, no danger of perversion, and no express or implicit signification of a false worship or of any approbation of a false religion.[6] For example, one could enter a schismatic church to use it as a protection against the weather, or in the time of war to use it as a bomb shelter, and in other similar emergencies.

Servants could enter a schismatic church in consequence of the nature of their work, if it were necessary for them to accompany their master or his family while attending services. De Lugo cited Hurtado as holding the opinion that, when a servant accompanied the king, he could genuflect when the king genuflected and stand when the king stood, since this was done not for the sake of religion but in consideration of the regal honor to be paid to the sovereign.[7] De Lugo agreed with Hurtado in all points except in regard to genuflecting, since, as De Lugo contended, such an act is not executed out of honor solely for the king. The same was to be said in regard to such an action as the striking of the breast. These actions under the circumstances were always invested with a religious signification.

When the entering of a non-Catholic church had been commanded by a governing power in support of a non-Catholic religion, the action could no longer be considered an indifferent action. A law of this nature had been issued by Queen Elizabeth of England (1558-1603). Catholics were obliged under grave penalties to enter Protestant churches and to be present at the religious services. Some theologians held the opinion that Catholics could obey the law and be present materially in order to

5 *Manuale Theologiae Moralis*, I, n. 527, p. 373.

6 De Lugo, *De Virtute Fidei Divinae*, disp. XIV, sect. 6 — *Disputationes*, Tom. I, 560, 561.

7 De Lugo, *loc. cit.*

escape the penalties.[8] However, the practice was declared illicit in a motu proprio of Paul V (1605-1621). In explaining this prohibition the authors argued that the reasons for it were extrinsic. De Lugo preferred to consider the reasons as being intrinsic. Although the action of entering a church could of itself be totally indifferent, yet in the given circumstances it was an act of religion signifying sacred worship. If it were licit to enter a non-Catholic church under these circumstances, then it would be likewise licit to receive communion from the Calvinists.[9]

Although this question concerned attendance at heretical ceremonies, the same conclusions obtain with reference to schismatic rites.

In explaining the words *"ratione civilis officii"* of canon 1258, §2, Blat by way of example points to those domestic servants who are required to accompany their master, or to those who must be present in consequence of civil laws, such as are in force in Oriental countries.[10] Several authors mention the situation in which soldiers and prisoners frequently find themselves when they are required to attend non-Catholic services for the sake of discipline and order, and say that it is permissible for them to attend these services.[11] It would, however, be illicit to attend if such attendance were commanded *in odium fidei.*

In a recent article on the question of religious communication in the Orient, a Catholic officer of the British army, who was stationed in Egypt for four or five years, was quoted as saying: "Provided each Catholic hears Mass or Liturgy in a church in union with the Holy See, he is free to wander into a dissident

8 Cf. De Lugo, *De Virtute Fidei Divinae,* disp. XIV, sect. 6 — *Disputationes,* Tom. I, 562.

9 De Lugo, *loc. cit.*

10 *Commentarium,* IV, 166. Cf. also Davis, *Moral and Pastoral Theology,* I, 283.

11 Prummer, *Manuale Theologiae Moralis,* I, n. 527; Sabetti-Barrett, *Compendium Theologiae Moralis quae continet Addenda Recognita a Daniele F. Creeden* (34. ed., New York: Frederick Pustet Co., 1939), n. 154, p. 159; Davis, *op. cit.,* I, 283; Jone, *Moral Theology,* n. 126.

church on Sunday."[12] The officer evidently referred to attendance during the time religious services were in progress. From the tenor of the entire article it seems that the author of the article is in agreement with the quoted statements of the officer. The statement of the British officer seems very broad if not ultra-liberal, and certainly stands contrary to the mind of the Church. Canon 1258, §2, merely *tolerates* a passive presence for a grave reason. In view of this language of the Code one could hardly state without qualification that a Catholic is free to visit a dissident church on Sunday.

Article II — Singing in Church or Playing the Organ

The music or chant which accompanies a religious service constitutes a very important part of the act of worship. Music is certainly not essential to a religious service, but it embellishes the service, adds beauty and sublimity to the worship, and is inseparable from the act of worship. Consequently, to play the organ or to sing at a schismatic religious service would constitute an active participation in a forbidden act of worship. This is the mind of the Holy See and the general opinion of the authors.

The Sacred Congregation for the Propagation of the Faith stated with the approval of Pope Leo XIII (1878-1903) that it was illicit to play the organ in churches of heretics when they were performing acts of false worship.[13] This reply was given in answer to the question whether it could be permitted to play the organ in Protestant churches on feast days, so that the organist could provide a livelihood for himself. There would seldom be a situation in which one would be required to play the organ in a non-Catholic church for a reason more serious than that of providing a livelihood for oneself. If the Holy See declared the practice illicit in this case, certainly it is illicit in practically every case.

12 "On Conducting Oneself in an Orthodox Church" — *The Voice of the Church,* December, 1944, p. 17; *The Eastern Churches Quarterly,* V (1944), July-September, 351 ff.

13 S. C. de Prop. Fide, litt., 8 iul. 1889 — *Coll. S. C. P. F.,* n. 1713.

Laymann[14] seemed ready to excuse a recent convert to the faith if he continued to play the organ in a non-Catholic church. He was not bound, so Laymann stated, to relinquish his position at once if he was in grave necessity, but at the same time it had to be evident that he was performing his task as a purely indifferent action. Davis[15] expressed the same opinion, adding that there must be no scandal. The absence of scandal is always a necessary condition when exceptions are made to the general principle which forbids religious communication with non-Catholics.

Kenrick (1797-1863), speaking with reference to Protestant churches in America, stated that those who sing hymns, who play the organ, or who make the responses in these churches are obviously participators in the religious service, and so in a certain sense are betraying the faith.[16] But it seemed to him that no offense against the faith was committed by Catholics who in the company of Protestants sang publicly outside these churches when there was no semblance of any religious worship, as in various kinds of social gatherings. On the part of Catholics he considered their participation as lawful even though the songs were written by Protestants, as long as they contained nothing contrary to faith. The principle could analogously be applied to a similar communication of Catholics with schismatics.

What has been forbidden by the Holy See as also in the doctrine of the authors is the playing of the organ or the singing of hymns as part of the non-Catholic religious services. When these actions are not part of a religious service, then one would be permitted to participate as long as the hymns do not reflect anything that is contrary to the faith, and provided always that the occasion of scandal and the danger of perversion are effectively precluded.[17] Hence, one could play the organ or sing for the ruler of a country in a non-Catholic church, as long as the act

14 *Theologiae Moralis*, Lib. 2, tr. 3, c. 13, n. 5.

15 *Op. cit.*, I, 286.

16 *Theologiae Moralis* (2. ed., 2 vols., Baltimorae: Murphy, 1866), II, 48.

17 Vermeersch-Creusen, *Epitome Iuris Canonici*, II, 406, ftn. 1.

did not constitute part of a religious service.[18] One could likewise take part in a musical festival held in a non-Catholic church.[19]

A non-Catholic could more readily be permitted to play the organ in a Catholic church than a Catholic could be permitted to play the organ at the religious services of any heretical or schismatical sect.[20]

Article III — Processions

Sacred processions designate the solemn supplications made by the faithful under the leadership of the clergy when all the participants move in an orderly manner from one sacred place to another for the purpose of promoting devotion, of commemorating God's benefits, of thanking Him, and of imploring the divine assistance.[21] A procession, as distinct from a parade or a civic demonstration, postulates the presence of the clergy in their official capacity, the participation of a fairly large number of people marching from one sacred place to another, and a motivation that looks to a pious purpose.[22] This is the notion of a procession according to the Catholic concept, but analogously the same is true of the processions of schismatics. The principal factor of concern is the religious characteristic of processions. They constitute an act of religious worship, a *res sacra*, and consequently are comprehended within the scope of canon 1258.

It is forbidden to take an active part in a schismatic procession. From the very nature of a procession, the mere presence of anyone among those who form in procession constitutes an active participation. In reference to this matter the Sacred Congregations have issued several responses.

On March 12, 1789, the Sacred Congregation for the Propagation of the Faith declared it illicit for Catholics on the occasion of the respective feasts of the Blessed Mother and of the

18 Merkelbach, *op. cit.*, I, n. 758, p. 586.

19 Davis, *op. cit.*, I, 286.

20 Merkelbach, *op. cit.*, I, 586, ftn. 2.

21 Can. 1290, §1.

22 Ayrinhac, *Administrative Legislation*, p. 161.

Saints to carry to schismatic churches the pictures and the icons of the Blessed Mother or of the Saints which they treasured in their homes, to burn lamps in schismatic churches, to offer public prayer with schismatics, to assist out of curiosity at their functions, and to go in procession with them, unless there was question of the procession which takes place at the time of a funeral.[23]

Clerics were instructed by the Holy Office[24] that, if they took part in the procession which accompanied the king under the baldachino to the Greek church, they were not to wear any sacred vestments or a surplice, and they were to use a baldachino different from the one traditionally used at sacred functions. Also, the baldachino was to be carried by laymen.

It is apparent from these responses that, when a participation in sacred processions was permitted, the practice was tolerated for reasons of civil duty or honor. Even in these cases anything which savored of a religious communication was forbidden. Consequently, it was not permissible to carry lighted candles, or, in the case of clerics, to wear sacred vestments.

Article IV — Communication in Prayer

It was forbidden for Catholics to be present at the Masses and official public prayers of schismatics, even when the prayers contained nothing that was contrary to the faith or opposed to the Catholic rite.[25]

When Catholics were guests at a dinner, they could not offer up prayers for those who had died impenitent or as apostates from the faith. It seems to have been a custom to offer such prayers at meals, according to a response of the Sacred Congregation for the Propagation of the Faith.[26]

Sometimes Catholics invited heretics or schismatics to dinner, and when the guests saw that the Catholics did not bless the food or give thanks, they were scandalized, since they knew it was a custom among Catholics to say such prayers. However,

23 *Fontes,* n. 4626; *Fonti,* II, 111.

24 22 iun. 1864 — *Fontes,* n. 977; *Fonti,* I, 101.

25 S. C. S. Off., 7 aug. 1704, ad 1 — *Fontes,* n. 770; *Fonti,* II, 83.

26 3 aug. 1818 — *Fontes,* n. 4711; *Coll. S. C. P. F.,* n. 729.

the Sacred Congregation for the Propagation of the Faith commended those missionaries who omitted the prayers in this case, since they thus avoided a forbidden religious communication.[27]

In the Acts of the Sacred Congregation for the Propagation of the Faith of 1769 is also found an exhortation which called upon the bishops to prohibit their priests and the faithful from communicating with schismatics in their prayers. The exhortation stated that this prohibition had been decreed by all the Sacred Councils.[28]

However, when the prayers are private, namely, such as are said by private individuals and without any official recognition or direction by an ecclesiastical authority, the authors allow greater liberty than is permitted in respect to public prayer. When the prayers are private and contain nothing against faith, and when there is present no danger of perversion or scandal, it is permissible to join with schismatics in such prayers. It is not only permissible but even laudable for a Catholic and a schismatic who are husband and wife to join in family prayer under these conditions.[29]

Article V — Sermons

The preaching of the word of God is also considered as a sacred function, and consequently it is forbidden Catholics to assist at sermons preached in a schismatic church. Ordinarily the preaching of a sermon constitutes a part of some solemnity or religious service, so that one will seldom have occasion to be present merely for a sermon. If one has reason to be present for the principal service, he will also be permitted to remain for the preaching of the sermon.

Externally there is no difference between active or passive assistance during a sermon. In assisting at the preaching of a sermon by a schismatic the principal danger to Catholics is that of perversion in the faith. Precautions must be taken against

27 20 aug. 1826 — *Fonti*, II, 123.

28 *Fonti*, XII, 227.

29 Cf. Beste, *Introductio in Codicem*, p. 615; De Meester, *Compendium*, III, 153, ftn. 3.

this danger, and in so far as it is possible one should try to pay no attention to the instruction of the preacher. The Holy Office on May 10, 1770, stated that it was regularly illicit for Catholics to be present at the sermons of schismatics and heretics.[30]

The authors likewise point to the practice of assisting at non-Catholic sermons as being forbidden.[31] However, presence during a sermon is permitted within the restriction of the principles stated in canon 1258, §2. Prümmer stated that for a sufficient reason one could enter a heretical church to view the pictures, or also to hear the music or a sermon, if there was no danger of perversion.[32] A likely reason to warrant one's presence at a sermon could inhere in the purpose of refuting the errors, but one would have to be careful that scandal was not occasioned. Ordinarily, if one is well known in the community, there will be great danger of scandal.

Those Catholics who listen to sermons and services of non-Catholic worship which are broadcast over the radio are not guilty of a forbidden *communicatio in sacris* in the strict sense of the term because they are not physically present at the service. However, the local ordinary could forbid the faithful to listen to non-Catholic radio services. In fact, to listen to non-Catholic radio services is forbidden by the natural law when there is present the danger of perversion or of giving scandal to others.[33]

A rather unique difficulty arose in regard to the point of preaching, and though it is only remotely related to the present question, it is not irrelevant to mention it here. The question arose whether Catholic missionaries upon invitation could preach in schismatic churches. The answer was given in the affirmative, contingent on the fact that the missionaries found it possible to preach the whole Catholic truth and freely to show the errors of

30 *Fontes*, n. 828; *Fonti*, II, 109.

31 Noldin-Schmitt, *Summa Theologiae Moralis*, II, n. 39; Sipos, *Enchiridion Iuris Canonici*, p. 699; Genicot-Salsmans, *Institutiones Theologiae Moralis*, I, n. 200; Woywod, *Practical Commentary*, II, 60; Davis, *Moral and Pastoral Theology*, I, 284.

32 *Manuale Theologiae Moralis*, I, n. 527, p. 373.

33 Berutti, *Institutiones Iuris Canonici* (Taurini-Romae: ex Officina Libraria Marietti, IV [1940]), IV, 232.

the schismatics. They were not permitted to accept the invitation if in their preaching they were restricted to a consideration of those virtues and vices which were of common concern to Catholics and schismatics alike.[34]

Article VI — Oaths

An oath is an act by which one calls God to witness to the truth of one's assertions or the sincerity of one's actions. Thereby one pays homage to His infinite truthfulness and adds strength to one's own word, as a religious man would not appeal to God in support of falsehood or deceit.[35] The oath of its nature is a sacred act, and consequently it is illicit to communicate with schismatics in the taking of an oath.

In Quebec, where Protestant officials were in power at the time, it was required of everyone who took an oath to touch and to kiss the Bible, the copies in use being heretical versions of the Sacred Scriptures. Priests were excepted, for they were allowed to hold their hand over their heart. It was asked whether the faithful should be disquieted in the matter of the established usage. The Holy Office on February 23, 1820, answered in the negative.[36]

A similar problem arose in the case of schismatics among whom a civil oath had to be taken before a Greek schismatic priest. To this difficulty the Holy Office replied that when the schismatic minister assisted at the oath of Catholics by means of a mere passive and political presence, without a stole or any other signs of the ministry, and thus not in a religious capacity, the practice could be licitly continued; but not otherwise.[37]

Merkelbach stated that when the Protestant Bible is used, the Bible is not considered as an unlawfully issued or perhaps falsified publication but as a holy book.[38]

34 Souarn, *Praxis Missionarii,* p. 208; cf. *Coll. S. C. P. F.* (1893), n. 1674.

35 Ayrinhac, *Administrative Legislation,* p. 188.

36 *Fontes,* n. 858; *Fonti,* II, 123.

37 S. C. S. Off. (Zacynt.), 1 apr. 1857 — *Fontes,* n. 940; *Fonti,* II, 133.

38 *Summa Theologiae Moralis,* I, 586, ftn. 1.

Article VII — Co-operation in Schismatic Worship

As explained in the treatment on the notion of communication, the term co-operation denotes a genus in relation to which the term communication exists as a species. Hence, co-operation is the more general term and designates any action in which one acts jointly with another, whether that joint operation be very closely or only remotely interrelated. In all co-operation there is at least a moral union of actions. That union is very evident in a case of active religious communication when one simultaneously places an action together with a schismatic in a schismatic rite. However, there are other actions which show favor or support to a schismatic sect, but which because of their mediate and remote connection with the actual worship are considered not a religious communication but a more remote form of co-operation.

Certain forms of co-operation are closely related to the question of religious communication, and consequently are pertinent to the matter at hand. Illicit co-operation, as it is generally understood under its moral aspect, is the concurrence with another in an illicit action. The problem of illicit co-operation involves principally a moral consideration. Here the question will be considered only in so far as the co-operation is related to an illicit form of worship with specific reference to the schismatic sects.

There are various types of co-operation. Co-operation may be formal or material, immediate or mediate, proximate or remote.[39] It is formal when one concurs not only in the evil action, but also in the evil intention. It is material when one concurs simply in the evil action. The co-operation is immediate if there is a participation in the evil action itself; mediate, if it is secondary or subservient, and thus merely facilitates the execution of the principal action. Mediate co-operation may again be either proximate or remote, depending on the degree of closeness in the relation between the principal and the secondary action.

Formal co-operation is never licit. The licitness of material

[39] Cf. Genicot-Salsmans, *op. cit.*, I, n. 235; Noldin-Schmitt, *op. cit.*, II, n. 117; pp. 117, 118; Merkelbach, *op. cit.*, I, n. 761; Davis, *op. cit.*, I, 341.

co-operation receives its determination from the accompanying circumstances. Even for a material co-operation in an illicit action one always needs a just cause, and the nature and the seriousness of the requisite cause receives its determination in relation to the proximity of the co-operation and the gravity of the illicit action. The act of material co-operation also must be at least indifferent, for it is never licit to place an illicit action, even if good will result. It is difficult to give any specific general principles in regard to the licitness of material co-operation. Each case must be examined on its own merits if one is properly to determine whether the accompanying circumstances justify material co-operation.

A. *Building of Schismatic Churches*

A question of practical importance arises when in view of his trade a Catholic artisan is called upon to assist in the building of a schismatic place of worship. Unless one's services were demanded out of hatred for the Catholic faith, one could assist materially for a sufficient cause.[40] Those whose co-operation is more essential, such as the architect or the contractor, would need a grave cause. The common laborer would need a less serious cause, but in no case should one co-operate merely in order to earn money. If the sect is not established in the territory, an architect would need a very grave reason for accepting the work.[41] If the sect is already established in the locality, the architect and the contractor could accept the work for a just reason, such as that of averting a possible boycott occasioned by their refusal.

In Constantinople it was fully permissible to co-operate proximately in the building or restoration of mosques, as long as it was not done out of a motive of hatred for the true religion. However, such intimate material co-operation was not permis-

40 Woywod, *Practical Commentary,* II, 59; Noldin-Schmitt, *op. cit.,* II, n. 122.

41 Genicot-Salsmans, *op. cit.,* I, n. 237; Noldin-Schmitt, *op. cit.,* II, n. 122.

sible in Rome, where there were so comparatively few non-Catholics.[42]

Konings (1821-1884) stated that in our country the work of building a non-Catholic church is licit, since it is not considered a *communicatio in sacris* and implies only a remote form of co-operation.[43] However, if the co-operation of Catholics would be looked upon as an approval of a schismatic sect, the co-operation would be forbidden because of the scandal that would be given.

B. *Furnishing Articles Necessary for Worship*

Closely related to the question of co-operating in the building of schismatic churches is that of supplying schismatics with other objects necessary for divine worship. The more closely the object is related to divine worship, the more proximate is the co-operation, and consequently the more serious must be the reason that can serve as a requisite for permitting such co-operation. To sell benches, tables, linens, lights, and similar articles would point to a remote co-operation, and the profit motive would prove a sufficient reason for selling these objects to schismatics.

A more serious reason would be required when there is a question of supplying the organ, bells, altar, chalice, vestments, and liturgical books. In this instance the co-operation is more closely connected with the actual sacrifice, and the profit motive alone does not prove sufficient for justifying such co-operation.[44]

On April 30, 1831, an interesting difficulty was solved by the Sacred Congregation for the Propagation of the Faith.[45] The question was asked whether it was licit to send a miter to the Metropolitan of Iberia (Transcaucasian Georgia), who was a schismatic. The reason for this gesture was that by this gift the people subject to him would be drawn to the faith. The Fathers

42 Souarn, *Praxis Missionarii*, p. 211.

43 *Theologia Moralis* (7. ed., 2 vols., New York: Benziger, 1888), I, n. 314.

44 Cf. Noldin-Schmitt, *op. cit.*, II, n. 122.

45 *Fonti*, I, 91.

of the Congregation disagreed in the manner of the solution. Those who held to the negative view maintained that the act implied a *communicatio in sacris,* especially since it was a gift whose principal use would be linked with the celebration of sacred functions and especially of the Mass, in the celebration of which the presence of grave sin was to be presumed on the part of schismatic priests in view of their suspension *a divinis.* However, a final agreement was reached. Such gifts could be presented by the missionaries in their own name. The reason which stated that there was a co-operation in the sin of schismatics could not be considered as a valid objection, since the missionaries were in no way a proximate cause of the sin.

To sell the bread or wine which is to be used in the sacrifice would require a very serious reason, since such co-operation is proximate. Davis states that it would be scandalous to bake altar breads in order to supply them for use in the Anglican Communion, in which these hosts are thought to lend themselves for a valid consecration.[46] Konings held the opinion that co-operation would be more easily permitted in relation to schismatic priests than in relation to Anglican clergymen, since the latter are not true priests.[47]

In the light of these general principles, would it be licit for a Catholic priest to give the neighboring schismatic pastor some wine or hosts for the sacrifice? Undoubtedly the refusal on the part of the Catholic priest would produce much animosity between the Catholics and the schismatics in that locality, but unless more serious harm would result, it could hardly be permitted the Catholic to supply the schismatic with these articles. Scandal could hardly be forestalled, if the fact became publicly known that the Catholic priest gave the wine or the hosts to the schismatic. In the given case the co-operation of the Catholic priest is of a necessary and proximate character, and though the schismatic sacrifice is valid, it is nevertheless celebrated illicitly, and one could not co-operate so directly in this illicit action.

46 *Op cit.,* I, 286.

47 *Op. cit.,* I, n. 314, p. 144.

C. *Contributing toward the Support of a Schismatic Sect*

In answer to a doubt the Sacred Congregation for the Propagation of the Faith on January 29, 1828, replied that it was illicit to give alms for a schismatic church.[48]

In the ninth canon of the Greek-Melkite Synod of Ain-Traz (1835)[49] it was stated that one could not call into doubt the fact that the offering of gifts to churches and holy places *ex voto* implied an act of worship and an adoration of God, even if sometimes the gifts were used in honor of certain Saints. Religion forbade the Catholic faithful to communicate *in divinis* with heretics and schismatics, or to support as ministers of the Church of Christ those who were separated from the Church, or to petition their prayers as though they were priests of the Universal Church. And so it was absolutely forbidden to Catholics to make offerings, no matter of what nature, to the churches and monasteries outside the Catholic communion. Penalties were threatened for the violation of this canon.

The Sacred Congregation for the Propagation of the Faith also declared it illicit for Catholics to make an offering for the Masses or prayers offered by schismatics.[50]

One is not permitted of his own accord to contribute money towards the building of a heretical church.[51] If one is forced to pay a tax, as it were, toward a common fund from which a schismatic church also benefited, it is permissible to pay this tax, since the money can be used also for indifferent purposes. If one is forced to pay money directly toward the support of a schismatic religion, he should protest in order to show that he has no intention of supporting or approving a false religion by this act of contributing. Under the same conditions he could also contribute money for the erection of a schismatic church. Although he knows the money will be used only for an evil purpose, the

48 *Fonti,* I, 91.

49 *Coll. Lac.,* II, 585; *Fonti,* XV, 67.

50 12 mart. 1789, ad 2 — *Fontes,* n. 4626; *Fonti,* II, 111.

51 Woywod, *Practical Commentary,* II, 59.

action itself is not intrinsically bad, since it does not necessarily connote the approval of a false sect.[52]

In this matter there is a particular reply of the Sacred Penitentiary[53] which stated that it was licit to offer money for the erection of a heretical church only on condition that by such an action Catholics who worshipped in the same church as the Protestants could free themselves from such a scandalous simultaneous use of the same church. Noldin-Schmitt draw two conclusions from this reply: 1) The act of donating money is not in itself evil, and 2) the Sacred Penitentiary has judged that only the cause of offsetting a common danger is sufficient to permit such co-operation. Nevertheless, some authors consider that the consequence of a serious private loss or injury would also excuse one in furnishing such co-operation.[54]

In regions where both Catholics and schismatics live together it would be licit for Catholics to contribute financial aid for the building and sustaining of schismatic schools and orphanages or similar institutions, since the principal purpose of these institutions is not a religious one. However, two conditions are necessary to justify this aid, namely, that the contributions would not be considered as a sign of adherence to a false sect, and that the money would not be used for the perversion of Catholics who are admitted to these institutions.[55]

A difficulty commonly arising is that of the Catholic merchant or professional man who is called upon to contribute to various churches as a business gesture. To give money directly toward the support of a schismatic church would not be licit. A Catholic merchant does not wish to refuse to contribute, for by so doing he incurs the displeasure of his schismatic patrons, and if he has a large number of them, it may mean a serious decrease in his trade. However, he can usually obviate this by making an

52 Genicot-Salsmans, *Institutiones Theologiae Moralis,* I, n. 237; Noldin-Schmitt, *Summa Theologiae Moralis,* II, n. 122.

53 Cf. Noldin-Schmitt, *loc. cit.;* Genicot-Salsmans, *loc. cit.*

54 Cf. Noldin-Schmitt, *loc. cit.;* Genicot-Salsmans, *loc. cit.*

55 Noldin-Schmitt, *loc. cit.;* Genicot-Salsmans, *loc. cit.;* Davis, *op. cit.,* I, 287; Merkelbach, *op. cit.,* I, n. 766.

indirect contribution. He will gain the good will of the people and at the same time co-operate only remotely in the support of a schismatic sect. If he donates some articles which have a good or at least an indifferent use, such as school desks, library books, desk lamps, or similar objects, or even gives money to be used for these purposes, his co-operation will be remote and will be permissible for any reasonable cause.

D. *Calling a Schismatic Minister*

One is often placed in a difficult position in regard to schismatics as a result of one's responsibility as a nurse or as an attendant in a hospital. Such persons are frequently requested by non-Catholic patients to call their respective priest or minister for spiritual assistance. If a nurse calls a schismatic priest to administer the last rites to a dying schismatic, she will be co-operating in the illicit administration of the sacraments in a schismatic rite.

The Holy Office has declared this co-operation on the part of nuns assisting the sick to be inherently illicit. It stated that the former were obliged to assume a passive attitude when requested by the patient to send for a non-Catholic minister.[56] They would manifest a passive attitude if they permitted some non-Catholic to call the schismatic priest for the dying patient. They could also tell the patient to ask some non-Catholic to send for a schismatic priest. For a grave reason of necessity they could even call the schismatic priest, but then should merely tell him that there is a sick person who wishes the priest to visit him.[57] The act in itself is indifferent, but it is proximate co-operation, and in the light of the attending circumstances can all too readily be given a wrong interpretation. Hence, only for a grave reason of necessity would such an action be permitted.[58] But it is never

[56] S. C. S. Off., 14 mart. 1848 — *Coll. S. C. P. F.*, n. 2030, note 2.

[57] Ferreres, *Casus Conscientiae* (5. ed., 2 vols., Barcinone: Eugenius Subirana, 1926), I, n. 211.

[58] Noldin-Schmitt, *op. cit.*, II, n. 122; Genicot-Salsmans, *op. cit.*, I, n. 201.

licit to call the minister directly for the administration of the schismatic rites.

For grave reasons it is also permitted a Catholic nurse to set a table and prepare the patient for the visit of the schismatic priest, but she cannot take any active part in any of the rites.[59]

The authors usually treat this subject with reference to non-Catholic ministers in general. With schismatics there is some difference, and a possible exception could be allowed when the patient is in danger of death, and when the schismatic priest is the only priest who is available. As explained previously in the consideration of the sacrament of penance, the schismatic priest is authorized to administer the sacraments under these circumstances. Hence, it is certainly licit to call him directly to administer to the dying. In practice, however, the case would be rare with the possible exception of those dying on the battlefield in time of war.

What has been said of co-operation in the ministrations of a schismatic priest to the sick may be applied also with regard to the burying of the dead. If a schismatic relative dies, the best practice is to leave the funeral arrangements in the hands of other schismatic relatives, and thus to remain passive.[60]

Article VIII — Ecclesiastical Sanctions

In the treatment which dealt with the sacraments of baptism and of matrimony some mention was made of ecclesiastical penalties attaching to the acts of a forbidden religious communication.[61] Apart from these there are other enacted penalties which receive mention in the Code.

If a person were actually guilty of schism, he would be subject to the penalties enacted in canon 2314, among which is the *ipso facto* incurred excommunication which is reserved to the

59 Prümmer, *Manuale Theologiae Moralis*, I, n. 526; Davis, *op. cit.*, I, 284.

60 Genicot-Salsmans, *op. cit.*, I, n. 201; Konings, *Theologia Moralis*, I, n. 313.

61 Cf. *supra*, pages 64, 110, 111.

Apostolic See in a special way. When there is no profession of schism, but merely an external participation in the sacred rites of schismatics, one would not be subject to the same penalties.

Canon 2316 states that a person who of his own accord and knowingly helps in any manner to propagate heresy, or who communicates in sacred rites with heretics contrary to the prescriptions of canon 1258, incurs the suspicion of heresy. The orthodoxy in his faith on the part of one who incurs this penalty is questioned, and he is subject to further penalties if upon warning he does not remove the suspicion. If he does not amend his ways within six complete months after having incurred these penalties, he is to be considered as a heretic and as subject to the penalties for heresy.[62]

Since penalties are to be interpreted strictly,[63] the terms *heresy* and *heretic* are to be taken in the strict sense. There is a definite distinction between heresy and schism as also between the heretic and the schismatic.[64] Although authors consider schismatics to be guilty also of heresy, the Holy See still uses the term schismatic and refers to the Oriental dissidents as schismatics. Since the delict of canon 2316 is the communication *in divinis* with heretics contrary to the prescriptions of canon 1258, one who communicates with schismatics contrary to the prescriptions of canon 1258 will not incur the ecclesiastical penalty of suspicion of heresy. Not all that is condemned in canon 1258 falls under the penalty of canon 2316, but merely religious communication with *heretics* contrary to the prescriptions of canon 1258. Canon 1258 determines what manner of positive communication with non-Catholics is licit and what manner is illicit. It uses the terms, *in sacris acatholicorum,* whereas the penalty of canon 2316 is restricted by the terms, *cum haereticis.*

The only other penalties attached to forbidden religious communication are those which are enacted in canon 2319. Those Catholics who attempt marriage before a non-Catholic minister contrary to the prescriptions of canon 1063, §1, incur a *latae*

62 Cf. can. 2315.

63 Cf. can. 19.

64 Cf. can. 1325, §2.

sententiae excommunication reserved to the ordinary. This censure has already been given sufficient consideration in the treatment of communication with schismatics in regard to matrimony.[65]

A *latae sententiae* excommunication reserved to the ordinary is also incurred by those Catholic parents who knowingly presume to offer their own children to non-Catholic ministers for baptism.[66] Only the parents and not the guardians would incur this excommunication, since the canon states specifically *liberos suos*.[67] Ignorance, even though it be crass, as also fear would excuse one from incurring this penalty.[68]

A further penalty of the suspicion of heresy is incurred by those Catholics who attempt marriage before a non-Catholic minister[69] and by those parents who presume to offer their children for baptism to non-Catholic ministers.[70] In both these cases the penalty would be incurred even though the minister were a schismatic, since canon 2319 uses the more general term, "non-Catholic," and not merely the term, "heretic," as canon 2316 does. Chelodi (1880-1922) stated that canon 2319 is entirely directed against heresy or schism.[71]

It should also be noted here that an irregularity arising from crime is contracted by those who in any way permit baptism to be conferred on them by non-Catholics except in the case of extreme necessity.[72] Irregularities, however, have not the juridical nature of a penalty. They are impediments specifying negatively the qualifications the Church demands in her ministers for admission to the services of the altar.[73]

65 Cf. *supra*, pages 110, 111.

66 Can. 2319, §3.

67 Beste, *Introductio in Codicem*, p. 939.

68 Chelodi, *Ius Canonicum de Delictis et Poenis et de Iudiciis Criminalibus* (5. ed., recognita et aucta a Pio Ciprotti, Vicenza: Società Anonima Tipografica, 1943), n. 60, p. 81.

69 Can. 2319, §1, 1°.

70 Can. 2319, §1, 3°.

71 *Op. cit.*, n. 60, p. 80, ftn. 1.

72 Can. 985, 2°.

73 Woywod, *Practical Commentary*, I, 522.

CHAPTER VIII

RELIGIOUS COMMUNICATION OF SCHISMATICS WITH CATHOLICS

Thus far the question of religious communication has been considered under a positive aspect, namely, in reference to the communication of Catholics in the sacred rites of non-Catholics. There is, however, a religious communication which is negative in character, but which is, nevertheless, a true religious communication. As has already been explained in the introduction, negative communication is that which occurs when non-Catholics participate in the sacred rites and ceremonies of Catholics. This participation is active when non-Catholics take an active part in the services, as when, for example, they receive the sacraments from a Catholic priest. It is passive when they are merely present in a material way at Mass celebrated in a Catholic church.

Canon 1258 does not directly consider the problem of negative religious communication, and there is no other canon in the Code which states a general prohibition against negative religious communication as does canon 1258 in regard to positive religious communication. However, there are individual canons which take up particular phases of negative communication, e.g., in regard to the sacraments (c. 731, §2) and the sacramentals (c. 1149), in reference to the use of sponsors at baptism (c. 765, n. 2) and confirmation (c. 795, n. 2). The legislation of the Code is also supplemented by the responses of the Sacred Congregation of the Holy Office and of the Sacred Congregation for the Propagation of the Faith. These responses will be cited where they are relevant.

It is to be noted that not all the authors use the same terminology. The majority of them refer to negative communication as passive communication.[1] But the already suggested terminol-

[1] Cf. Wernz-Vidal, *Ius Canonicum*, V, 437; Noldin-Schmitt, *Summa Theologiae Moralis*, II, n. 34.

ogy seems preferable, since it eliminates all confusion between a passive presence and a negative communication.

In general it is to be observed concerning negative communication that the admission of non-Catholics to an active participation in Catholic worship would be a violation of the bond of unity which should exist among the faithful. The unity of the faithful must consist in their participation in the same sacraments and in the same religious worship. If one were to admit a non-Catholic to an active participation in the sacraments of Catholics, it would signify that a unity and agreement in religious profession existed between Catholics and non-Catholics, as though Catholic worship did not differ substantially from heretical worship. When from the circumstances it is sufficiently evident that by an act of negative religious communication there is no signification of unity and compromise in religious worship between Catholics and non-Catholics, but rather, on the contrary, that the heretic recognizes the truth of the Catholic religion, the Church more readily tolerates such religious communication. Hence it is that the Church permits the celebration of a mixed marriage before a Catholic priest, while it most severely forbids its celebration before a non-Catholic minister.[2]

There are certain helps to salvation which of their nature are ordained for the reconciling of non-Catholics to the Church. These can be communicated to them. Other gifts which the Church dispenses are symbols of ecclesiastical communion which presuppose dispositions which non-Catholics lack. These goods of the Church regularly are not to be conferred on non-Catholics.[3] What these objects are and under what circumstances it is licit to confer them, or obligatory to deny them, to non-Catholics will be seen in the following articles.

2 Wernz-Vidal, *Ius Canonicum,* V, 437; Beste, *Introductio in Codicem,* p. 615.

3 Sipos, *Enchiridion Iuris Canonici,* p. 700.

Article I — Administering the Sacraments to Schismatics

It is forbidden to administer the sacraments of the Church to heretics or schismatics, even though they err in good faith and ask for them, unless they have first renounced their errors and been reconciled with the Church.[4]

Prümmer stated that the reason for the prohibition of canon 731, §2, lies in the fact that heretics and schismatics are considered public sinners.[5] However, Vermeersch-Creusen rightly conclude that the reason is found not in the general principle that the sacraments are to be denied to the unworthy, but in the fact that heretics and schismatics are separated from the Church, which possesses the sacraments as its very own.[6] Those schismatics who err in good faith could be more worthy of the sacraments than some Catholics to whom the sacraments are given.

A. *Outside the Danger of Death*

The prohibition of canon 731, §2, is general. It admits of no exceptions when a schismatic is not in danger of death.[7] When one has to deal with formal schismatics, namely, with those who err in bad faith, it is evident that they are in a state of sin, which in and of its nature is most grievous. As such they are absolutely unworthy and accordingly must be excluded from the reception of the sacraments. Those schismatics who are in good faith but are not in any danger of death are likewise to be excluded from the sacraments, since the administration of the sacraments has been committed to the Church by Christ, and only those who are of the body of Christ's Church are entitled to the reception of the sacraments. Heretics and schismatics, as long as they have not been reconciled with the Church, in no way pertain to the body of the Church. Hence they must be excluded from the reception of the sacraments of the Church.[8]

4 Canon 731, §2.

5 *Manuale Iuris Canonici*, p. 369.

6 *Epitome Iuris Canonici*, II, n. 15.

7 Vermeersch-Creusen, *Epitome Iuris Canonici*, II, n. 16; Woywod, *Practical Commentary*, I, 323.

8 Cappello, *De Sacramentis*, I, n. 62, p. 54.

The Holy Office has always forbidden the administration of the sacraments to schismatics if they were not in danger of death. According to a reply under date of August 28, 1669,[9] it could not be tolerated that converted Nestorian priests be authorized by their ordinary to hear the confessions of their schismatic nationals. Least of all could such toleration be granted in favor of heretics and schismatics. Even though the non-accommodation of the request of a penitent who desired to make his confession would, besides revealing them as Catholics, subject them to the payment of fines and deprive them of all the financial help that constituted their means of sustenance, it still could not be tolerated that they administer the sacrament of penance.

The same prohibition was contained in a later response of the Holy Office on May 15, 1709.[10]

Cardinal Bellarmine (1542-1621) seemed to hold an opinion that allowed an exception to this general rule. He stated that if separated Greeks came to confession to a Catholic priest, they had first to make an abjuration of their errors in the matter of religion. Then, with much caution, he made an exception in favor of the unlettered and uninstructed: "Si dicant se nihil scire (de controversiis graecorum cum latinis) et vere appareant rudes et incapaces, fortasse poterunt audiri et relinqui in ignorantia."[11] The doctrine was indeed couched in very careful language, which seemed implicitly to acknowledge for the opposite opinion a larger measure of security.

When a schismatic is in danger of death, the situation is somewhat altered. In these circumstances the Church, in its efforts to save all men, allows some exceptions to its general prohibition.

9 *Fontes*, n. 740; *Fonti*, I, 87.

10 "Non licere catholicos communicare cum haereticis et schismaticis et eorum confessiones audire, nec coram illis emittere, nec iis sacram Eucharistiam conferre." — *Fontes*, n. 773.

11 G. Hofmann, "Il Beato Roberto Bellarmino e gli Orientali" — *Orientalia Christiana*, VIII (1926-1927), 270.

B. *In Danger of Death*

The circumstances under which one can be considered to be in danger of death have already been explained in connection with the treatment of positive communication.[12] What has been said there can be applied to the present question.

1. Schismatic in Full Possession of His Senses

When a formal schismatic is in possession of his senses, even though he be in danger of death, he cannot be given absolution if he does not retract his errors and submit to the Church, and consequently he cannot receive any of the other sacraments. If he is a purely material schismatic or, as they say, in good faith, the situation is a very delicate one and must be handled with great prudence. Whether such a schismatic can be absolved is a disputed question among the authors.

Such a schismatic must have the proper dispositions before he can be absolved. He must at least manifest contrition for his sins and be prepared to do all those things which are ordained by God for the attainment of everlasting happiness. If he is so disposed, some theologians hold that he can be absolved conditionally.[13]

In support of this opinion is the fact that neither the validity nor the licitness of such an absolution can be impugned. The necessary requirements for the administration of the sacrament are present. There are present the proper intention, the proper dispositions, and the required Catholic faith.[14] There is no absence of the proper intention, for all that is needed is an implicit intention, and this is contained in the sincere and explicit will to profess and to employ all the means ordained by God for the attainment of salvation. The schismatic is also properly disposed, since a confession made in general is sufficient for the

12 Cf. *supra*, pages 96, 97.

13 Cappello, *De Sacramentis*, I, n. 62, p. 55; Genicot-Salsmans, *Institutiones Theologiae Moralis*, II, n. 298, p. 262; cf. Noldin-Schmitt, *Summa Theologiae Moralis*, III, n. 297, p. 302.

14 Cappello, *loc. cit.*

validity of the absolution. In the present case the schismatic should be advised to confess that he is a sinner or that he has sinned, and that with the hope of receiving forgiveness he asks God to forgive him his sins. There will then be present the necessary confession and contrition which is required for a valid absolution. Finally, since it is possible especially for a material schismatic to have a supernatural faith, the required faith in relation to the reception of the sacraments will most probably be present. Cappello is of the opinion that this view can be sustained notwithstanding the prohibition of canon 731, §2, which states the safe and ordinary norm to be followed. In any event scandal must be avoided.[15]

When there is a reasonable belief that a dying schismatic will abjure his errors if he is warned, then the warning must be given. Once he has abjured his errors and is properly disposed, he may be absolved, anointed, and then be given any other sacraments according to his needs and dispositions. However, if it is prudently feared that the warning would be useless and would only disturb the good faith of the schismatic, it should be omitted.[16]

In this matter there are several responses of the Holy Office which are pertinent. They are frequently cited, and at times also quoted, by the authors. The general practice of conferring absolution on all schismatics in danger of death and of presuming them to be in good faith was declared illicit. The Holy Office furnished an answer to this specific question on January 13, 1864.[17] The question pointed to the fact of the presumably good faith of many who had been reared in heresy or in schism, and who, when death was imminent, could no longer place an act that would at least implicitly betoken their reconciliation with the Church. The question postulated also that the conditional absolution would be granted only when it could be accorded in harmony with the principles that regulate the conditional administration of the sacrament. With such circumstances obtain-

15 Cappello, *loc. cit.*

16 Regatillo, *Ius Sacramentarium,* I, n. 23, p. 18.

17 *Fontes,* n. 975; *Fonti,* II, 135.

ing in the case, was it allowable for a priest to grant a conditional absolution, even though with regard to the penitent's previous reconciliation with the Church he had held his silence, either because he found it impossible to speak of it, or because he was desirous of doing nothing that could perturb the dying person's conscience?

The Holy Office disapproved strongly of the usage in line with which, in the circumstances as mentioned, a conditional absolution would be imparted. With a special caution it stressed the need of some token that could establish at least a reasonable doubt in favor of the heretic's or the schismatic's expressed desire for reconciliation. When the presence of such a token could be assumed with at least a degree of reasonable probability, then the priest could hold to the indicated norms of the accredited authors in the question of granting or withholding the act of conditional absolution. In the earlier responses the Holy Office did not consider this question in detail, and one had to depend chiefly on the opinions of authors to determine what course to follow.

However, the later replies took into consideration justifying circumstances, and at least implicitly granted some exceptions to the general prohibition. There are three principal responses touching on this matter, those of: 1) July 20, 1898;[18] 2) May 26, 1916;[19] and 3) November 15, 1941.[20]

The first of these responses had resulted from a case which had been presented to the Holy Office in which Boniface, a Catholic priest, absolved Agatha, a schismatic penitent. The schismatic had gone to confession to the priest, but was going to receive Communion in the schismatic church. Because of the schismatic's sincerity and good faith the priest did not wish to disturb her good faith, and so he absolved her. In connection with this case several questions were proposed. To the question,

18 *Fontes*, n. 1203.

19 *Archiv für katholiches Kirchenrecht* (Innsbruck, 1857-1861; Mainz, 1862 —), XCVII (1917), 84 ff. (hereafter cited *AKK)*.

20 *Il Monitore Ecclesiastico*, tom. 67, p. 114 — cf. Regatillo, *Ius Sacramentarium*, I, 20.

"An aliquando absolvi possint schismatici materiales, qui in bona fide versantur?" the answer was given, "Cum scandalum nequeat vitari, negative; praeterquam in mortis articulo; et tunc efficaciter remoto scandalo." The Holy Office was also asked to pass judgment on the case in question. As was to be expected, it replied that Boniface had acted erroneously.

The second reply was a private response of the Holy Office to the Bishop of Linz. It was published in a diocesan paper, and not in the *Acta Apostolicae Sedis*. In this reply the following pronouncements were made:

> 1) An schismaticis materialibus in mortis articulo constitutis, bona fide sive absolutionem sive Extremam Unctionem petentibus, ea Sacramenta conferri possint sine abiuratione errorum.
>
> Reply: Negative, sed requiri, ut, meliori quo fieri possit modo, errores reiiciant et professionem fidei faciant.
>
> 2) An schismaticis in mortis articulo sensibus destitutis absolutio et Extrema Unctio conferri possit.
>
> Reply: Sub conditione *affirmative,* praesertim, si ex adiunctis coniicere liceat, eos implicite saltem errores suos reiicere, remoto tamen scandalo, manifestando scilicet adstantibus, Ecclesiam supponere eos in ultimo momento ad unitatem rediisse.
>
> 3) Quoad sepulturam ecclesiasticam, standum Rituali Romano.
>
> 4) Quoad baptismum infantium a parentibus schismaticis oblatorum: Non esse baptizandos, extra mortis periculum nisi probabilis affulgeat spes catholicae eorum educationis.

What was stated in this response was confirmed and further clarified by the response of the Holy Office of November 15, 1941, to the Apostolic Visitator for the Ukrainians in Germany. Because of its importance it may well be reproduced here in its entirety:

> 1. Sacerdos catholicus commendatos sibi habeat schismaticos qui, deficiente ministro acatholico, catholicum vocent. Infirmos visitet, et praesertim in mortis periculo versantes ad orationem, contritionem, et submissionem divinae voluntati excitet (c. 1350, §1).
>
> 2. Etiam in periculo mortis, ut sacramenta eis ministrentur, requiritur ut meliori quo fieri possit modo, pro adiunctis

saltem implicite errores reiiciant et fidei professionem emittant.

3. Bona fide errantibus iam sensibus destitutis sacramenta conferri possunt sub conditione, praesertim si coniicere liceat eos *implicite saltem* errores reiecisse.

4. Semper curandum est ut scandalum vel suspicio interconfessionalismi vitetur. Quo minus est periculum in mora eo magis explicita retractatio errorum et fidei professio exigi debent.

5. Quoad sepulturam standum est c. 1240. Sacerdos tamen sine veste sacra, sine ullo ritu sacro coram cadavere domi exposito preces privatim fundere, officii civilis causa funus sequi et in coemeterio apud tumulum orare poterit, remoto scandalo.

6. Pueri schismatici a parentibus oblati ut baptizentur *extra mortis periculum* generatim non sunt baptizandi, nisi probabilis spes sit catholicae educationis.[21]

According to the last two responses quoted above it is evident that the Holy See requires an abjuration of error and a profession of faith from a schismatic even in danger of death when he is in the possession of his senses. These acts must be express, but they need not be explicit. The abjuration of error and the profession of faith are contained implicitly in acts of the penitent by which he manifests at least attrition for sin and shows himself prepared to do all things necessary for salvation. This opinion is sustained by weighty authors.[22] Some authors[23] consider the question particularly in reference to Protestants, and are inclined to be a little more strict in their opinions. Here one is considering dying schismatics, who admit the necessity of the sacraments for salvation, and hence certain presumptions can be made in their favor that would not be available in the case of Protestants.

In reference to this question there are some interesting state-

21 *Il Monitore Ecclesiastico*, tom. 67, p. 114 — cf. Regatillo, *Ius Sacramentarium*, I, 20.

22 Coronata, *De Sacramentis*, I, n. 72, p. 52; Cappello, *De Sacramentis*, I, n. 62, p. 55; Regatillo, *Ius Sacramentarium*, I, p. 19, n. 23. Cf. Vermeersch-Creusen, *Epitome Iuris Canonici*, II, n. 16; Moriarty, *The Extraordinary Absolution from Censures*, p. 80.

23 Cf. Woywod, *Practical Commentary*, I, 323, 324.

ments made by the late Bishop Neveu (✠1946), Administrator Apostolic of Moscow, at that time residing in Paris. He issued an instruction to the army chaplains as to how to minister to Orthodox soldiers at the front.[24] Among other things he stated that there are nine presumptions against one that an Orthodox Christian (Russian schismatic) has not committed the sin of schism. Consequently he is not a formal schismatic and has not incurred the excommunication of canon 2314. He presented several arguments in favor of his assertions, and finally concluded the instruction in the following terms:

> Dear soldier priests, you have only to deal with a man who has recourse to your ministry as you would deal with a Catholic and brother in the faith. If he is wounded or gravely ill, make sure of his good faith, which you may anyhow presume. Make him make an act of faith as explicitly as possible in the authority of the visible head of the Church, and hear his confession as well as you can. A decree of the Holy Office of July 20, 1898, allows the absolution of material schismatics in good faith, provided there be no scandal. All the more may we absolve a Christian who declares that he wants to live and die in communion with the Universal Church and the Vicar of Christ. You may then content yourselves with the general and ordinary formula of absolution. . . . Then give him extreme unction and the Viaticum, if there is time, and have no hesitation in giving him the honor of a Catholic funeral . . .

This instruction is of interest both because of the official source from which it comes and inasmuch as it seems to encourage the priest to take a broad view of the phrase "as explicitly as possible."[25] This instruction was given to army chaplains, but similar problems are not uncommon in hospital practice in the United States. This instruction is a further confirmation of the views expressed by Vermeersch-Creusen, Coronata, Cappello, and others.[26]

24 Cf. *The Tablet*, November 11, 1939, pp. 548-549.

25 ". . . meliori quo fieri possit modo" — cf. S. C. S. Off., 26 maii 1916 — *AKK*, XCVII (1917), 84 ff.

26 Cf. John C. Ford, "Current Moral Theology and Canon Law" — *Theological Studies*, II (1941), 543.

The authors state that at least a conditional absolution should be given. However, if there is no prudent doubt concerning the dispositions of the penitent, there is no reason why absolution should not be given absolutely. If a devout schismatic ardently desires Viaticum from a Catholic priest who alone is present, Vermeersch-Creusen think that in the usual circumstances *(per se)* it is to be denied him.[27] However, there can be circumstances in which from the very denial there will be danger that his good faith will be disturbed. In this case some are of the opinion that there is room for *epikeia,* if scandal is removed.[28]

If the dying schismatic refuses to manifest a sorrow for sin or to show his willingness to do all things necessary for salvation, he will not be disposed and consequently cannot be given the sacraments.

2. Schismatic Bereft of His Senses

When a dying schismatic is unconscious, the circumstances are again changed. The more common opinion holds that one cannot absolve a formal schismatic who is bereft of his senses.[29] St. Alphonsus, in speaking of heretics in danger of death, stated that even though they gave signs of contrition, such persons could never prudently be presumed to have given the requisite signs in respect of confession, since with the heretics the sacrament of penance is held in detestation.[30] However, this is a general presumption which certainly would not find equal application in the case of schismatics. Accordingly there are authors who hold that even formal schismatics who are bereft of their senses can be given conditional absolution. Cappello states that this opinion enjoys a true probability of correctness for the case in which scandal is duly removed and that this opinion is also confirmed by the response of the Holy Office of May 26, 1916.[31] However,

27 *Epitome Iuris Canonici,* II, n. 16.

28 Vermeersch-Creusen, *loc. cit.;* Regatillo, *Ius Sacramentarium,* I, 20.

29 Cappello, *De Sacramentis,* I, n. 62, p. 54.

30 *Theologia Moralis,* Lib. VI, n. 483 — Tom. II, 501.

31 Cf. *supra,* page 157.

this opinion cannot be sustained in view of the later response of November 15, 1941,[32] which permits the giving of conditional absolution and extreme unction only to material schismatics bereft of their senses and makes no concessions in favor of formal schismatics.

In the particular response of May 26, 1916, it is to be noted that no distinction is made between formal and material schismatics. The Holy Office also uses the word *praesertim* which indicates that even an implicit reconciliation was not required for the licit administration of the sacrament in a conditional manner. In interpreting this response King (1895-1926) offered some very pertinent remarks.[33] He stated that in the case of those destitute of their senses no sign of reconciliation is mentioned or demanded in the decree. It is quite clear that none in the knowledge of the minister has been given. The sacraments are to be administered conditionally, especially *"si ex adiunctis coniicere liceat eos implicite saltem errores suos reiicere,"* about which there would be no doubt if signs had been given. Scandal is to be removed by making it known to the bystanders that the Church supposes such to have returned to the unity of the Church in their last moments. However, there would be more than a supposition if definite signs had been given.[34]

The response of May 26, 1916, as is evident, was issued before the promulgation of the Code, but sufficient proof that it is still in effect is found in the fact that the principles enunciated in this response were repeated and confirmed by the Holy Office in its response of November 15, 1941, to the Apostolic Visitator for the Ukrainians in Germany.[35]

However, the latter response, in speaking of those who are bereft of their senses, mentions specifically only material schismatics, and in so doing seems to restrict the more general termi-

32 Cf. *supra,* page 157.

33 *The Administration of the Sacraments to Dying Non-Catholics,* The Catholic University of America Canon Law Studies, n. 23 (Washington, D. C.: The Catholic University of America, 1924), p. 81.

34 King, *loc. cit.*

35 Cf. *supra,* page 157.

nology of the response of May 26, 1916. The opinion which stated that even formal schismatics who are in danger of death and are at the same time bereft of their senses could be given conditional absolution and extreme unction cannot be sustained in view of the response of November 15, 1941. It is evidently the mind of the Holy See not to grant the sacraments even conditionally to formal schismatics under any circumstances.

Since the Church permits the conditional administration of the sacraments to material schismatics in danger of death, and since the subject is evidently in need of the sacraments, the Catholic priest should not hesitate to administer the sacraments as long as scandal can effectively be precluded. Under these circumstances the Catholic priest would not only be permitted, but he would be obliged by a grave obligation in justice or charity to administer the sacraments to the dying schismatic.

Both the sacrament of penance and the sacrament of extreme unction are to be administered conditionally to the material schismatic who is dying and is bereft of his senses. The condition that is to be made in conferring both of these sacraments is, *si es capax,* and not, *si es dispositus.* This is in accordance with the general principle that the condition be in regard to the validity of the sacrament, and should not concern the dispositions which are necessary for the fruitful reception of the sacrament, in order that the reviviscence of the sacrament may not be prevented.[36]

There is some difference of opinion as to whether extreme unction should be administered conditionally or absolutely in the present case. According to the principles given by Noldin-Schmitt, it seems that in this case extreme unction should be administered absolutely.[37] However, Cappello is of the opinion that the sacrament of extreme unction is to be administered conditionally in the present case.[38] This latter opinion is more in accordance with the replies of the Holy Office of May 26, 1916, and of November 15, 1941, both of which state that the

[36] Merkelbach, *Summa Theologiae Moralis,* III, n. 705, p. 685.

[37] Noldin-Schmitt, *Summa Theologiae Moralis,* III, n. 446.

[38] *De Sacramentis,* III — *De Extrema Unctione,* n. 110.

sacraments of penance and extreme unction are to be administered conditionally.

Article II — Reception and Use of the Sacramentals by Schismatics

As a rule the sacramentals were not to be administered or given to schismatics. This was the general principle which formed the basis of the replies of the Sacred Congregations, although in some instances it allowed of exceptions.

In certain localities Bulgarian dissidents desired that the Latin missionary come to bless their homes on the Feast of the Epiphany. The Sacred Congregation for the Propagation of the Faith on April 17, 1758, replied that it was to be tolerated that a priest bless the homes of schismatics on the Feast of the Epiphany, if under constraint of fear he had been called to them to do so, as long as it remained evident that he did not communicate with them in prayer.[39]

In an Instruction of the Holy Office for the United States on June 22, 1859,[40] it was declared to be wrong to invite heretics to the choir for sacred functions, to sing the psalms alternately with them, to give them the *pax,* blessed ashes, candles, blessed palms, and other like things which form part of the external worship, all of which are properly considered as indications of an interior bond and of the union of mind and heart among the worshippers, either in the active, or also in the passive sense. Not only were Catholics forbidden to give these sacramentals to heretics, but they were likewise forbidden to receive similar objects from heretics in their sacred functions. In either case such actions would be tantamount to welcoming them and to communicating with them in their evil works.

According to another Instruction it was also forbidden to give the nuptial blessing in a mixed marriage.[41]

The Code has mitigated somewhat the severity of these pro-

39 *Fontes,* n. 4525; *Fonti,* II, 99.

40 *Fontes,* n. 952; *Fonti,* II, 133.

41 S. C. S. Off., 3 ian. 1871, ad 3 — *Fontes,* n. 1013.

hibitions. According to the present law[42] blessings are to be given primarily to Catholics, and when there exists no prohibition of the Church they may also be given to non-Catholics, in order that they may obtain the light of faith, or together with it bodily health.

Canon 1144 furnishes a definition of a sacramental: Sacramentals are sacred objects and actions which the Church, in a certain imitation of the Sacraments, is accustomed to employ in order to obtain through her intercession favors which are especially spiritual. The sacred objects are, for example, blessed ashes, holy water, blessed candles. Actions are ceremonies or blessings, such as the nuptial blessing, the churching of women, the blessing of homes.

Although the Code treats here simply of blessings, the prescription is a general one which applies to other sacramentals, namely, to sacramental objects and exorcisms.[43]

There is no general prohibition of the Church against the reception of sacramentals by non-Catholics, but generally the latter are not to be admitted publicly to the use of the sacramentals on account of the forbidden religious communication.[44] Vermeersch-Creusen state that the faculty given in canon 1149 of conferring blessings also on non-Catholics is restricted by the Instruction of June 22, 1859.[45] Consequently, even though it is permitted to give the sacramentals to schismatics, they should not be given publicly. When the sacramentals are given to schismatics they should be given only privately.[46] Regatillo adds that they can be given privately and *extra ecclesiam*.[47]

These are the opinions of authors and they are based principally on the responses of the Holy See to particular questions. However, there is no general prohibition in the Code against administering sacramentals even publicly but outside of sacred

42 Cf. canon 1149.

43 Coronata, *De Sacramentis*, III, n. 736, p. 1022.

44 Coronata, *loc. cit.*

45 *Epitome Iuris Canonici*, II, n. 577, p. 406, ftn. 6.

46 Cf. Woywod, *Practical Commentary*, I, 735.

47 *Ius Sacramentarium*, II, p. 439, n. 681.

functions to schismatics. As a guide in this matter one has to depend largely on the principles of the divine law and the practice of the Church. If no scandal is occasioned through the administration of the sacramentals to schismatics, then there is nothing to forbid the practice.

The Instruction of June 22, 1859,[48] forbade the administration of certain sacramentals during sacred functions. But there would be nothing to forbid a Catholic to take home a blessed palm or some holy water to give it to a schismatic friend, as long as there is no scandal or danger of irreverence. Lest there be any superstitious use of these articles among the uninstructed, they should be informed that these articles do not confer any infallible protection against lightning, disease, or any other misfortunes.[49]

It is presumed also that when it is permitted to give the sacramentals to non-Catholics there is absent the danger of scandal, of contempt, and of superstition in their use.[50] When the sacramentals are given to schismatics there will hardly be any danger of contempt or superstition, but there may be present the danger of scandal. It will more readily be permitted to give blessed articles which in themselves have a certain material value, as, for example, blessed food or medals, than those which have no particular use or value without the blessing, such as blessed ashes, oil, or water.[51]

According to canon 1152 exorcisms can be exercised not only over the faithful and catechumens, but also over non-Catholics and excommunicates.

Canon 2260 forbids the reception of the sacramentals by persons under declaratory or condemnatory sentence of excommunication. But the ordinary schismatic, even though he may have incurred the *latae sententiae* excommunication enacted in canon 2314, is not thereby under declaratory or condemnatory sentence. Hence he is not included in the prohibition of canon 2260.

48 *Fontes,* n. 952.

49 Vermeersch-Creusen, *Epitome Iuris Canonici,* II, p. 322, n. 467.

50 Sipos, *Enchiridion Iuris Canonici,* p. 659.

51 Sipos, *loc. cit.*

Non-Catholics are prohibited from receiving the nuptial blessing when they contract marriage.[52] However, it seems from the wording of canon 1102 that in order to neutralize more serious evils the ordinary could permit even this blessing to be given. To grant this exception is not the practice of the Church, for the conferral of this blessing was expressly forbidden in an Instruction of the Holy Office.[53] According to Sipos the blessing of a woman after childbirth is also a sacramental whose reception is forbidden to schismatics.[54]

The state of grace is not necessary for the reception of the sacramentals. However, since the dispositions of the subject play a great part in producing the effect of the sacramentals, the subject should be exhorted to elicit an act of perfect contrition.[55]

The primary purpose of conferring sacramentals on non-Catholics is that they obtain the light of faith. This purpose should always be present, for one cannot obtain other graces without this fundamental grace, namely, the gift of faith.[56] Although the Code mentions solely the health of the body as a secondary motive inherent in the reception of a sacramental, it seems that all temporal favors must be understood as comprised under this general designation.[57]

In connection with this matter an interesting incident was related by Bishop Neveu, the Administrator Apostolic of Moscow.[58] Its circumstances were known personally to him. The Holy Father, Pius XI, who knew the extent of his duties and rights, and would certainly not have given his blessing to excommunicated people in a state of mortal sin, nevertheless gave his paternal blessing to a pious Russian Bishop then still Orthodox. The Holy Father said that he considered him as a son, and this so moved the Bishop that he decided to make at once his official

52 Can. 1102.

53 3 ian. 1871, ad 3 — *Fontes*, n. 1013.

54 *Enchiridion Iuris Canonici*, p. 700.

55 Coronata, *De Sacramentis*, III, n. 736, p. 1023.

56 Blat, *Commentarium*, II, pars I, p. 711.

57 Coronata, *loc. cit.*

58 Cf. *The Tablet*, November 11, 1939, pp. 548, 549.

submission to the Sovereign Pontiff. This Bishop died as a confessor of the faith in a Communist dungeon in 1935. Pius XI also blessed as his own Catholic children, Orthodox Christians, still separated from the Roman communion, but who suffered for the Christian Church. Bishop Neveu concluded with the remark: "Have we, then, a right to be more Catholic than the Pope?"

Article III — Presence of Schismatics at Catholic Functions

Passive assistance by schismatics at the sacred functions of Catholics is not forbidden, but schismatics are to be repelled from active participation. According to a reply of the Holy Office Mass could be celebrated in the presence of schismatics.[59] The Sacred Congregation for the Propagation of the Faith also permitted schismatic soldiers to attend Catholic services and to assist at the sacred functions if they were not heretics or schismatics who were notoriously excommunicated. They could not be admitted to the sacraments, however, until they had abjured their heresy, abandoned their schism, and returned to the Church.[60]

The practice of having Russian schismatics at Catholic functions, and present also by invitation at meals with Catholics, could be tolerated as long as schismatics and heretics demonstrated their presence to be a mere material presence dictated by reason of the civil honor due them, and provided that they did not join in the prayers and rites of the Catholics. But if they practiced their own rites, or joined in the Catholic rite, their presence could not licitly be permitted. The Sacred Congregation commended the missionaries who omitted on such occasions all functions involving prayer.[61]

Such active assistance as that which is given by one who serves the Mass could not be permitted a schismatic. This was

59 26 nov. 1665 — *Coll. S. C. P. F.*, n. 164; *Fonti*, II, 79.
60 30 iul. 1806 — *Fontes*, n. 850.
61 12 aug. 1826 — *Fonti*, II, 123.

expressly forbidden in a reply of the Holy Office on November 20, 1850.[62]

Although the Holy See in its responses takes a rather severe attitude toward the communication of schismatics in the sacred functions of Catholics, there are many instances, even in modern times, in which the directives of the Holy See were not adhered to strictly in practice. It is evident that under the circumstances the actions had the support of important ecclesiastical authorities.

According to information received by Dr. Ploechl from a high dignitary of the Archdiocese of Vienna, the following incidents occurred in very recent times. At the home of His Eminence, Cardinal Innitzer, there lived the Russian Orthodox Bishop of Zytomir, Leontij, who on the occasion of all solemn feasts was present at the services in the Cathedral of St. Stephen. He had his place in the stall of the former imperial family. Pious orthodox archimandrites even participated in the Eucharistic processions in the cathedral on the Feast of Corpus Christi.

Perhaps in the case presented there was no danger of scandal or of perversion because of the accompanying circumstances, and there may have been some grave reason for permitting such communication, but without a doubt such a religious communication could hardly be permitted here in the United States.

Many particular questions in regard to this matter have been presented to the Sacred Congregations for deliberation, and these will be presented under their respective headings.

A. *Schismatic Sponsor at Baptism and Confirmation*

The Code clearly states that those who are members of a schismatic sect cannot act as sponsor at the baptism (canon 765, 2°) or confirmation (canon 795, 2°) of Catholics. The language of the Code is not identical in regard to both sacraments. Canon 765 forbids him who belongs to a schismatic sect, whereas canon 795 forbids him who is enrolled in a schismatic sect, from acting validly as a sponsor. Canon 765 appears to be more comprehen-

[62] *Coll. S. C. P. F.*, n. 1053; *Fonti*, II, 131.

sive, though in practice there would be little difference between the two restrictions. In any event the person would have to be a member or a defender of the sect and not merely one who had schismatic tendencies.[63]

This prohibition is imposed in the Code under pain of invalidity, although prior to the law of the Code a schismatic could act validly but illicitly as sponsor.[64] The responses of the Sacred Congregations throw some light on this matter and present some interesting cases which determine the mode of procedure in actual difficult circumstances.

In regard to non-Catholic sponsors, the first response was that of October 14, 1676, which forbade heretical schismatics in Bosnia to act as sponsors at Catholic baptism.[65]

A very learned response in regard to this question was given to the missionaries in Egypt by Pope Benedict XIV (1740-1758) on December 9, 1745.[66] The response is fortified with references which support its assertions. If no one but a heretic was present to act as sponsor, then the baptism was to be conferred without a sponsor. The displeasure on the part of the heretic, no matter how great, was not a sufficient reason to permit him to act as sponsor. He could be tolerated as a sponsor in a given case only when a refusal would entail danger to one's life, or give rise to some other imminent grave danger.

Benedict XIV quoted Verricelli (✠1656) as commending the Franciscan missionaries who, in order to meet the tragic situation to which the Albanians were subject if they repulsed the Turks from acting as sponsors, arranged the matter in such a fashion that the child was placed on the shoulders of or actually held by some Christian, with the result that the Turk was not in principal active contact with the child. Thus, though the Turk

63 Coronata, *De Sacramentis*, I, n. 178, p. 132.

64 Cf. Vermeersch-Creusen, *Epitome Iuris Canonici*, II, n. 577; Sipos, *Enchiridion Iuris Canonici*, p. 447; Salmanticenses, *Cursus Theologiae Moralis* (6 vols. in 3, Venetiis: apud Nicolaum Pezzana, 1722), Tom. I, tract. 2, c. 7, n. 46; Sporer, *Theologia Moralis*, I, tr. II, c. 2, sect. 3, n. 31.

65 S. C. S. Off., ad 1 — *Fontes*, n. 753.

66 *Fontes*, n. 798.

assumed that he was acting as sponsor, he was not in reality the sponsor.

On the other hand, the National Albanian Synod of 1703,[67] approved in 1705 under Pope Clement IX (1700-1721), adverted to the current custom, which it called detestable, of admitting infidels or schismatics as sponsors at baptism. The Synod ruled that bishops were to impose severer penalties than theretofore against the practice.

In view of this and other authorities, Benedict XIV declared that infidels, heretics, or schismatics were not permitted to act as sponsors at a baptism which was administered to the children of Catholics.

An implicit prohibition against the use of schismatic sponsors was also contained in the Acts of the Congregation for the Propagation of the Faith in the year 1769.[68]

In spite of the numerous decrees to the contrary, in some instances and as late as 1855 schismatics were still admitted as sponsors at the baptism of the children of Catholics. Notice of this was brought to the attention of the Bishop of Tenas, and he was instructed to eradicate the abuse to the best of his power.[69]

In a response to the Bishop of Smyrna in 1864[70] the prohibition of the practice of having a non-Catholic sponsor at baptism was reiterated.

Following this response the Holy Office issued a more detailed Instruction[71] in order to remove further doubts concerning the sponsorship of heretics and schismatics at Catholic baptisms. Heretics or schismatics could neither themselves nor through a Catholic proxy, neither alone nor together with Catholics, licitly perform the office of sponsor. There is no evidence of any later

67 *Coll. Lac.*, I, 298c.

68 *Fonti*, XII, 227.

69 *Fonti*, I, 99. The diocese of Tenas, created in the ninth century, eventually became united with the archdiocese of Naxas, one of the larger of the Cyclades Islands in the Aegean Sea.

70 Ad 4 — *Fontes*, n. 978.

71 S. C. S. Off., instr. (ad Archiep. Corcyren.), 3 ian. 1871, ad 1 — *Fontes*, n. 1013.

replies concerning the admission of schismatic sponsors. However, at a later date, the Holy Office again treated the question of the sponsorship of heretics.[72] In this reply it was made clear that a heretic could not be considered merely as one who was notoriously under censure when there was a question of admitting a heretic to act as sponsor at a Catholic baptism.

The Holy Office demands that the priest inform the non-Catholic that he cannot be sponsor properly so called, but can assist at most as a witness.[73]

Cappello[74] states that if a heretic or a schismatic is designated by the parents and cannot be repulsed without grave inconvenience, the pastor can tolerate his presence as a witness who does not touch the infant during the actual baptism. But if the pastor cannot forestall this, then with a view to averting greater evil he can tolerate this also, since there is no question here of an act that is intrinsically evil.

It is interesting to note that in the recent granting to pastors of the faculty of confirming in danger of death, a reference is made to the communication of heretics or schismatics at the rite of confirmation. The priest who is confirming is to take precautions lest he perform the rite of confirmation in the presence of heretics or schismatics, much less with their assistance.[75]

B. *Matrimony*

1. Mixed Marriages

Mixed marriages open the way for the ultimate result of a communication with schismatics. On August 1, 1821, the Holy Office forbade priests when assisting at a mixed marriage to employ the customary form, to pronounce the accompanying prayers, or to bless the ring of the heretical spouse.[76]

It was forbidden also to allow a heretic or a schismatic the

[72] S. C. S. Off., 3 maii 1893 — *Fontes*, n. 1163.

[73] Woywod, *Practical Commentary*, I, 348; cf. S. C. S. Off., instr. (ad Praef. Mission. Tripol.), mense ian. 1763 — *Fontes*, n. 812.

[74] *De Sacramentis*, I, n. 177, p. 155.

[75] *AAS*, XXXVIII (1946), 356.

[76] *Fontes*, n. 863; *Fonti*, II, 126.

use of one's home as a place for the contracting of his marriage. This prohibition was evidenced in a response in 1864.[77]

In an Instruction of the Holy Office of January 3, 1871,[78] there was presented a detailed explanation as to what conditions were required if a mixed marriage was to be contracted licitly. According to the Instruction it was stated that the Church traditionally has abhorred the marriages of Catholics with heretics or schismatics, but that such marriages can be permitted for just and grave reasons under the conditions

1) that a dispensation be obtained from the Holy See, which alone has the right to dispense;
2) that the marriage take place outside the church building and without the blessing of the pastor or any other ecclesiastical rite; and
3) that the conditions required by the natural and the positive divine law be present, namely, that there be no danger of perversion for the Catholic spouse, that the Catholic education of all the offspring be safeguarded, and that the Catholic party endeavor earnestly to lead the non-Catholic to the true faith.

At one time in the past it had been held by some authors that mixed marriages could be licitly contracted without a dispensation of the Holy See, but the untenableness of that opinion had since been demonstrated.[79] The practice of blessing such marriages in church could be tolerated wherever it was so deeply entrenched that it could not be abolished without the provocation of graver evil consequences in its stead. The presence of the set conditions was so essential that a dispensation therefrom was inadmissible. The pastor was in duty bound to tell people of their obligation if they declined to make the needed promises. He could not entertain the idea of letting a party remain in good faith, for the very possibility of its presence was unthinkable.

These regulations of the Holy Office in reference to the marriage ceremony are summed up in canon 1102, which states that

[77] S. C. S. Off. (Smyrnen.), 30 iun., 7 iul. 1864, ad 3 — *Fontes*, n. 978.
[78] Instr. (ad Archiep. Corcyren.), nn. 2-7 — *Fontes*, n. 1013.
[79] Benedictus XIV, *De Synodo Dioecesana*, Lib. IX, c. 2.

all sacred rites are forbidden, and that the marriage ceremony is not to take place in the church. If from this prohibition greater evils are anticipated, the ordinary may allow some of the usual sacred ceremonies, but never the celebration of Mass. There are to be employed only those ceremonies which are essential to the validity of the marriage contract.

2. Assistance at Marriage

With reference to the marriage of Catholics before a Catholic priest, a schismatic as a rule was forbidden to assist. However, according to an Instruction of the Holy Office for the United States[80] it was permitted for heretics to assist at a Catholic marriage according to the following conditions, namely, those who merely stood at the side of the spouses, and neither said nor did anything which could be regarded as a sign of forbidden participation, could be allowed to engage in this function if no scandal was to be feared as a result of their material presence. The Instruction did not positively state that a heretic could act as one of the official witnesses of the marriage.

When asked whether heretics, schismatics, or infidels could be invited to the wedding ceremony of Catholics or to the celebration of mixed marriages when these were being contracted licitly, the Holy Office replied that for a reasonable cause this could be tolerated, as long as there was no *communicatio in sacris* and no reasonable fear of scandal.[81]

On August 19, 1891, the Holy Offive gave an answer on this point concerning the witnesses.[82] When asked whether those who were not of the faith could act as witnesses at the marriages of Catholics, the Holy Office replied that they should not be employed as witnesses. However, the ordinary could for a grave reason tolerate their presence in the capacity of witnesses, as long as no scandal resulted.

It is not permitted to have a schismatic act as an official

80 22 iun. 1859 — *Fontes*, n. 952; *Fonti*, II, 133.
81 14 ian. 1874 — *Fontes*, n. 1028.
82 *Fontes*, n. 1144.

witness at the marriage ceremony without the consent of the ordinary. However, it can be permitted for a schismatic to be among those whose presence merely adds dignity to the wedding ceremony.[83] This, at least, is the custom which is followed in this country.

C. *Funerals and Burials*

Numerous responses were issued by the Sacred Congregations in reference to assistance at funerals. Anything that savored of an active participation was always forbidden. The Holy Office stated that it could be tolerated for Greek priests, heretical or schismatic, to attend the funerals of Catholics as a mark of civil honor, but they were forbidden to take part in the Catholic prayers or rites.[84] The Sacred Congregation for the Propagation of the Faith, a few years after this response of the Holy Office, issued an answer of similar import.[85] A reply of the Holy Office on January 14, 1874, cited the decree of May 10, 1753, and substantially repeated its import.[86]

Catholics were permitted to accompany the corpse of a heretic to the cemetery, and to be present while the exequies were performed in the heretical rite.[87] It was also permitted for heretics to be present at the exequies of Catholics. This interchange of presence at funerals reflected a time-honored custom which could not be obviated without grave harm to Catholics, and besides it possessed the character of a merely civil or political act.

The office of pall-bearer, if strictly considered, constitutes an active participation in the Catholic burial rite, since the *trans-*

[83] Vermeersch-Creusen, *Epitome Iuris Canonici*, II, n. 577.

[84] S. C. S. Off. (Mission. Tenas in Peloponneso), 10 maii 1753, ad 1 — *Fontes*, n. 804; *Fonti*, II, 95.

[85] 17 apr. 1758 — *Fontes*, n. 4525 — *Fonti*, II, 99.

[86] Ad 4: "— 2. Urgendum ne haeretici, aut infideles, in cadaverum fidelium humatione, cum catholicis et praesertim clericis quoquo modo se immisceant." — *Fontes*, n. 1028.

[87] S. C. S. Off., litt. (ad. Vic. Ap. Algeriae), 21 ian. 1751 — *Fontes*, n. 803; *Fonti*, II, 87.

latio cadaveris is an essential part of the funeral service.[88] However, there is a legitimate custom in the United States to permit non-Catholics to act as pall-bearers at a Catholic funeral, since the office is considered here merely in the nature of a civil duty. In practice, when preparations for the funeral are being made, no questions are asked as to who the pall-bearers will be, and if non-Catholics act in that capacity, their presence is tolerated. There is hardly any question of scandal, and hence such assistance can easily be permitted.

There was a problem, too, regarding the place of burial of schismatics. The Sacred Congregation for the Propagation of the Faith forbade the Maronite Patriarch to grant to schismatics a place among the church's tombs for the burial of their dead.[89] On March 29, 1830, the same Sacred Congregation forbade the burial of non-Catholics in a Catholic cemetery as long as there was another cemetery in that locality.[90] If there was no other cemetery, then a division of the cemetery was to be made with separate entrances.

The Holy Office was asked whether deceased non-Catholics could by reason of the bond of consanguinity or marriage be lawfully placed in the family sepulchers of Catholic relatives. The Holy Office replied that the bishops were to see that all things be done according to the sacred canons. However, if this could not be accomplished without scandal and danger, the practice could be tolerated.[91]

It has been the practice of the Church to have its own distinct cemetery separate from the burial places of non-Catholics, and this has been incorporated in the law of the Code in canon 1206. This has been sufficiently explained in the earlier treatment given to the consideration of positive communication.

88 Cf. canon 1204.

89 8 iul. 1774 — *Fonti,* I, 89.

90 *Fontes,* n. 4747; *Fonti,* II, 125.

91 30 mart. 1859 — *Fontes,* n. 949; *Fonti,* II, 133.

D. *Schismatic Chanters and Organists*

Singing sacred music with Catholics or playing the organ at Catholic religious services is a religious communication, and generally it is forbidden schismatics to participate in both these actions. However, under certain circumstances both the admitting of schismatics to sing together with Catholics at Catholic services and the playing of the organ by a non-Catholic have been permitted by the Holy See.

On May 1, 1889, the Holy Office[92] considered as an abuse to be eliminated the custom of admitting non-Catholics, even boys who attended a Catholic school, to sing with Catholics in Catholic churches. When the question concerning the lawfulness of admitting them was presented to the Holy Office, adequate reasons for the toleration of the practice were not indicated, and consequently the Holy Office declared the practice illicit. It seems the principal reason for permitting the practice was the scarcity of Catholic choir boys. This reason could and was to be neutralized through the training of Catholic boys.

However, on January 24, 1906, in consideration of the peculiar circumstances of the case presented, the Holy Office declared that a similar practice could be tolerated.[93] The case was presented by the Vicar Apostolic of Sophia and Philippopolis in Bulgaria. Certain religious, the Sisters of Wisdom, conducted an institute for girls, to which schismatics were admitted together wth Catholics. The custom prevailed that in ecclesiastical functions, and especially at the exposition of and benediction with the Blessed Sacrament, as also before or after it, the schismatic girls joined in the chanting with the Catholics in the parochial church. Accordingly it was asked whether this practice could be tolerated, in the light of the following circumstances:

1) This usage obtained in a place where the number of Catholics in relation to the schismatics was very small.
2) There was no danger of scandal, since the same practice was observed in almost all the regions of the Orient.

92 *Coll. S. C. P. F.*, n. 1703.

93 *Fontes*, n. 1276; *Coll. S. C. P. F.*, n. 2227.

3) On the contrary, the practice furnished good hope for the conversion of the non-Catholics.
4) It would be difficult for the Sisters who conducted the institute to impose silence on the schismatics who of their own ready accord and desire sang along in church with the Catholics.
5) Finally, with reference to the same schismatic girls, inasmuch as they lived in good faith in their schismatical status, it appeared that they should not be considered as excommunicated.

To this the Holy Office replied that in the light of the circumstances attending the case the mentioned practice could be tolerated. This decision was specifically approved and confirmed within the same month by Pope Pius X (1903-1914).

On February 23, 1820, the Holy Office gave an answer to the following question: In the absence of a Catholic man to play the organ in a Catholic church, could a non-Catholic be admitted temporarily for this function? The Holy Office replied that if all scandal and danger of scandal were obviated in the case, the non-Catholic could be admitted.[94]

In regard to this question an interesting incident occurred on the occasion of the peace celebration after the defeat of Napoleon. The Russians were allies of the Austrians, and they joined with them in celebrating the victory. On November 8, 1809, the chanters of Count Rozumovsky, the Ukrainian Ambassador to Austria, sought permission to sing during the Divine Liturgy in the Church of St. Barbara in Vienna, since the chapel of the Russian Delegation was closed. They were granted the permission in order to show that there was no feeling of animosity between the Uniates and the schismatics, and that the schismatics might observe that there was no difference in the ceremonies of the Catholics, and also because the Russians had been the allies of the Austrians in the war against Napoleon. It was remarked that because of the beauty of the chant many were

94 S. C. S. Off. (Quebec), ad 3 — *Fontes*, n. 858; *Fonti*, II, 125.

drawn into the Church *(cantus suavitas plurimos in Ecclesiam allicuit)*.[95]

E. *Sermons*

Not only are schismatics permitted to be present for sermons preached in a Catholic church, but they should even be invited to attend.[96] The reason for this is obvious. To forbid schismatics to attend sermons preached in a Catholic church would be to cut them off from the source of truth, which is in opposition to the divine mission of the Church to teach all nations. The preaching of the gospel is a channel through which the reception of the gift of faith is made possible.

F. *Processions*

On the occasion of a Corpus Christi procession schismatics and Catholics had joined in the procession, and it was doubted whether this constituted a *communicatio in sacris*. Pope Benedict XIV stated that such an action could not be proclaimed absolutely illicit in every case. If injury and harm, altercation and strife, or other similar grave evils could prudently be feared as a result of the positive exclusion of the schismatics, their act of joining in the procession could be tolerated.[97]

Article IV — Miscellaneous Questions

A. *Offering of Mass or Prayers for Schismatics*

According to canon 809 a priest is free to apply Holy Mass for any living person and also for the poor souls in purgatory. However, this faculty is restricted by the rules enacted in canon 2262, §2, 2°, concerning excommunicates. This canon allows Mass to be applied privately for an excommunicated person if

[95] MS, Parish Chronicle of St. Barbara's, Vienna, Austria, Vol. I (1809), page 104 (cited with the permission of Dr. Ploechl).

[96] McHugh-Callan, *Moral Theology*, I, n. 957.

[97] S. C. S. Off., 24 febr. 1752 — *Fonti*, II, 91.

there be no scandal. But if the person is a *vitandus,* Mass may be said only for his conversion.

The Code grants greater freedom in this matter than was allowed by the Holy Office in its various earlier responses. According to the questions presented to the Sacred Congregation for the Propagation of the Faith by the Archbishop of Antivari (Jugoslavia),[98] it seems that the Latin priests were receiving Mass offerings from schismatics who wished Masses to be celebrated for their dead. The priests accepted the stipends, but applied the Masses for the donors' ancestors who at one time had been Catholics. The Sacred Congregation forbade the practice.

The mind of the Holy See was further clarified by a response of the Holy Office on April 19, 1837.[99] The question was this: Could a Mass be celebrated and a stipend for it be accepted from a Greek schismatic who insisted very strongly that Mass be applied for him, The answer was given that the Mass could not be said, unless it was expressly evident that the offering was made for the sake of petitioning a conversion to the true faith.

The Synod of Lwów (1891) grieved at the practice of some of the laity who were unashamed to offer stipends to schismatic priests to procure the exercise of sacred functions for the salvation of the soul of some Ruthenian poet or some schismatic political figure, inasmuch as they seemed to consider all these things as licit or at least indifferent. Consequently the Synod strictly warned all priests, catechists, and others engaged in the care of souls, on all suitable occasions to instruct their subjects concerning these things, and to dissuade them from their earlier practice.[100]

In treating this question the authors distinguish between schismatics who are living and those who are dead. In regard to the living it can be said that the ordinary schismatic is not a *vitandus,* and hence according to canon 2262, §2, 2°, Mass can be said privately not only for his conversion, but for any other

98 18 apr. 1757 — *Fonti,* II, 109, 111.
99 *Fontes,* n. 876; *Fonti,* II, 127.
100 *Fonti,* XI, 159.

intention which he may designate. Before the Code the authors held that Mass could be said only for the conversion of the schismatic, and they based their opinion on the response of the Holy Office of April 19, 1837.[101] However, this restriction is evidently removed by the Code in canon 809. But, although Mass can be said for any legitimate intention which a schismatic may request, the application of the Mass for that particular intention must be private, and there must be no scandal as a result of it.

It is to be noted that the Mass itself need not be a private Mass, but the application of the Mass for the specific intention must be private. Some of the authors consider a private application to be synonymous with a private celebration.[102] However, canon 2262 speaks of a private application of the Mass. The application is private when the intention for which the Mass is being offered is known to no one but the celebrant and the petitioner or the donor of the stipend, or to very few other persons.[103] Hence, even a Solemn Mass could be celebrated for a schismatic as long as the specific intention for which the Mass is being offered is not publicly known. But an announced Mass could not be said for a schismatic.

The primary purpose of canon 2262 in prohibiting publicity in this matter is the avoidance of scandal. The Church wants to avoid this publicity lest the faithful regard the penalty of excommunication lightly and believe that one can save his soul and serve God equally well in a non-Catholic sect as in the Catholic Church.[104]

The prohibition is against offering the Mass publicly for excommunicates. Hence, if a schismatic wished to have Mass offered for a Catholic, such an intention could be made public.

101 *Fontes*, n. 876; cf. *supra*, p. 179.

102 Cappello, *De Sacramentis*, I, nn. 590, §2, p. 542; Augustine, *A Commentary on Canon Law*, IV, 144.

103 Beste, *Introductio in Codecim*, p. 919; cf. Noldin-Schmitt, *Summa Theologiae Moralis*, III, 178.

104 Genicot-Salsmans, *Institutiones Theologiae Moralis*, II, n. 221, p. 191.

Prudence, however, may dictate that the name of the donor of the stipend be left unannounced.

When Mass is offered privately for a schismatic, scandal is removed when every likelihood of publicity with reference to the application or the nature of the Mass, the acceptance of the stipend, or the solemnity of its celebration is duly neutralized. Any publicity which would give offense to the faithful must be precluded.[105]

When the schismatic for whom the Mass is to be offered is a deceased person, the Code is more specific in its regulations. If the schismatic gave signs of repentance before death, he is even entitled to Christian burial,[106] and Mass can be offered for him publicly if scandal is duly obviated. But if he gave no signs of repentance, then Mass can still be said for him, but only privately and in the absence of scandal.[107]

Canon 1241 contains a special prohibition with reference to those who have been denied Christian burial. Such persons must also be denied the funeral Mass, an anniversary Mass, or any other public burial services. The term "funeral Mass" must be interpreted strictly. It does not include the concept of a private Mass not connected with the funeral services.[108]

Cappello raises the question whether a Requiem Mass could be said privately for those denied Christian burial, and, if it could, whether the special oration for the deceased person may be said.[109] Unless the Mass be a funeral Mass or part of the funeral service, there is no express prohibition in law against it, and as long as the application of the Mass is private, no scandal would be present. In practice it is counseled to omit saying the Requiem Mass, or at least the special oration.[110]

Since Mass can be applied privately for a schismatic, for a greater reason can prayers be offered up privately for schis-

105 Beste, *loc. cit.*

106 Can. 1240.

107 Cappello, *De Sacramentis,* I, n. 591, p. 543.

108 Augustine, *A Commentary on Canon Law,* IV, 145.

109 Cappello, *loc. cit.*

110 Regatillo, *Ius Sacramentarium,* I, n. 134, p. 82.

matics.[111] The public prayers of the Church are those which the ministers, deputed by the Church, offer to God in the name of the Church, such as the divine office, processions prescribed by the rubrics, and the prayers recited at Mass. Private prayers are those which the laity or clergy offer up in their own name.[112]

Private prayers can be said licitly for individuals and for everyone in general. Public prayers, however, can be said only for all non-Catholics in general, but not for individuals except for living rulers of nations.[113]

B. *Commemorating Schismatics in the Liturgy*

The question of mentioning the names of heretics or of schismatics in the liturgy and at sacred functions arose quite frequently in those territories where schismatics predominated.

On August 30, 1636, a doubt was settled by the Sacred Congregation for the Propagation of the Faith concerning the so called *"Laus Graecorum."*[114] The *Laus Graecorum* consisted of the praises and acclamations made to the Roman Pontiff and to the Patriarch of Constantinople by the Greek clergy. In the instance here in question the praises and acclamations were sung in the Latin cathedral and in the presence of the Latin bishop. The Sacred Congregation instructed the bishop to repel from his church the Greeks who sang these acclamations, if indeed he could effectively do so, for the Patriarchs of Constantinople were not only schismatics, but also heretics, and consequently were deserving rather of imprecation.

A deacon, even if he had the best of intentions, was not permitted to sing out the names of heretics in the liturgy.[115] Nor was it permitted for a priest at Mass to name the Patriarch of the Armenians, a schismatic, for the sake of having public prayers offered for him, even though by such an action that

111 Cf. canon 2262, §2, 1°.

112 Vermeersch-Creusen, *Epitome Iuris Canonici*, III, n. 464, p. 278.

113 Sipos, *Enchiridion Iuris Canonici*, p. 700.

114 *Fonti*, I, 79.

115 S. C. S. Off. (Mesopotamiae), 28 aug. 1669, ad 2 — *Fontes*, n. 740; *Fonti*, I, 89.

nation would have been won to a kindlier attitude for the Latins.[116]

Benedict XIV, in an encyclical letter of March 1, 1756, condemned the practice of mentioning liturgically the name of the Bishop or of the Patriarch when he was recognized as a heretic or a schismatic.[117] However, a favorable reply was given by the Holy Office on February 23, 1820, for the Archdiocese of Quebec.[118] It was revealed in this case that prayers were said for the Pope, for the Bishop, and for the King, at Benediction of the Blessed Sacrament. And at a solemn Mass there was sung the *"Domine, salvum fac Regem."* The continuance of both practices was tolerated. Here, then, there was question of a heretical monarch, but the same principle of tolerance could also find application when there was question of a schismatic.

The foregoing answer was evidently within the memory of the Holy See in the following case. The President of the Greek States had asked that prayers be said for him. The Bishop had prescribed the words, *Domine, salvum fac Praesidem"* after the *"Domine, salvum fac Regem."* The Holy See replied that the arrangement could stand.[119]

In another instance the Catholic Latin bishops were asked by the local governor to solemnize the feasts of the courts in their churches. They limited the solemnity to the Ambrosian hymn and Benediction of the Blessed Sacrament, after which the accustomed triple acclamation, *"Viva il Re,"* was made. In its response to the Bishop of Santorin the Holy Office recalled former similar instructions, and stated that the prayers were to be directed not only for the temporal welfare of the governor, but also for his true happiness, namely, that he receive the precious gift of faith.[120]

116 S. C. S. Off., 7 iun. 1673 — *Fonti*, I, 89.

117 *Fontes*, n. 438; *Fonti*, II, 97.

118 *Fontes*, n. 858; *Fonti*, II, 121.

119 2 aug. 1830 — *Fonti*, II, 127.

120 S. C. S. Off., instr. (ad Ep. Sanctorien.), 12 maii 1841, ad 3 — *Fontes*, n. 885; *Fonti*, II, 127. Santorin, later united with Naxas, was a diocese in the group of islands known as the Cyclades, in the Aegean Sea.

C. *Ringing Church Bells During Schismatic Celebrations*

The principal purpose of church bells is to call the faithful to the religious services. They were also used to announce deaths and funerals, as also the greater liturgical feasts, to remind the people on the eve of a fast day of their obligation on the following day, or to invite them to pray for the dead. Bells were rung for the visit of a bishop or sometimes of secular princes, and for such occasions as solemn processions, marriages, days of national rejoicing, or when a storm or impending danger threatened the community.[121]

The Church has always claimed exclusive control of blessed or consecrated bells, and has prohibited the use of them for purely secular purposes. The Code reaffirms this principle,[122] but it permits the ringing of bells for purposes not strictly religious, if with the approval of the bishop a stipulation to that effect had been made by the founder, or in cases of necessity, or with the approval of the ordinary on the occasion of a national victory or similar event, and whenever legitimate custom sanctions the practice.[123]

There did not exist any positive Church law that prohibited the ringing of church bells on the occasion of a non-Catholic celebration, but the ringing of the bells on such an occasion was to be regarded as an active communication *in divinis,* which consequently stood forbidden. Such a ringing of the bells naturally led the Catholics to join in the celebration, which in turn brought with it at least the danger of scandal. On the other hand, if the ringing of the bells connoted merely an act of civil duty, then there was implied the profane use of a sacred thing. In view of these circumstances, then, the practice could hardly be permitted.[124]

Bells are sacred objects, even though they be somewhat re-

121 Ayrinhac, *Administrative Legislation,* p. 18.

122 Cf. can. 1169.

123 Ayrinhac, *op. cit.,* pp. 18, 19.

124 Cf. Bock, "Communicatio in divinis cum schismaticis" — *Theologisch-praktische Quartalschrift,* LXVIII (1915), 111.

motely connected with divine services, and consequently should not be used for the benefit of a schismatic sect. They are not to be used in connection with the funerals of heretics. Since a schismatic is denied Christian burial, he is also to be denied the tolling of bells at the time of burial.[125] Since bells are not to be used for purely secular purposes, it must be concluded *a fortiori* that they should not be used for schismatic religious functions. However, if a denial of the use of the church bells would bring serious harm or inconvenience to the community, the use of church bells for schismatic functions could be tolerated.[126]

125 Cf. Noldin-Schmitt, *Summa Theologiae Moralis,* II, n. 39, p. 41; can. 1241.

126 Noldin-Schmitt, *loc. cit.*

CONCLUSIONS

1. Pure schism was rarely found, for the majority of schismatics adhered to some heretical doctrine in order to justify their separation from the Catholic Church. Especially since the definition of Papal Infallibility by the Vatican Council it is practically impossible for one to be guilty of schism without being simultaneously guilty of heresy. From the pronouncements of the Holy See it is also evident that in many respects schismatics were also considered as heretics.

2. In the early centuries of the Church the juridical status of schismatics was uncertain. The first explicit excommunication against schismatics in general is contained in the *Bulla Coenae* of Paul IV in 1559.

3. Schismatics in large majority were material schismatics, and consequently did not incur the censure of excommunication.

4. Prior to the XVI century there was very little legislation that treated specifically or exclusively of *communicatio in divinis* with schismatics.

5. The General Councils decreed practically nothing concerning the communication *in divinis;* the norms and principles governing the communication *in divinis* were illustrated in the Instructions and the Responses of the Holy See.

6. According to a solidly probable opinion an active communication in the rites of schismatics, as long as these rites are of their nature Catholic, is not contrary to the divine law. However, in practically all cases such communication is forbidden in view of the accompanying danger of perversion from the faith and of the occasion of scandal for others.

7. In the light of this opinion canon 1258, §1, implies more than a mere statement of the divine law, since its legislation is more comprehensive than that which the divine law comprises within its scope, for according to this canon there is forbidden not only the active participation with schismatics in rites that are of their nature non-Catholic, but also the communication

with them in rites which, though peculiarly Catholic, are exercised under the auspices of a non-Catholic sect.

8. The present law of the Church is concerned solely with *public* religious communication. *Private* religious communication is governed by the principles of the divine law.

9. *Communcatio in profanis* is forbidden by ecclesiastical law only in the case of the *excommunicatus vitandus*.

10. The principal factors in the light of which the licitness of religious communication can be determined are those which preclude the danger of perversion from the faith and the occasioning of scandal for others. The presence or the absence of the elements of danger for one's faith and of likely scandal for others is ascertainable through a due consideration of the accompanying circumstances. However, even when scandal and the danger of perversion are duly precluded, the law of canon 1258 must still be obeyed. According to this law one must have a serious reason to participate even materially in a schismatic ritual ceremony or function.

11. It is a general principle that the sacraments cannot licitly be requested or received from the hands of schismatics outside the case of extreme necessity. In extreme necessity only thoss sacraments which are necessary for salvation (baptism, penance, extreme unction) may be received from a schismatic minister.

12. A presumption regularly exists in favor of the validity of the sacraments administered by schismatics. This presumption probably obtains even in regard to the administration of those sacraments which require the possession of jurisdiction for their valid administration, provided of course that there are fulfilled those conditions through the existence of which jurisdiction is supplied in consequence of the principles enunciated in canon 209.

13. It is never permitted for a Catholic to act as sponsor, either himself or through a proxy, at the baptism of the children of schismatics when that sacrament is conferred by a schismatic minister.

14. Catholics are permitted to visit the Blessed Sacrament in the churches of schismatics and pray before the images of the Saints outside of the times when services are being held, provided

that no scandal results, provided that there be no danger of perversion from the faith, and provided that the Catholics do not join in prayer with the schismatics.

15. A Catholic in danger of death can licitly request absolution from a schismatical priest as long as no scandal is given to others, provided that no Catholic priest is available, provided that there is no danger of the Catholic's perversion from the faith, and provided finally that there is a probable basis for believing that the schismatical priest will administer the sacrament according to the rites of the Church.

16. When a Catholic in danger of death requests the sacraments, he is to prefer all other priests to the schismatic. However, if confession to another priest entails considerable repugnance or difficulty (as, for example, when the priest does not understand the language of the penitent), the penitent can licitly request absolution from the schismatic.

17. Catholics are forbidden to act as the official witnesses or as the maid of honor or first bridesmaid or as the best man at a schismatic wedding ceremony. However, for serious reasons of civil duty or honor one could act in a secondary capacity as an attendant for the bride or the groom, as long as the danger of scandal is effectively precluded and the action is tolerated with the permission of the ordinary.

18. The material presence of Catholics at schismatic functions is not evil in itself, for there is no formal co-operation in the non-Catholic rite, but even the act of being merely materially present is regularly forbidden by the Church because of the accompanying dangers of perversion from the faith and of giving scandal to others.

18. One's curiosity is not a sufficient reason for entering a schismatic church while services are in progress. Canon 1258, §2, tolerates a merely material presence. Even for such a presence this canon demands that one have a grave reason for the act of materially taking part in the services.

20. The sacraments must not be administered even to material schismatics if they are not in danger of death, unless they have abjured their schism and have become reconciled with the

Church. When material schismatics while in danger of death are fully conscious, they can according to a solidly probable opinion be given the sacraments at least conditionally, if they have manifested contrition for their sins and have shown themselves prepared to do all things which are ordained by God for the attainment of everlasting happiness. When material schismatics while in danger of death are bereft of their senses, they can be given the sacraments conditionally, especially if it can be presumed they have at least implicitly rejected their errors. In all cases the emergence of scandal must be effectively obviated.

BIBLIOGRAPHY

Sources

Acta Apostolicae Sedis, Commentarium Officiale, Romae, 1909 —.

Acta et Decreta Concilii Plenarii Baltimorensis Tertii, A. D. 1884, Baltimorae: Typis Joannis Murphy Sociorum, 1886.

Acta et Decreta Sacrorum Conciliorum Recentiorum, Collectio Lacensis, 7 vols., Friburgi Brisgoviae: Herder, 1870-1890.

Acta Sanctae Sedis, 41 vols., Romae, 1865-1908.

Bruns, Hermann T., *Canones Apostolorum et Conciliorum Saeculorum IV, V, VI, VII*, 2 vols., Berolini, 1839.

Bullarum Diplomatum et Privilegiorum Sanctorum Pontificum Taurinensis Editio, 24 vols. et Appendix, Augustae Taurinorum, 1857-1872.

Codex Iuris Canonici Pii X Pontificis Maximi iussu digestus Benedicti Papae XV auctoritate promulgatus, Romae: Typis Polyglottis Vaticanis, 1917.

Codex Theodosianus, ed. Krueger, Berolini: Weidmann, 1928.

Codicis Iuris Canonici Fontes, cura Emi Petri Card. Gasparri editi, 9 vols., Romae (postea Civitate Vaticana): Typis Polyglottis Vaticanis, 1923-1939. (Vols. VII-IX ed. curà et studio Emi Iustiniani Card. Serédi.)

Codificazione Canonica Orientale, Fonti, Serie I-III, Civitate Vaticana: Tipografia Poliglotta Vaticana, 1930 —.

Collectanea S. Congregationis de Propaganda Fide, Romae: Typographia Polyglotta S. C. de Propaganda Fide, 1893.

Collectanea S. Congregationis de Propaganda Fide, 2 vols., Romae: Typographia Polyglotta S. C. de Propaganda Fide, 1907. (Vol. I, nn. 1-1299; Vol. II, nn. 1300-2317.)

Corpus Iuris Canonici, editio Lipsiensis secunda, post Aemilii Richteri curas, instruxit Aemilius Friedberg, 2 vols., Lipsiae, 1879-1881.

Decretales D. Gregorii Papae IX suae integritati una cum glossis restitutae, Romae, 1582.

Decretum Gratiani emendatum et observationibus illustratum una cum glossis, Gregorii XIII Pont. Max. iussu editum, 2 vols., Romae, 1582.

Enchiridion Symbolorum, Definitionum, et Declarationum de Rebus Fidei et Morum, Denzinger-Bannwart-Umberg, editio 21-23, Friburgi Brisgoviae: Herder and Co., 1937.

Jaffé, Phillipus, *Regesta Pontificum Romanorum ab condita Ecclesia ad annum post Christum natum MCXCVIII*, 2. ed., correctam et auctam auspiciis Gulielmi Wattenbach curaverunt S. Löwenfeld, F. Kaltenbrunner, P. Ewald, 2 tomes in 1 vol., Lipsiae, 1885-1888.

Liber Sextus Decretalium D. Bonifacii Papae VIII una cum Clementinis et extravagantibus tum D. Ioannis XXII tum Communibus, una cum earum glossis, Romae, 1582.

Mansi, Joannes, *Sacrorum Conciliorum Nova et Amplissima Collectio*, 53 vols. in 60, Parisiis, Arnhem, Lipsiae, 1901-1927.

Potthast, Augustus, *Regesta Pontificum Romanorum inde ab anno post Christum natum MCXCVIII ad annum MCCCIV*, 2 vols., Berolini, 1874-1875.

Religious Bodies: 1936, 2 vols. in 3, Washington: U. S. Government Printing Office, 1941.

Schroeder, H. J., *Canons and Decrees of the Council of Trent*, St. Louis: B. Herder, 1941.

Reference Works

Aertnys, J. - Damen, C. A., *Theologia Moralis secundum doctrinam S. Alfonsi de Ligorio Doct. Ecclesiae*, 13. ed., 2 vols., Romae: Marietti, 1939.

Algermissen, Konrad, *Christian Denominations* (translated by Rev. Joseph W. Grundner), St. Louis: Herder, 1945.

Alphonsus M. de Liguori, St., *Theologia Moralis*, ed. L. Gaudé, 4 vols., Romae, 1905-1912.

Augustine, Charles, *A Commentary on the New Code of Canon Law*, 2. ed., 8 vols., St. Louis, Mo.: B. Herder Book Co., 1918-1924. Vol. IV, 2. ed., 1921, Vol. VIII, 2. ed., 1924.

Ayrinhac, H. A., *Administrative Legislation in the New Code of Canon Law*, New York: Longmans, Green and Co., 1930.

Ayrinhac, H. A. - Lydon, P. J., *Marriage Legislation in the New Code of Canon Law*, new revised edition, New York: Benziger Brothers, 1940.

——, *Penal Legislation in the New Code of Canon Law*, New York: Benziger Brothers, 1936.

Bancroft, John, *Communication in Religious Worship with Non-Catholics*, The Catholic University of America Studies in Sacred Theology, n. 75, Washington, D. C.: The Catholic University of America Press, 1943.

Benedictus XIV, *De Synodo Dioecesana*, 2. ed., 2 vols., Parmae, 1764.

Berutti, Christophorus, *Institutiones Iuris Canonici*, Vol. IV, Taurini-Romae: ex Officina Libraria Marietti, 1940.

Beste, Udalricus, *Introductio in Codicem*, 2. ed., Collegeville, Minn.: St. John's Abbey Press, 1944.

Blat, Albertus, *Commentarium Textus Codicis Iuris Canonici*, 5 vols. in 6, Romae: ex Typographia Pontificia in Instituto Pii IX, 1921-1934; Lib. II, 2. ed., 1921; Lib. III, Partes II-VI, 2. ed., 1934.

Bouscaren, T. Lincoln, *The Canon Law Digest*, 2 vols., Milwaukee, Wis.: The Bruce Publishing Co., 1934-1943.

Cappello, Felix M., *Tractatus Canonico-Moralis De Censuris iuxta Codicem Iuris Canonici*, 3. ed., Taurinorum Augustae: Marietti, 1933.

——, *Tractatus Canonico-Moralis De Sacramentis*, 3 vols. in 6, Romae: Domus Editorialis Marietti, 1935-1945. Vol. I, 4. ed., 1945; Vol. II, pars I, 4. ed., 1944; Vol. II, pars II, 2. ed., 1942; Vol. II, pars III, 1935; Vol. III, partes I, II, 4. ed., 1939.

Castropalao, Ferdinandus de, *Opera Omnia,* 7 tomes in 3 vols., Lugduni: Anisson & Joannis Posuel, 1700.

Chelodi, Ioannes, *Ius Canonicum de Delictis et Poenis et de Iudiciis Criminalibus,* 5. ed. recognita et aucta a Pio Ciprotti, Vicenza: Società Anonima Tipografica, 1943.

Cocchi, Guido, *Commentarium in Codicem Iuris Canonici ad Usum Scholarum,* 8 vols. in 5, Taurinorum Augustae: Ex Officina Libraria Marietti, Vol. V, 4. ed., 1938.

Coronata, Matthaeus Conte A., *Institutiones Iuris Canonici ad usum utriusque cleri et scholarum,* 5 vols., Romae: Domus Editorialis Marietti, Vol. II, 2. ed., 1939.

——, *Institutiones Iuris Canonici ad usum utriusque cleri et scholarum "De Sacramentis,"* 3 vols., Romae: Domus Editorialis Marietti, 1943-1946.

Davis, Henry, *Moral and Pastoral Theology,* 4. ed., 4 vols., London: Sheed and Ward, 1945.

De Lugo, Joannes, *Disputationes Scholasticae et Morales,* editio nova, 8 vols., Parisiis: apud Ludovicum Vivès, 1868-1869.

De Meester, A., *Juris Canonici et Juris Canonico-Civilis Compendium,* nova editio, 3 vols. in 4, Brugis: Desclée de Brouwer et Soc., 1921-1928.

Dictionnaire de Droit Canonique, commencé sous la direction de A. Villien et E. Magnin (1924), continué sous la direction de A. Amanieu (1926), publié sous la direction de R. Naz (1934), 3 vols., Paris: Letouzey et Ané, 1924 —.

Fagnanus, Prosper, *Commentaria in Decretales Gregorii IX,* Venetiis: apud Paulum Balleonium, 1708.

Ferraris, L., *Prompta Bibliotheca Canonica, Juridica, Moralis, Theologica, necnon Ascetica, Polemica, Rubricistica, Historica,* 8 vols., Parisiis, 1852-1857.

Ferreres, Joannes, *Casus Conscientiae,* 5. ed., 2 vols., Barcinone: Eugenius Subirana, 1926.

Genicot, Eduardus - Salsmans, I., *Institutiones Theologiae Moralis,* 14. ed., 2 vols., Bruxellis: L'edition Universelle, S.A., 1939.

Goodwine, Joseph, *The Reception of Converts,* The Catholic University of America Canon Law Studies, n. 198, Washington, D. C.: The Catholic University of America Press, 1944.

Graesse, J. G., *Orbis Latinus,* Berlin, 1909.

Hefele, Karl, and Le Clercq, Henri, *Histoire des Conciles,* 10 vols. in 19, Paris: Letouzey and Ané, 1907-1938.

Hostiensis, Cardinalis (Henricus de Segusio), *Commentaria in Quinque Libros Decretalium,* 3 vols., Venetiis, 1581.

——, *Summa Aurea,* Venetiis, 1570.

Hyland, F. E., *Excommunication, Its Nature, Historical Development and Effects,* The Catholic University of America Canon Law Studies, n. 49, Washington, D. C.: The Catholic University of America, 1928.

Janin, Raymond, *The Separated Eastern Churches,* trans. by P. Boylan, St. Louis: B. Herder, 1933.

Jone, Heribert, *Moral Theology,* translated by Urban Adelman, Westminster, Md.: Newman Bookshop, 1945.

Jugie, Martin, *Theologia Dogmatica Christianorum Orientalium ab Ecclesia Catholica Dissidentium,* 4 vols., Parisiis: Letouzey et Ané, 1926-1933.

Kenrick, Franciscus, *Theologia Moralis,* 2. ed., 2 vols., Baltimorae: Murphy, 1866.

Kilker, Adrian J., *Extreme Unction,* St. Louis: B. Herder, 1927.

King, James Ignatius, *The Administration of the Sacraments to Dying Non-Catholics,* The Catholic University of America Canon Law Studies, n. 23, Washington, D. C.: The Catholic University of America, 1924.

Kober, F., *Der Kirchenbann nach den Grundsätzen des canonischen Rechts,* Tübingen, 1863.

Konings, A., *Theologia Moralis,* 7. ed., 2 vols., New York: Benziger, 1888.

La Croix, Claudius, *Theologia Moralis,* 2 tomes in 1 vol., Coloniae: ex officina Noetheniana, 1729.

Laymann, Paulus, *Theologia Moralis,* 2 vols. in 1, in epitomen redacta a Joanne Domenico Mansi, Patavii: sumptibus Remondinianis, 1760.

Leech, George L., *A Comparative Study of the Constitution "Apostolicae Sedis" and the "Codex Iuris Canonici,"* The Catholic University of America Canon Law Studies, n. 15, Washington, D. C.: The Catholic University of America, 1922.

McHugh, John A. - Callan, Charles J., *Moral Theology,* 2 vols., New York City: Joseph F. Wagner, 1929.

MacKenzie, Eric F., *The Delict of Heresy in Its Commission, Penalization, Absolution,* The Catholic University of America Canon Law Studies, n. 77, Washington, D. C.: The Catholic University of America, 1932.

Marbach, Joseph F., *Marriage Legislation for the Catholics of the Oriental Rites in the United States and Canada,* The Catholic University of America Canon Law Studies, n. 243, Washington, D. C.: The Catholic University of America Press, 1946.

Maritain, Jacques, *Ransoming the Time,* translated by Harry Lorin Binsse, New York: Charles Scribner's Sons, 1941.

Merkelbach, Benedictus Henricus, *Summa Theologiae Moralis ad Mentem D. Thomae et ad Normam Iuris Novi,* 3. ed., 3 vols., Parisiis: Typis Desclée de Brouwer et Soc., 1938-1939.

Migne, Jacques P., *Patrologiae Cursus Completus, Series Latina,* 221 vols., Parisiis, 1844-1864.

Moriarty, F. E., *The Extraordinary Absolution from Censures*, The Catholic University of America Canon Law Studies, n. 113, Washington, D. C.: The Catholic University of America, 1938.

Noldin, H. - Schmitt, A., *Summa Theologiae Moralis*, 27. ed., 3 vols., Oeniponte Lipsiae: Sumptibus et Typis Feliciani Rauch, 1940-1941.

Petrovits, J., *The New Church Law on Matrimony*, 2. ed., Philadelphia: John Joseph McVey, 1926.

Pignatelli, G., *Consultationes Canonicae*, 6 vols., Coloniae Allobrogum, 1700.

Prümmer, Dominicus, *Manuale Iuris Canonici in Usum Scholarum*, 6. ed., Friburgi Brisgoviae: Herder and Co., 1933.

——, *Manuale Theologiae Moralis*, 5. ed., 3 vols., Friburgi Brisgoviae: Herder and Co., 1928.

Regatillo, Eduardus F., *Institutiones Iuris Canonici*, 2 vols., Sal Terrae, Santander: Aldus, S.A. de Artes Graficas, Vol. I, 2. ed., 1946; Vol. II, 1942.

——, *Ius Sacramentarium*, 2 vols., Sal Terrae, Santander: Talleres Tipograficos J. Martinez, 1945-1946.

Reiffenstuel, Anacletus, *Jus Canonicum Universum*, 5 vols. in 3, Maceratae, 1760.

Sabetti, Aloysius - Barrett, Timotheus, *Compendium Theologiae Moralis*, 34. ed., New York: Frederick Pustet Co., 1939.

Salmanticenses, *Cursus Theologiae Moralis*, 6 vols. in 3, Venetiis: apud Nicolaum Pezzana, 1722.

Schenk, Francis J., *The Matrimonial Impediments of Mixed Religion and Disparity of Cult*, The Catholic University of America Canon Law Studies, n. 51, Washington, D. C.: The Catholic University of America, 1929.

Schmalzgrueber, Franciscus, *Jus Ecclesiasticum Universum*, 5 vols. in 12, Romae, 1843-1845.

Schmitz, Ignatius, *De Effectibus Sacramenti Extremae Unctionis*, Friburgi Brisgoviae: Sumptibus Herder, 1893.

Sipos, Stephanus, *Enchiridion Iuris Canonici*, 4. ed., Pécs: ex typographis "Haladas R. T.," 1940.

Smith, S. B., *Elements of Ecclesiastical Law*, 3 vols., New York: Benziger Brothers, 1887-1888. Vol. III, 3. ed., 1888.

Souarn, Romuald, *Memento de Theologie Morale a L'usage des Missionaires*, Paris: Librairie Victor Lecoffre, 1907.

——, *Praxis Missionarii in Oriente Servata*, Parisiis, 1911.

Sporer, Patritius, *Theologia Moralis*, 3 vols. in 2, Venetiis: apud Nicolaum Pezzana, 1731.

Suarez, Franciscus, *Opera Omnia*, 28 vols., Parisiis, 1856-1866.

Tanquerey, A., *Synopsis Theologiae Dogmaticae*, 24. ed., 3 vols., Parisiis: Typis Societatis Sancti Joannis Evangelistae, Desclée et Socii, 1933-1938.

Van Espen, Zegerus, *Ius Ecclesiasticum Universum*, 5 vols. in 4, Lovanii, 1778.

——, *Ius Ecclesiasticum Universum in Epitomen Redactum*, 5 vols. in 2, Bassani, 1784.

Vecchiotti, S. M., *Institutiones Canonicae ex Operibus Cardinalis Soglia Excerptae*, 2 vols., Augustae Taurinorum, 1867.

Vermeersch, A. - Creusen, J., *Epitome Iuris Canonici*, 3 vols., Mechliniae-Romae: Dessain, 1936-1940. Vol. I, 6. ed., 1937; Vol. II, 6. ed., 1940; Vol. III, 5. ed., 1936.

Waldron, Joseph F., *The Minister of Baptism*, The Catholic University of America Canon Law Studies, n. 170, Washington, D. C.: The Catholic University of America Press, 1942.

Wernz, Franciscus X., *Ius Decretalium*, 2. ed., 6 vols., Romae et Prati, 1906-1913.

Wernz, Franciscus X. - Vidal, Petrus, *Ius Canonicum ad Codicis Normam Exactum*, 7 tomes in 8 vols., Romae: apud aedes Universitatis Gregorianae, Tom. IV, Vol. I, 1934, Vol. II, 1935.

Woywod, Stanislaus, *A Practical Commentary on the Code of Canon Law*, 9. printing, 2 vols., New York: Joseph F. Wagner, 1945.

Periodicals

American Ecclesiastical Review, The, Philadelphia, 1889-1943: Washington, D. C., 1944 —. Vol. XXXIII (1905) — Vol. CIX (1943), *The Ecclesiastical Review*.

Analecta Ecclesiastica, Romae, 1893-1911.

Analecta Iuris Pontificii, Romae, 1855-1869; Parisiis, 1872-1891.

Apollinaris, Romae, 1928 —.

Archiv für katholiches Kirchenrecht, Innsbruck, 1857-1861; Mainz, 1862 —.

Eastern Churches Quarterly, The, London, 1936 —.

Orientalia Christiana, Romae, 1922-1935; ab anno 1935; *Orientalia Christiana Anacleta et Orientalia Christiana Periodica*, Romae, 1935 —.

Periodica de Religiosis et Missionariis, Brugis, 1905-1919; *Periodica de Re Canonica et Morali*, Brugis, 1920-1927; *Periodica de Re Canonica, Morali, Liturgica*, Brugis, 1927 —.

Tablet, The, London, 1840 —.

Theological Studies, New York: The America Press, 1940 —.

Theologisch-praktische Quartalschrift, Linz, 1832 —.

Voice of the Church, The, Lisle, Ill., 1937 —.

Articles

Bock, J. P., "Communicatio in divinis cum schismaticis" — *Theologisch-praktische Quartalschrift*, LXVIII (1915), 105-115.

Bouscaren, T. Lincoln, "Co-operation with Non-Catholics" — *Theological Studies*, III (1942), 475-512.

Ford, John C., "Current Moral Theology and Canon Law" — *Theological Studies*, II (1941), 543.

Herman, Aemilius, "Regunturne Orientales dissidentes legibus matrimonialibus Ecclesiae latinae?" — *Periodica*, XXVII (1938), 7-20.

Hofmann, G., "Il Beato Roberto Bellarmino e Gli Orientali" — *Orientalia Christiana*, VIII (1926-1927), 270.

Neveu, P. E., "Instruction to the Army Chaplains as to how to deal with Orthodox soldiers at the front." — *The Tablet*, November 11, 1939, pp. 548, 549.

"On Conducting Oneself in an Orthodox Church" — *The Voice of the Church*, December, 1944, pp. 14-17. (The name of the author of the article was not published. The article is a reprint from the *Stoudion*, a Review published in Rome and edited by Father Cyril Korolevsky, a Catholic priest of the Byzantine rite and a consultor of the Oriental Congregation.)

Ploechl, Willibald, "The Church Laws for Orientals of the Austrian Monarchy in the Age of Enlightenment" — (Reprinted from the *Quarterly Bulletin of the Polish Institute of Arts and Sciences in America*, April, 1944).

Unpublished Material

MS, Parish Chronicle of St. Barbara's, Vienna, Austria, Vol. I (1809), page 104 — quoted with the permission of Dr. Ploechl.

Information received by Dr. Ploechl from a high dignitary of the Archdiocese of Vienna.

Abbreviations

AAS — *Acta Apostolicae Sedis.*

AKK — *Archiv für katholiches Kirchenrecht.*

ASS — *Acta Sanctae Sedis.*

Coll. S. C. P. F. (1893) — *Collectanea S. C. de Propaganda Fide* (1893).

Coll. S. C. P. F. — *Collectanea S. C. de Propaganda Fide* (1907).

Coll. Lac. — *Collectio Lacensis.*

Denzinger — *Enchiridion Symbolorum, Definitionum et Declarationum de Rebus Fidei et Morum.*

Fontes — *Codicis Iuris Canonici Fontes*, cura . . . Gasparri editi.

Fonti — *Codificazione Canonica Orientale*: Fonti, Serie I.

Jaffé — *Regesta Pontificum Romanorum*, etc.

Mansi — *Sacrorum Conciliorum Nova et Amplissima Collectio.*

MPL — Migne, *Patrologia, Series Latina.*

S. C. de Prop. Fide — Sacra Congregatio de Propaganda Fide.

S. C. S. Off. — Sacra Congregatio Sancti Officii.

ALPHABETICAL INDEX

BIOGRAPHICAL NOTE

Ignatius Joseph Szal was born January 30, 1918, in Minersville, Pennsylvania. He received his primary education in the Saint Stanislaus Parochial School and the Minersville Public Schools. After graduating from Minersville High School in 1935 he was admitted to Saint Charles Seminary, Overbrook, Philadelphia, Pennsylvania. In June, 1940, he received the degree of Bachelor of Arts. He was ordained to the Sacred Priesthood by His Excellency, the Most Reverend Bishop Hugh Lamb, at the Cathedral of Saints Peter and Paul in Philadelphia on June 3, 1944. In October of the same year he entered the Graduate School of Canon Law at the Catholic University of America. He received the degree of Bachelor of Canon Law in May, 1945, and the degree of Licentiate in Canon Law in June, 1946.

CANON LAW STUDIES*

1. Freriks, Rev. Celestine A., C.PP.S., J.C.D., Religious Congregations in Their External Relations, 121 pp., 1916.
2. Galliher, Rev. Daniel M., O.P., J.C.D., Canonical Elections, 117 pp., 1917.
3. Borkowski, Rev. Aurelius L., O.F.M., J.C.D., De Confraternitatibus Ecclesiasticis, 136 pp., 1918.
4. Castillo, Rev. Cayo, J.C.D., Disertacion Historico-Canonica sobre la Potestad del Cabildo en Sede Vacante o Impedida del Vicario Capitular, 99 pp., 1919 (1918).
5. Kubelbeck, Rev. William J., S.T.B., J.C.D., The Sacred Penitentiaria and Its Relation to Faculties of Ordinaries and Priests, 129 pp., 1918.
6. Petrovits, Rev. Joseph, J.C., S.T.D., J.C.D., The New Church Law on Matrimony, X-461 pp., 1919.
7. Hickey, Rev. John J., S.T.B., J.C.D., Irregularities and Simple Impediments in the New Code of Canon Law, 100 pp., 1920.
8. Klekotka, Rev. Peter J., S.T.B., J.C.D., Diocesan Consultors, 179 pp., 1920.
9. Wanenmacher, Rev. Francis, J.C.D., The Evidence in Ecclesiastical Procedure Affecting the Marriage Bond, 1920 (Printed 1935).
10. Golden, Rev. Henry Francis, J.C.D., Parochial Benefices in the New Code, IV-119 pp., 1921 (Printed 1925).
11. Koudelka, Rev. Charles J., J.C.D., Pastors, Their Rights and Duties According to the New Code of Canon Law, 211 pp., 1921.
12. Melo, Rev. Antonius, O.F.M., J.C.D., De Exemptione Regularium, X-188 pp., 1921.
13. Schaaf, Rev. Valentine Theodore, O.F.M., S.T.B., J.C.D., The Cloister, X-180 pp., 1921.
14. Burke, Rev. Thomas Joseph, S.T.D., J.C.D., Competence in Ecclesiastical Tribunals, IV-117 pp., 1922.
15. Leech, Rev. George Leo, J.C.D., A Comparative Study of the Constitution "Apostolicae Sedis" and the "Codex Juris Canonici," 179 pp., 1922.
16. Motry, Rev. Hubert Louis, S.T.D., J.C.D., Diocesan Faculties According to the Code of Canon Law, II-167 pp., 1922.
17. Murphy, Rev. George Lawrence, J.C.D., Delinquencies and Penalties in the Administration and the Reception of the Sacraments, IV-121 pp., 1923.

* From nn. 1-100 inclusive only n. 25 is still obtainable.
From n. 101 onward all numbers are available except the following: nn. 101-114 inclusive; also nn. 116, 118, 120, 122.

18. O'Reilly, Rev. John Anthony, S.T.B., J.C.D., Ecclesiastical Sepulture in the New Code of Canon Law, II-129 pp., 1923.
19. Michalicka, Rev. Wenceslas Cyril, O.S.B., J.C.D., Judicial Procedure in Dismissal of Clerical Exempt Religious, 107 pp., 1923.
20. Dargin, Rev. Edward Vincent, S.T.B., J.C.D., Reserved Cases According to the Code of Canon Law, IV-103 pp., 1924.
21. Godfrey, Rev. John A., S.T.B., J.C.D., The Right of Patronage According to the Code of Canon Law, 153 pp., 1924.
22. Hagedorn, Rev. Francis Edward, J.C.D., General Legislation on Indulgences, II-154 pp., 1924.
23. King, Rev. James Ignatius, J.C.D., The Administration of the Sacraments to Dying Non-Catholics, V-141 pp., 1924.
24. Winslow, Rev. Francis Joseph, O.F.M., J.C.D., Vicars and Prefects Apostolic, IV-149 pp., 1924.
25. Correa, Rev. Jose Servelion, S.T.L., J.C.D., La Potestad Legislativa de la Iglesia Catolica, IV-127 pp., 1925.
26. Dugan, Rev. Henry Francis, A.M., J.C.D., The Judiciary Department of the Diocesan Curia, 87 pp., 1925.
27. Keller, Rev. Charles Frederick, S.T.B., J.C.D., Mass Stipends, 167 pp., 1925.
28. Paschang, Rev. John Linus, J.C.D., The Sacramentals According to the Code of Canon Law, 129 pp., 1925.
29. Piontek, Rev. Cyrillus, O.F.M., S.T.B., J.C.D., De Indulto Exclaustrationis necnon Saecularizationis, XIII-289 pp., 1925.
30. Kearney, Rev. Richard Joseph, S.T.B., J.C.D., Sponsors at Baptism According to the Code of Canon Law, IV-127 pp. 1925.
31. Bartlett, Rev. Chester Joseph, A.M., LL.B., J.C.D., The Tenure of Parochial Property in the United States of America, V-108 pp., 1926.
32. Kilker, Rev. Adrian Jerome, J.C.D., Extreme Unction, V-425 pp., 1926.
33. McCormick, Rev. Robert Emmet, J.C.D., Confessors of Religious, VIII-266 pp., 1926.
34. Miller, Rev. Newton Thomas, J.C.D., Founded Masses According to the Code of Canon Law, VII-93 pp., 1926.
35. Roelker, Rev. Edward G., S.T.D., J.C.D., Principles of Privilege According to the Code of Canon Law, XI-166 pp., 1926.
36. Bakalarczyk, Rev. Richardus, M.I.C., J.U.D., De Novitiatu, VIII-208 pp., 1927.
37. Pizzuti, Rev. Lawrence, O.F.M., J.U.L., De Parochis Religiosis, 1927. (Not Printed).
38. Bliley, Rev. Nicholas Martin, O.S.B., J.C.D., Altars According to the Code of Canon Law, XIX-132 pp., 1927.

39. BROWN, MR. BRENDAN FRANCIS, A.B., LL.M., J.U.D., The Canonical Juristic Personality with Special Reference to its Status in the United States of America, V-212 pp., 1927.
40. CAVANAUGH, REV. WILLIAM THOMAS, C.P., J.U.D., The Reservation of the Blessed Sacrament, VIII-101 pp., 1927.
41. DOHENY, REV. WILLIAM J., C.S.C., A.B., J.U.D., Church Property: Modes of Acquisition, X-118 pp., 1927.
42. FELDHAUS, REV. ALOYSIUS H., C.PP.S., J.C.D., Oratories, IX-141 pp., 1927.
43. KELLY, REV. JAMES PATRICK, A.B., J.C.D., The Jurisdiction of the Simple Confessor, X-208 pp., 1927.
44. NEUBERGER, REV. NICHOLAS J., J.C.D., Canon 6 or the Relation of the Codex Juris Canonici to the Preceding Legislation, V-95 pp., 1927.
45. O'KEEFE, REV. GERALD MICHAEL, J.C.D., Matrimonial Dispensations, Powers of Bishops, Priests, and Confessors, VIII-232 pp., 1927.
46. QUIGLEY, REV. JOSEPH A. M., A.B., J.C.D., Condemned Societies, 139 pp., 1927.
47. ZAPLOTNIK, REV. JOHANNES LEO, J.C.D., De Vicariis Foraneis, X-142 pp., 1927.
48. DUSKIE, REV. JOHN ALOYSIUS, A.B., J.C.D., The Canonical Status of the Orientals in the United States, VIII-196 pp., 1928.
49. HYLAND, REV. FRANCIS EDWARD, J.C.D., Excommunication, Its Nature, Historical Development and Effects, VIII-181 pp., 1928.
50. REINMANN, REV. GERALD JOSEPH, O.M.C., J.C.D., The Third Order Secular of Saint Francis, 201 pp., 1928.
51. SCHENK, REV. FRANCIS J., J.C.D., The Matrimonal Impediments of Mixed Religion and Disparity of Cult, XVI-318 pp., 1929.
52. COADY, REV. JOHN JOSEPH, S.T.D., J.U.D., A.M., The Appointment of Pastors, VIII-150 pp., 1929.
53. KAY, REV. THOMAS HENRY, J.C.D., Competence in Matrimonial Procedure, VIII-164 pp., 1929.
54. TURNER, REV. SIDNEY JOSEPH, C.P., J.U.D., The Vow of Poverty, XLIX-217 pp., 1929.
55. KEARNEY, REV. RAYMOND A., A.B., S.T.D., J.C.D., The Principles of Delegation, VII-149 pp., 1929.
56. CONRAN, REV. EDWARD JAMES, A.B., J.C.D., The Interdict, V-163 pp., 1930.
57. O'NEIL, REV. WILLIAM H., J.C.D., Papal Rescripts of Favor, VII-218 pp., 1930.
58. BASTNAGEL, REV. CLEMENT VINCENT, J.U.D., The Appointment of Parochial Adjutants and Assistants, XV-257 pp., 1930.
59. FERRY, REV. WILLIAM A., A.B., J.C.D., Stole Fees, V-136 pp., 1930.
60. COSTELLO, REV. JOHN MICHAEL, A.B., J.C.D., Domicile and Quasi-Domicile, VII-201 pp., 1930.

61. Kremer, Rev. Michael Nicholas, A.B., S.T.B., J.C.D., Church Support in the United States, VI-136 pp., 1930.
62. Angula, Rev. Luis, C.M., J.C.D., Legislation de la Iglesia sobre la intencion en la application de la Santa Misa, VII-104 pp., 1931.
63. Frey, Rev. Wolfgang Norbert, O.S.B., A.B., J.C.D., The Act of Religious Profession, VIII-174 pp., 1931.
64. Roberts, Rev. James Brendan, A.B., J.C.D., The Banns of Marriage, XIV-140 pp., 1931.
65. Ryder, Rev. Raymond Aloysius, A.B., J.C.D., Simony, IX-151 pp., 1931.
66. Campagna, Rev. Angelo, Ph.D., J.U.D., Il Vicario Generale del Vescovo, VII-205 pp., 1931.
67. Cox, Rev. Joseph Godfrey, A.B., J.C.D., The Administration of Seminaries, VI-124 pp., 1931.
68. Gregory, Rev. Donald J., J.U.D., The Pauline Privilege, XV-165 pp., 1931.
69. Donohue, Rev. John F., J.C.D., The Impediment of Crime, VII-110 pp., 1931.
70. Dooley, Rev. Eugene A., O.M.I., J.C.D., Church Law on Sacred Relics, IX-143 pp., 1931.
71. Orth, Rev. Clement Raymond, O.M.C., J.C.D., The Approbation of Religious Institutes, 171 pp., 1931.
72. Pernicone, Rev. Joseph M., A.B., J.C.D., The Ecclesiastical Prohibition of Books, XII-267 pp., 1932.
73. Clinton, Rev. Connell, A.B., J.C.D., The Paschal Precept, IX-108 pp., 1932.
74. Donnelly, Rev. Francis B., A.M., S.T.L., J.C.D., The Diocesan Synod, VIII-125 pp., 1932.
75. Torrente, Rev. Camilo, C.M.F., J.C.D., Las Procesiones Sagradas, V-145 pp., 1932.
76. Murphy, Rev. Edwin J., C.PP.S., J.C.D., Suspension Ex Informata Conscientia, XI-122 pp., 1932.
77. MacKenzie, Rev. Eric F., A.M., S.T.L., J.C.D., The Delict of Heresy in its Commission, Penalization, Absolution, VII-124 pp., 1932.
78. Lyons, Rev. Avitus E., S.T.B., J.C.D., The Collegiate Tribunal of First Instance, XI-147 pp., 1932.
79. Connolly, Rev. Thomas A., J.C.D., Appeals, XI-195 pp., 1932.
80. Sangmeister, Rev. Joseph V., A.B., J.C.D., Force and Fear as Precluding Matrimonial Consent, V-211 pp., 1932.
81. Jaeger, Rev. Leo A., A.B., J.C.D., The Administration of Vacant and Quasi-Vacant Episcopal Sees in the United States, IX-229 pp., 1932.
82. Rimlinger, Rev. Herbert T., J.C.D., Error Invalidating Matrimonial Consent, VII-79 pp., 1932.

83. BARRETT, REV. JOHN D. M., S.S., J.C.D., A Comparative Study of the Councils of Baltimore and the Code of Canon Law, X-223 pp., 1932.
84. CARBERRY, REV. JOHN J., PHD., S.T.D., J.C.D., The Juridical Form of Marriage, X-177 pp., 1934.
85. DOLAN, REV. JOHN L., A.B., J.C.D., The Defensor Vinculi, XII-157 pp., 1934.
86. HANNAN, REV. JEROME D., A.M., S.T.D., LL.B., J.C.D., The Canon Law of Wills, IX-517 pp., 1934.
87. LEMIEUX, REV. DELISE A., A.M., J.C.D., The Sentence in Ecclesiastical Procedure, IX-131 pp., 1934.
88. O'ROURKE, REV. JAMES J., A.B., J.C.D., Parish Registers, VII-109 pp., 1934.
89. TIMLIN, REV. BARTHOLOMEW, O.F.M., A.M., J.C.D., Conditional Matrimonial Consent, X-381 pp., 1934.
90. WAHL, REV. FRANCIS X., A.B., J.C.D., The Matrimonial Impediments of Consanguinity and Affinity, VI-125 pp., 1934.
91. WHITE, REV. ROBERT J., A.B., LL.B., S.T.B., J.C.D., Canonical Ante-Nuptial Promises and the Civil Law, VI-152 pp., 1934.
92. HERRERA, REV. ANTONIO PARRA, O.C.D., J.C.D., Legislacion Ecclesiastica sobra el Ayuno y la Abstinencia, XI-191 pp., 1935.
93. KENNEDY, REV. EDWIN J., J.C.D., The Special Matrimonial Process in Cases of Evident Nullity, X-165 pp., 1935.
94. MANNING, REV. JOHN J., A.B., J.C.D., Presumption of Law in Matrimonial Procedure, XI-111 pp., 1935.
95. MOEDER, REV. JOHN M., J.C.D., The Proper Bishop for Ordination and Dimissorial Letters, VII-135 pp., 1935.
96. O'MARA, REV. WILLIAM A., A.B., J.C.D., Canonical Causes for Matrimonial Dispensations, IX-155 pp., 1935.
97. REILLY, REV. PETER, J.C.D., Residence of Pastors, IX-81 pp., 1935.
98. SMITH, REV. MARINER T,. O.P., S.T.Lr., J.C.D., The Penal Law for Religious, VII-169 pp., 1935.
99. WHALEN REV. DONALD W., A.M., J.C.D., The Value of Testimonial Evidence in Matrimonal Procedure, XIII-297 pp., 1935.
100. CLEARY, REV. JOSEPH F., J.C.D., Canonical Limitations on the Alienation of Church Property, VIII-141 pp., 1936.
101. GLYNN, REV. JOHN C., J.C.D., The Promoter of Justice, XX-337 pp., 1936.
102. BRENNAN, REV. JAMES H., S.S., M.A., S.T.B., J.C.D., The Simple Convalidation of Marriage, VI-135 pp., 1937.
103. BRUNINI, REV. JOSEPH BERNARD, J.C.D., The Clerical Obligations of Canons 139 and 142, X-121 pp., 1937.
104. CONNOR, REV. MAURICE, A.B., J.C.D., The Administrative Removal of Pastors, VIII-159 pp., 1937.
105. GUILFOYLE, REV. MERLIN JOSEPH, J.C.D., Custom, XI-144 pp., 1937.

106. HUGHES, REV. JAMES AUSTIN, A.B., A.M., J.C.D., Witnesses in Criminal Trials of Clerics, IX-140 pp., 1937.

107. JANSEN, REV. RAYMOND J., A.B., S.T.L., J.C.D., Canonical Provisions for Catechetical Instruction, VII-153 pp., 1937.

108. KEALY, REV. JOHN JAMES, A.B., J.C.D., The Introductory Libellus in Church Court Procedure, XI-121 pp., 1937.

109. MCMANUS, REV. JAMES EDWARD, C.SS.R., J.C.D., The Administration of Temporal Goods in Religious Institutes, XVI-196 pp., 1937.

110. MORIARITY, REV. EUGENE JAMES, J.C.D., Oaths in Ecclesiastical Courts, X-115 pp., 1937.

111. RAINIER, REV. ELIGIUS GEORGE, C.SS.R., J.C.D., Suspension of Clerics, XVII-249 pp., 1937.

112. REILLY, REV. THOMAS F., C.SS.R., J.C.D., Visitation of Religious, VI-195 pp., 1938.

113. MORIARITY, REV. FRANCIS E., C.SS.R., J.C.D., The Extraordinary Absolution from Censures, XV-334 pp., 1938.

114. CONNOLLY, REV. NICHOLAS P., J.C.D., The Canonical Erection of Parishes, X-132 pp., 1938.

115. DONOVAN, REV. JAMES JOSEPH, J.C.D., The Pastor's Obligation in Prenuptial Investigation, XII-322 pp., 1938.

116. HARRIGAN, REV. ROBERT J., M.A., S.T.B., J.C.D., The Radical Sanation of Invalid Marriages, VIII-208 pp., 1938.

117. BOFFA, REV. CONRAD HUMBERT, J.C.D., Canonical Provisions for Catholic Schools, VII-211 pp., 1939.

118. PARSONS, REV. ANSCAR JOHN, O.M.Cap., J.C.D., Canonical Elections, XII-236 pp., 1939.

119. REILLY, REV. EDWARD MICHAEL, A.B., J.C.D., The General Norms of Dispensation, XII-156 pp., 1939.

120. RYAN, REV. GERALD ALOYSIUS, A.B., J.C.D., Principles of Episcopal Jurisdiction, XII-172 pp., 1939.

121. BURTON, REV. FRANCIS JAMES, C.S.C., A.B., J.C.D., A Commentary on Canon 1125, X-222 pp., 1940.

122. MIASKIEWICZ, REV. FRANCIS SIGISMUND, J.C.D., Supplied Jurisdiction According to Canon 209, XII-340 pp., 1940.

123. RICE, REV. PATRICK WILLIAM, A.B., J.C.D., Proof of Death in Prenuptial Investigation, VIII-156 pp., 1940.

124. ANGLIN, REV. THOMAS FRANCIS, M.S., J.C.D., The Eucharistic Fast, VIII-183 pp., 1941.

125. COLEMAN, REV. JOHN JEROME, J.C.D., The Minister of Confirmation, VI-153 pp., 1941.

126. DOWNS, REV. JOHN EMMANUEL, A.B., J.C.D., The Concept of Clerical Immunity, XI-163 pp., 1941.

127. ESSWEIN, REV. ANTHONY ALBERT, J.C.D., Extrajudicial Penal Powers of Ecclesiastical Superiors, X-144 pp., 1941.

128. FARREL, REV. BENJAMIN FRANCIS, M.A., S.T.L., J.C.D., The Rights and Duties of the Local Ordinary Regarding Congregations of Women Religious of Pontifical Approval, V-195 pp., 1941.
129. FEENEY, REV. THOMAS JOHN, A.B., S.T.L., J.C.D., Restitutio in Integrum, VI-169 pp., 1941.
130. FINDLEY, REV. STEPHEN WILLIAM, O.S.B., A.B., J.C.D., Canonical Norms Governing the Deposition and Degradation of Clerics, XVII-279 pp., 1941.
131. GOODWINE, REV. JOHN, A.B., S.T.L., J.C.D., The Right of the Church to Acquire Property, VIII-119 pp., 1941.
132. HESTON, REV. EDWARD LOUIS, C.S.C., PH.D., S.T.D., J.C.D., The Alienation of Church Property in the United States, XII-222 pp., 1941.
133. HOGAN, REV. JAMES JOHN, A.B., S.T.L., J.C.D., Judicial Advocates and Procurators, XIII-200 pp., 1941.
134. KEALY, REV. THOMAS M., A.B., Litt.B., J.C.D., Dowry of Women Religious, IX-152 pp., 1941.
135. KEENE, REV. MICHAEL JAMES, O.S.B., J.C.D., Religious Ordinaries and Canon 198, V-164 pp., 1942.
136. KERIN, REV. CHARLES A., S.S., M.A., S.T.B., J.C.D., The Privation of Christian Burial, XVI-279 pp., 1941.
137. LOUIS, REV. WILLIAM FRANCIS, M.A., J.C.D., Diocesan Archives, X-101 pp., 1941.
138. McDEVITT, REV. GILBERT JOSEPH, A.B., J.C.D., Legitimacy and Legitimation, X-247 pp., 1941.
139. McDONOUGH, REV. THOMAS JOSEPH, A.B., J.C.D., Apostolic Administrators, X-217 pp., 1941.
140. MEIER, REV. CARL ANTHONY, A.B., J.C.D., Penal Administrative Procedure Against Negligent Pastors, XI-240 pp., 1941.
141. SCHMIDT, REV. JOHN ROGG, A.B., J.C.D., The Principles of Authentic Interpretation in Canon 17 of the Code of Canon Law, XII-331 pp., 1941.
142. SLAFKOSKY, REV. ANDREW LEONARD, A.B., J.C.D., The Canonical Episcopal Visitation of the Diocese, X-197 pp., 1941.
143. SWOBODA, REV. INNOCENT ROBERT, O.F.M., J.C.D., Ignorance in Relation to the Imputability of Delicts, IX-271 pp., 1941.
144. DUBÉ, REV. ARTHUR JOSEPH, A.B., J.C.D., The General Principles for the Reckoning of Time in Canon Law, VIII-299 pp., 1941.
145. McBRIDE, REV. JAMES T., A.B., J.C.D., Incardination and Excardination of Seculars, XX-585 pp., 1941.
146. KRÓL, REV. JOHN T., J.C.D., The Defendant in Ecclesiastical Trials, XII-207 pp., 1942.
147. COMYNS, REV. JOSEPH J., C.SS.R., A.B., J.C.D., Papal and Episcopal Administration of Church Property, XIV-155 pp., 1942.

148. BARRY, REV. GARRETT FRANCIS, O.M.I., J.C.D., Violation of the Cloister, XII-260 pp., 1942.
149. BOLDUC, REV. GATIEN, C.S.V., A.B., S.T.L., J.C.D., Les Études dans les Religions Clèricales, VIII-155 pp., 1942.
150. BOYLE, REV. DAVID JOHN, M.A., J.C.D., The Juridic Effects of Moral Certitude on Pre-Nuptial Guarantees, XII-188 pp., 1942.
151. CANAVAN, REV. WALTER JOSEPH, M.A., LITT.D., J.C.D., The Profession of Faith, XII-143 pp., 1942.
152. DESROCHERS, REV. BRUNO, A.B., PH.L., S.T.B., J.C.D., Le Premier Concile Plènier de Quebéc et le Code de Droit Canonique, XIV-186 pp., 1942.
153. DILLON, REV. ROBERT EDWARD, A.B., J.C.D., Common Law Marriage, X-148 pp., 1942.
154. DODWELL, REV. EDWARD JOHN, PH.D., S.T.B., J.C.D., The Time and Place for the Celebration of Marriage, X-156 pp., 1942.
155. DONNELLAN, REV. THOMAS ANDREW, A.B., J.C.D., The Obligation of the Missa pro Populo, VII-131 pp., 1942.
156. ELTZ, REV. LOUIS ANTHONY, A.B., J.C.D., Cooperation in Crime, XII-208 pp., 1942.
157. GASS, REV. SYLVESTER FRANCIS, M.A., J.C.D., Ecclesiastical Pensions, XI-206 pp., 1942.
158. GUINIVEN, REV. JOHN JOSEPH, C.SS.R., J.C.D., The Precept of Hearing Mass, XIV-188 pp., 1942.
159. GULCZYNSKI, REV. JOHN THEOPHILUS, J.C.D., The Desecration and Violation of Churches, X-126 pp., 1942.
160. HAMMIL, REV. JOHN LEO, M.A., J.C.D., The Obligations of the Traveler According to Canon 14, VIII-204 pp., 1942.
161. HAYDT, REV. JOHN JOSEPH, A.B., J.C.D., Reserved Benefices, XI-148 pp., 1942.
162. HUSER, REV. ROGER JOHN, O.F.M., A.B., J.C.D., The Crime of Abortion in Canon Law, XII-187 pp., 1942.
163. KEARNEY, REV. FRANCIS PATRICK, A.B., S.T.L., J.C.D., The Principles of Canon 1127, X-162 pp., 1942.
164. LINAHEN, REV. LEO JAMES, S.T.L., J.C.D., De Absolutione Complicis In Peccato Turpi, 114 pp., 1942.
165. MCCLOSKEY, REV. JOSEPH ALOYSIUS, A.B., J.C.D., The Subject of Ecclesiastical Law According to Canon 12, XVII-246 pp., 1942.
166. O'NEIL, REV. FRANCIS JOSEPH, C.SS.R., J.C.D., The Dismissal of Religious in Temporary Vows, XIII-220 pp., 1942.
167. PRINCE, REV. JOHN EDWARD, A.B., S.T.B., J.C.D., The Diocesan Chancellor, X-136 pp., 1942.
168. RIESNER, REV. ALBERT JOSEPH, C.SS.R., J.C.D., Apostates and Fugitives from Religious Institutes, IX-168 pp., 1942.

169. STENGER, REV. JOSEPH BERNARD, J.C.D., The Mortgaging of Church Property, 186 pp., 1942.
170. WALDRON, REV. JOSEPH FRANCIS, A.B., J.C.D., The Minister of Baptism, XII-197 pp., 1942.
171. WILLETT, REV. ROBERT ALBERT, J.C.D., The Probative Value of Documents in Ecclesiastical Trials, X-124 pp., 1942.
172. WOEBER, REV. EDWARD MARTIN, M.A., J.C.D., The Interpollations, XII-161 pp., 1942.
173. BENKO, REV. MATTHEW ALOYSIUS, O.S.B., M.A., J.C.D., The Abbot *Nullius*, XV-147 pp., 1943.
174. CHRIST, REV. JOSEPH JAMES, M.A., S.T.L., J.C.D., Dispensation from Vindicative Penalties, XIII-285 pp., 1943.
175. CLANCY, REV. PATRICK M. J., O.P., A.B., S.T.LR., J.C.D., The Local Religious Superior, X-229 pp., 1943.
176. CLARKE, REV. THOMAS JAMES, J.C.D., Parish Societies, XII-147 pp., 1943.
177. CONNOLLY, REV. JOHN PATRICK, S.T.L., J.C.D., Synodal Examiners and Parish Priest Consultors, X-223 pp., 1943.
178. DRUMM, REV. WILLIAM MARTIN, A.B., J.C.D., Hospital Chaplains, XII-175 pp., 1943.
179. FLANAGAN, REV. BERNARD JOSEPH, A.B., S.T.L., J.C.D., The Canonical Erection of Religious Houses, X-147 pp., 1943.
180. KELLEHER, REV. STEPHEN JOSEPH, A.B., S.T.B., J.C.D., Discussions with non-Catholics: Canonical Legislation, X-93 pp., 1943.
181. LEWIS, REV. GORDIAN, C.P., J.C.D., Chapters in Religious Institutes, XII-169 pp., 1943.
182. MARX, REV. ADOLPH, J.C.D., The Declaration of Nullity of Marriages Contracted Outside the Church, X-151 pp., 1943.
183. MATULENAS, REV. RAYMOND ANTHONY, O.S.B., A.B., J.C.D., Communication, a Source of Privileges, XII-225 pp., 1943.
184. O'LEARY, REV. CHARLES GERARD, C.SS.R., J.C.D., Religious Dismissed After Perpetual Profession, X-213 pp., 1943.
185. POWER, REV. CORNELIUS MICHAEL, J.C.D., The Blessing of Cemeteries, XII-231 pp., 1943.
186. SHUHLER, REV. RALPH VINCENT, O.S.A., J.C.D., Privileges of Religious to Absolve and Dispense, XII-195 pp., 1943.
187. ZIOLKOWSKI, REV. THADDEUS STANISLAUS, A.B., J.C.D., The Consecration and Blessing of Churches, XII-151 pp., 1943.
188. HENEGHAN, REV. JOHN JOSEPH, S.T.D., J.C.D., The Marriages of Unworthy Catholics: Canons 1065 and 1066, XVI-213 pp., 1944.
189. CARROLL, REV. COLEMAN FRANCIS, M.A., S.T.L., J.C.L., Charitable Institutions.
190. CIESLUK, REV. JOSEPH EDWARD, PH.B., S.T.L., J.C.L., National Parishes in the United States.

191. COBURN, REV. VINCENT PAUL, A.B., J.C.D., Marriages of Conscience, XII-172 pp., 1944.
192. CONNORS, REV. CHARLES PAUL, C.S.SP., A.B., J.C.D., Extra-Judicial Procurators in the Code of Canon Law, X-94 pp., 1944.
193. COYLE, REV. PAUL RAYMOND, A.B., J.C.D., Judicial Exemptions, X-142 pp., 1944.
194. FAIR, REV. BARTHOLOMEW FRANCIS, A.B., S.T.L., J.C.D., The Impediment of Abduction, XII-122 pp., 1944.
195. GALLAGHER, REV. THOMAS RAPHAEL, O.P., A.B., S.T.LR., J.C.D., The Examination of the Qualities of the Ordinand, X-166 pp., 1944.
196. GANNON, REV. JOHN MARK, S.T.L., J.C.D., The Interstices Required for the Promotion to Orders, XII-100 pp., 1944.
197. GOLDSMITH, REV. J. WILLIAM, B.C.S., S.T.L., J.C.D., The Competence of Church and State over Marriage—Disputed Points, X-128 pp., 1944.
198. GOODWINE, REV. JOSEPH GERARD, A.B., S.T.B., J.C.D., The Reception of Converts, XIV-326 pp., 1944.
199. KOWALSKI, REV. ROMUALD EUGENE, O.F.M., A.B., J.C.D., Sustenance of Religious Houses of Regulars, X-174 pp., 1944.
200. MCCOY, REV. ALAN EDWARD, O.F.M., J.C.D., Force and Fear in Relation to Delictual Imputability and Penal Responsibility, XII-160 pp., 1944.
201. MCDEVITT, REV. VINCENT JOHN, PH.B., S.T.L., J.C.L., Perjury.
202. MARTIN, REV. THOMAS OWEN, PH.D., S.T.D., J.C.D., Adverse Posession, Prescription and Limitation of Actions: The Canonical "Praescriptio," XX-208 pp., 1944.
203. MIKLOSOVIC, REV. PAUL JOHN, A.B., J.C.L., Attempted Marriages and Their Consequent Juridic Effects.
204. MUNDY, REV. THOMAS MAURICE, A.B., S.T.L., J.C.D., The Union of Parishes, X-164 pp., 1944.
205. O'DEA, REV. JOHN COYLE, A.B., J.C.D., The Matrimonial Impediment of Nonage, VIII-126 pp., 1944.
206. OLALIA, REV. ALEXANDER AYSON, S.T.L., J.C.D., A Comparative Study of the Christian Constitution of States and the Constitution of the Philippine Commonwealth, XII-136 pp., 1944.
207. POISSON, REV. PIERRE-MARIE, C.S.C., A.B., PH.L., THL., J.C.L., Droits Patrimoniaux des Maisons et des Églises Religieuses.
208. STADALNIKAS, REV. CASIMIR JOSEPH, M.I.C., J.C.D., Reservation of Censures, X-141 pp., 1944.
209. SULLIVAN, REV. EUGENE HENRY, S.T.L., J.C.D., Proof of the Reception of the Sacraments, X-165 pp., 1944.
210. VAUGHAN, REV. WILLIAM EDWARD, J.C.D., Constitutions for Diocesan Courts, X-210 pp., 1944.
211. PARO, REV. GINO, S.T.D., J.C.L., The Right of Apostolic Delegation.

212. BALZER, REV. RALPH FRANCIS, C.P., J.C.D., The Computation of Time in a Canonical Novitiate, X-227 pp., 1945.

213. DOUGHERTY, REV. JOHN WHELAN, A.B., S.T.L., J.C.D., De Inquisitione Speciali, XII-195 pp., 1945.

214. DZIOB, REV. MICHAEL WALTER, J.C.D., The Sacred Congregation for the Oriental Church, XII-181 pp., 1945.

215. EIDENSCHINK, REV. JOHN ALBERT, O.S.B., B.A., J.C.D., The Election of Bishops in the Letters of Pope Gregory the Great, VIII-200 pp., 1945.

216. GILL, REV. NICHOLAS, C.P., J.C.D., The Spiritual Prefect in Clerical Religious Houses of Study, X-140 pp., 1945.

217. HYNES, REV. HARRY GERARD, S.T.L., J.C.D., The Privileges of Cardinals, XII-183 pp., 1945.

218. MCDEVITT, REV. GERALD VINCENT, S.T.L., J.C.D., The Renunciation of an Ecclesiastical Office, XIV-179, pp., 1945.

219. MANNING, REV. JOSEPH LEROY, J.C.D., The Free Conferral of Offices, VIII-116 pp., 1945.

220. MEYER, REV. LOUIS G., O.S.B., A.B., S.T.B., J.C.D., Alms-gathering by Religious, XII-163 pp., 1945.

221. O'DONNELL, REV. CLETUS FRANCIS, M.A., J.C.D., The Marriage of Minors, XII-268 pp., 1945.

222. PRUNSKIS, REV. JOSEPH, J.C.D., Comparative Law, Ecclesiastical and Civil, in Lithuanian Concordat, X-161 pp., 1945.

223. SWEENEY, REV. FRANCIS PATRICK, C.SS.R., J.C.D., The Reduction of Clerics to the Lay State, X-199 pp., 1945.

224. VOGELPOHL, REV. HENRY JOHN, J.C.D., The Simple Impediments to Holy Orders, XVI-190 pp., 1945.

225. BROCKHAUS, REV. THOMAS AQUINAS, O.S.B., J.C.D., Religious who are known as *Conversi*, X-127 pp., 1945.

226. GRIESE, REV. N. ORVILLE, The Marriage Contract and the Procreation of Offspring, XVI-224 pp., 1946.

227. BOUDREAUX, REV. WARREN LOUIS, J.C.L., The "*ab acatholicis nati*" of Canon 1099, § 2.

228. BOWE, REV. THOMAS JOSEPH, A.B., J.C.L., Religious Superioresses.

229. DIEDERICHS, REV. MICHAEL FERDINAND, S.C.J., J.C.D., The Jurisdiction of the Latin Ordinaries over their Oriental Subjects, XIV-153 pp., 1946.

230. DINGMAN, REV. MAURICE JOHN, A.B., S.T.L., J.C.L., The Plaintiff in Contentious Trials.

231. FRISON, REV. BASIL, C.M.F., M.MUS., J.C.D., The Retroactivity of Law, X-221 pp., 1946.

232. GALVIN, REV. WILLIAM ANTHONY, M.A., J.C.D., The Administrative Transfer of Pastors, XII-288 pp., 1946.

233. Goracy, Rev. Joseph C., J.C.L., The Diriment Matrimonial Impediment of Major Orders.

234. Hale, Rev. Joseph Francis, M.A., S.T.L., J.C.L., The Pastor of Burial.

235. Henry, Rev. Joseph Arthur, A.B., J.C.D., The Mass and Holy Communion: Inter-Ritual Law, XII-138 pp., 1946.

236. Linenberger, Rev. Herbert, C.PP.S., J.C.L., The False Denunciation of an Innocent Confessor.

237. Lowry, Rev. James Martin, A.B., J.C.L., Dispensation from Private Vows.

238. Lynch, Rev. George Edward, A.B., S.T.L., J.C.D., Coadjutors and Auxiliaries of Bishops, X-107 pp., 1947.

239. Lynch, Rev. Timothy, M.S.SS.T., J.C.L., Contracts between Bishops and Religious Congregations.

240. McClunn, Rev. Justin David, A.B., S.T.L., J.C.D., Administrative Recourse, VII-142 pp., 1946.

241. Lohmuller, Rev. Martin Nicholas, A.B., J.C.D., The Promulgation of Law, XI-139 pp., 1947.

242. McGrath, Rev. James, A.B., J.C.D., The Privilege of the Canon, XII-156 pp., 1946.

243. Marbach, Rev. Joseph Francis, A.B., J.C.D., Marriage Legislation for the Catholics of the Oriental Rites in the United States and Canada, XIV-314 pp., 1946.

244. Shimkus, Rev. Bernard Aloysius, A.B., J.C.L., The Determination and Transfer of Rite.

245. Smith, Rev. Vincent Michael, A.B., S.T.L., J.C.L., Ignorance Affecting Matrimonial Consent.

246. Wachtrle, Rev. Paul Anthony, A.B., J.C.L., The Baptism of the Children of Non-Catholics.

247. Crotty, Rev. Matthew M., J.C.L., The Recipient of First Holy Communion.

248. Eagleton, Rev. George, J.C.L., The Quinquennial Faculties, Formula IV.

249. Gibbons, Rev. Marion L., C.M., LL.B., J.C.L., Domicile of the Wife Unlawfully Separated from Her Husband.

250. Kelly, Rev. Bernard M., S.T.L., J.C.L., The Functions Reserved to Pastors.

251. Kilcullen, Rev. Thomas J., LL.M., J.C.L., The Collegiate Moral Person as Party Litigant.

252. Lafontaine, Rev. Germain J., W.F., J.C.L., Relatiens Canoniques entre le Missionnaire et Ses Superieurs.

253. Lane, Rev. Loras T., A.B., S.T.L., J.C.L., Matrimonial Procedure in the Ordinary Court of Second Instance.

254. Lover, Rev. James F., C.SS.R., J.C.L., The Master of Novices.

255. McNICHOLAS, REV. TIMOTHY J., J.C.L., The *Septimae Manus* Witness.
256. MAROSITZ, REV. JOSEPH J., M.S.C., J.C.L., Obligations and Privileges of Religious Promoted to the Episcopal or Cardinalitial Dignities.
257. MURPHY, REV. FRANCIS J., A.B., J.C.L., Legislative Powers of the Provincial Council.
258. O'BRIEN, REV. ROMAEUS W., O.CARM., J.C.L., The Provincial Superior in Religious Orders of Men.
259. PFALLER, REV. BENEDICT A., O.S.B., J.C.L., The *Ipso Facto* Effected Dismissal of Religious.
260. POPEK, REV. ALPHONSE S., M.A., J.C.L., The Rights and Obligations of Metropolitans.
261. RISTUCCIA, REV. BERNARD J., C.M., J.C.L., Quasi-Religious.
262. SONNTAG, REV. NATHANIEL L., O.F.M. CAP., J.C.L., Censorship of Special Classes of Books.
263. STADLER, REV. JOSEPH N., J.C.L., Frequent Holy Communion.
264. SZAL, REV. IGNATIUS J., A.B., J.C.L., The Communication of Catholics with Schismatics.
265. WAGNER, REV. URBAN S., O.F.M. CONV., J.C.L., Parochial Substitute Vicars and Supplying Priests.

www.ingramcontent.com/pod-product-compliance
Lightning Source LLC
LaVergne TN
LVHW050245080826
844660LV00012B/597

* 9 7 8 0 8 1 3 2 2 4 4 2 8 *